Palgrave Studies in Utopianism

Series editor
Gregory Claeys
Royal Holloway, University of London
London, UK

Utopianism is an interdisciplinary concept which covers philosophy, sociology, literature, history of ideas, art and architecture, religion, futurology and other fields. While literary utopianism is usually dated from Thomas More's Utopia (1516), communitarian movements and ideologies proposing utopian ends have existed in most societies through history. They imagine varied ideal beginnings of the species, like golden ages or paradises, potential futures akin to the millennium, and also ways of attaining similar states within real time. Utopianism, in the sense of striving for a much improved world, is also present in many trends in contemporary popular movements, and in phenomena as diverse as films, video games, environmental and medical projections. Increasingly utopia shares the limelight with dystopia, its negative inversion, and with projections of the degeneration of humanity and nature alike. This series will aim to publish the best new scholarship across these varied fields. It will focus on original studies of interest to a broad readership, including, but not limited to, historical and theoretical narratives as well as accounts of contemporary utopian thought, interpretation and action.

More information about this series at
http://www.palgrave.com/gp/series/15242

Thomas Horan

Desire and Empathy in Twentieth-Century Dystopian Fiction

palgrave
macmillan

Thomas Horan
The Citadel
Charleston, SC, USA

Palgrave Studies in Utopianism
ISBN 978-3-319-70674-0   ISBN 978-3-319-70675-7   (eBook)
https://doi.org/10.1007/978-3-319-70675-7

Library of Congress Control Number: 2018933374

© The Editor(s) (if applicable) and The Author(s) 2018
This work is subject to copyright. All rights are solely and exclusively licensed by the Publisher, whether the whole or part of the material is concerned, specifically the rights of translation, reprinting, reuse of illustrations, recitation, broadcasting, reproduction on microfilms or in any other physical way, and transmission or information storage and retrieval, electronic adaptation, computer software, or by similar or dissimilar methodology now known or hereafter developed.
The use of general descriptive names, registered names, trademarks, service marks, etc. in this publication does not imply, even in the absence of a specific statement, that such names are exempt from the relevant protective laws and regulations and therefore free for general use.
The publisher, the authors and the editors are safe to assume that the advice and information in this book are believed to be true and accurate at the date of publication. Neither the publisher nor the authors or the editors give a warranty, express or implied, with respect to the material contained herein or for any errors or omissions that may have been made. The publisher remains neutral with regard to jurisdictional claims in published maps and institutional affiliations.

Cover illustration: Edvard Munch, Kiss IV (1902). © FineArt / Alamy Stock Photo

Printed on acid-free paper

This Palgrave Macmillan imprint is published by Springer Nature
The registered company is Springer International Publishing AG
The registered company address is: Gewerbestrasse 11, 6330 Cham, Switzerland

For Sarah

Acknowledgments

Although it reached somewhat different conclusions, my dissertation forms the kernel of this monograph. My director and advisor throughout graduate school, Pamela Cooper, was a great mentor and an even better friend. Special thanks to the other members of my dissertation committee: María DeGuzmán, J. Kimball King, Allan Life, and Thomas Reinert. I benefited so much from their expertise and guidance, and I will never forget my many conversations with them.

Thanks to Gregory Claeys, Carmel Kennedy, Emily Russell, the anonymous reader of my initial draft, and everyone else in Palgrave's Studies in Utopianism series for their feedback and assistance.

I should also like to thank The Citadel, Charleston, USA, for giving me a one-semester sabbatical to work on this project, and the staff of the Daniel Library, particularly Courtney McAllister, for tracking down so many secondary sources for me through interlibrary loan.

Thanks to Javier Martinez at the journal *Extrapolation* and Betsy Maury at Grey House Publishing for approving my request to include excerpts from two of my previously published articles.

Thanks to my sons, Adam and Nathan, for keeping me happy and grounded. Thanks to my in-laws, Tom and Dee Clere, for proofing so many of my chapter drafts.

Very special thanks to my mother, Marilyn Horan Kiley, for her limitless love and extraordinary support.

Finally, this book would not exist in its present form without several years of ongoing help and encouragement from my wife, Sarah Clere. Sarah's careful critiques of my claims, helpful suggestions, and line edits of my prose gave shape and definition to the rough manuscript. She sacrificed time and energy necessary to her own academic work to advance mine. I am both grateful and sorry for that. She is the best companion and collaborator anyone could have.

Sarah, I dedicate this book to you with all my love.

CONTENTS

1 Introduction 1

2 The Sexualized Proletariat in Jack London's *The Iron Heel* 25

3 Redemptive Atavism in Yevgeny Zamyatin's *We* 51

4 The Sexual Life of the Savage in Aldous Huxley's *Brave New World* 71

5 Katharine Burdekin's *Swastika Night*, a Gay Romance 93

6 Distortions of Queer Desire in Ayn Rand's *Anthem* 129

7 Desire and Empathy in George Orwell's *Nineteen Eighty-Four* 147

8 Ludic Perversions and Enduring Communities in Margaret Atwood's *The Handmaid's Tale* 169

9 Conclusion 203

Index 207

CHAPTER 1

Introduction

In her excellent study *Dystopian Fiction East and West*, Erika Gottlieb (2001) asserts that twentieth-century dystopian fiction is partially defined by a terrible and irrevocable finality: "It is one of the most conspicuous features of [...] dystopian fiction that once we allow the totalitarian state to come to power, there will be no way back" (p. 4). I argue instead that the major authors of twentieth-century dystopian fiction present sexual desire as an aspect of the self that can never be fully appropriated and therefore as a potential force for moral regeneration from within the totalitarian state. In a cross-section of twentieth-century dystopian novels, a sexual relationship gradually engenders revolutionary notions of social and personal responsibility. Though these sexual liaisons are frequently ill fated, they show that sexual desire has a propulsive ability to promote positive change even when both the sexual relationship and the resistance it elicits are curtailed. In this subgenre of speculative literature, sex works as a portal through which the citizen at the center of the dystopian world glimpses the idea of both political liberation and a transcendent human dignity.

To better denote how sexuality works in the particular type of dystopian fiction with which I am concerned, I have coined the term "projected political fiction," which refers to speculative dystopian literature that is primarily political in focus. As Gordon Browning (1970) notes, authors of dystopian literature frequently project a political system or philosophy with which they disagree into a futuristic story:

The author is, in one way or another, commenting on the nature of his own society by taking what he considers the most significant aspects of that society and projecting them into an imaginary environment. This projection reflects the author's dissatisfaction with the current state of affairs, but not to the extent that it is a prophecy of doom or a warning that we must brace ourselves for a certain disaster. It is instead a warning accompanied by faith or at least a hope that the situation will be improved if man will only accomplish a certain series of necessary reforms. (p. 18)

Setting their stories in the future allows writers of projected political fiction to explore immediate political concerns on a grand scale. These stories not only reach forward through the uncertain darkness to cast an image of what may lie ahead but also widen the scope of that image to encompass all aspects of cultural, political, and economic life.

In light of Donald Trump's election to the presidency of the USA, projected political fiction is ever more relevant to our daily lives. In the early years of the twenty-first century, however, the subgenre seemed past its heyday. Dystopian fiction remained popular and vibrant but, as Gregory Claeys (2017) observes, its "political content" had "diminished" since the 1990s (p. 489). Its focus shifted to technological and environmental concerns. Dystopian novels were increasingly written for a young-adult audience and paid less attention to political philosophy. Amid the entrenched partisan divisions determining Western government policy, political concerns and their relevance to cultural and scientific anxieties have retuned to the forefront of dystopian literature. Recent novels such as Omar El Akkad's *American War* and Lidia Yuknavitch's *The Book of Joan*, along with increased sales of and renewed interest in classic dystopias such as George Orwell's *Nineteen Eighty-Four* and Margaret Atwood's *The Handmaid's Tale*, indicate a remerging interest in the thematic and stylistic innovations of the projected political fiction of the twentieth century.

Dozens of projected political fictions have been written since the 1890s, but my analysis focuses chronologically on the seven most influential works of this genre from the twentieth century: Jack London's *Iron Heel* (1908), Yevneny Zamyatin's *We* (1924), Aldous Huxley's *Brave New World* (1932), Katharine Burdekin's *Swastika Night* (1937), Ayn Rand's *Anthem* (1938), George Orwell's *Nineteen Eighty-Four* (1949), and Margaret Atwood's *The Handmaid's Tale* (1985). These particular books are foundational because they guided and shaped the development of this subgenre of dystopian fiction, changing forever the climate of Western political thought. Through these writings, words and phrases such as "Big Brother," "Brave New Worldian, Doublethink," and "Orwellian," along with the concepts underlying them, became part of our common vocabulary.

These texts also exemplify the bias of Western political thought. The comparative paucity of acclaimed dystopian literature by nonwhite authors largely reflects the racism of the canon itself. Many nonwhite people did not have to imagine a political dystopia; institutional racism forced them to live in one. Fortunately, since the 1970s more dystopian literature by nonwhite novelists has been published and studied. Due to sexism, heterosexism, homophobia, and transphobia, most women and members of LGBTQ communities have undoubtedly felt at times that they face systems that are at best inequitable and at worst totalitarian. The same is undoubtedly true of non-Christians, particularly Jews, Muslims, and atheists. Given that my analysis includes three novels by women, at least one of whom was lesbian, I address concerns such as feminism and LGBTQ rights that are beyond my personal experience. These issues are as contested as they are crucial. As Sarah Webster Goodwin and Libby Falk Jones (1990) remind us, "One woman's utopia is another's nightmare; feminism itself takes on a range of meanings" (p. ix).

This ambiguity is manifest in the texts themselves. For example, while—like many critics—I read *The Handmaid's Tale* as a feminist novel, in her essay "*The Handmaid's Tale* and *Oryx and Crake* in Context," Atwood (2004) herself does not couch her first dystopia in these terms:

> I wanted to try a dystopia from the female point of view—the world according to Julia, as it were. However, this does not make *The Handmaid's Tale* a 'feminist dystopia,' except insofar as giving a woman a voice and an inner life will always be considered 'feminist' by those who think women ought not to have these things. (p. 516)

Rather than situating her first dystopia in relation to the work of other feminists, Atwood puts *The Handmaid's Tale* in dialogue with *Nineteen Eighty-Four*: "Orwell became a direct model for me much later in my life—in the real 1984, the year in which I began writing a somewhat different dystopia, *The Handmaid's Tale*" (p. 516). Moreover, while I draw upon feminist analyses of *Swastika Night*, I investigate the potential that the novel vests in gay desire.

Lyman Tower Sargent and Lucy Sargisson (2014) observe that classic dystopias testify to the liberating power of sex: "classic dystopias tend to suggest that sex is more powerful than the state" (p. 305), but they also concede the apparent limitations of this power: "Sex can take us a long way, but it cannot take us where we want to go" (p. 317). I argue that these novelists emphasize the enduring ethical value of sexual desire, which correctly orients us toward "where we want to go," even when the novel concludes before the journey toward utopia has begun.

Authors of projected political fiction have frequently been linked in the past, but mainly through the question of their influence on each other. Zamyatin not only read London's novels but also translated London's work into Russian. Orwell, who read and favorably reviewed *The Iron Heel* before beginning *Nineteen Eighty-Four*, admired London's critical perspective on what would ultimately be called fascism. He suspected that *Brave New World* was inspired by *We*. In a review of *We* which appeared in *Tribune* on January 4, 1946, Orwell (1946/1968d) writes: "The first thing anyone would notice about *We* is the fact—never pointed out, I believe—that Huxley's *Brave New World* must be partly derived from it" (p. 72). According to Jerome Meckier (2011), Huxley would later deny having read *We*, both to Drieu La Rochelle and to Zamyatin himself in 1932 (p. 229). Others have pointed out intriguing similarities between *We* and *Nineteen Eighty-Four*. For instance, In Meckier's opinion, "Orwell's borrowings resurrected Zamyatin's novel" (2011, p. 229). Atwood has acknowledged her debt to Orwell; and, as I discuss in Chap. 5, there is circumstantial evidence, though no conclusive proof, that Orwell may have been influenced by *Swastika Night*.

I make a different kind of comparison by exploring how sexual desire provides an opening out of the rigid structure of totalitarianism in the work of all of these authors. Drawing on the ideas of various cultural and literary theorists, I discuss how the methodology developed by these intellectuals helps illuminate the ethical concerns embedded in dystopian narratives. Indeed, projected political fictions often anticipate concepts subsequently explored by prominent theorists, as William Steinhoff (1975) notes in his analysis of the thematic similarities between Orwell and Hannah Arendt: "Hannah Arendt shows beautifully how the essence of totalitarianism is its unlimited and consistent logic, and it is remarkable how Orwell anticipated her detailed analysis of the destruction of the human person and the manner in which ideology may turn into insanity" (p. 209). M. Keith Booker (1994) perceptively argues that writers of dystopian literature and theorists frequently respond to one another in their writings, forming a kind of interdisciplinary discourse community: "In this sense, dystopian fiction is more like the projects of social critics like Nietzche, Freud, Bakhtin, Adorno, Foucault, Habermas, and many others" (p. 19).

Despite the informal dialogues between authors of twentieth-century dystopian narratives and political theorists, projected political fictions are, even now, occasionally referred to as science fiction, since there is a tendency to refer to any narrative set in the future as such. Booker points out that there is no definitive way to differentiate dystopian literature from science fiction; the two genres are not mutually exclusive: "Clearly there is a great deal of overlap between dystopian and science fiction, and many texts belong to both categories. But in general dystopian fiction differs from science fiction in the specificity of its attention to social and political critique" (1994, p. 19). As Booker observes, it is the author's emphasis on political and social satire that distinguishes dystopian literature from classic science fiction. Like Booker, Claeys (2011) defines dystopian fiction in a way that succinctly differentiates it even from science fiction with dystopian or utopian features:

> The term is used here in the broad sense of portraying feasible negative visions of social and political development, cast principally in fictional form. By 'feasible' we imply that no extraordinary or utterly unrealistic features dominate the narrative. Much of the domain of science fiction is thus excluded from this definition. (p. 109)

Projected political fiction is perhaps best understood as a form of soft science fiction with minimal science content.

Beyond placing the political ahead of the scientific, what defines projected political fiction as its own subgenre of dystopian literature is the way in which illicit sexual arousal always triggers moral awareness. Catríona Ní Dhúill (2010) recognizes that sexual desire permeates twentieth-century dystopian fiction, yet she presents it as just one of many transgressive impulses: "The dystopian fictions of Orwell, Zamyatin, Huxley, Margaret Atwood, and others are animated by a system that seeks to impose itself comprehensively and the unwarranted factors that persist despite it, be they transgressive sexual desire, individuality, imagination, feminist consciousness, or dirt" (p. 48). I argue that in these dystopian texts, individuality, imagination, feminist consciousness, dirt (symbolizing the natural world), and a range of other potentially liberating forces become possible through sexual passion. The most important of these liberating tendencies, though not mentioned by Ní Dhúill, is a new ethical framework catalyzed by erotic desire, one that makes opposition to the dominant order a moral imperative. Although he questions desire's ultimate efficacy, Booker rightly maintains that eroticism is a central concern of totalitarian regimes because it enables a diverse range of liberating energies: "But for both Freud and dystopian governments, sexuality functions as a central focus for repressive energies largely because it is also a potential source of powerful *subversive* energies" (1994, p. 12, emphasis in original).

Because sexual desire works as a hub for subversion, each projected political fiction is plotted around an unlawful erotic relationship, which may or may not develop into love, between two characters: an orthodox character who either believes in the existing political system or has submitted to it without hope of deliverance, and a subversive, lascivious radical. As the story progresses, the docile character is first overwhelmed with desire for the rebellious character and eventually won over to the hope provided by the renegade's heretical political philosophy, willfully defiant behavior, or some combination of the two. Since the legally and socially permissible method of sexual contact is different in each projected political fiction, the nature of these salacious relationships varies to the point where in some of these stories the eroticism depicted seems unremarkable by our own cultural standards.

Picking up on a related idea, Gottlieb sees the bond of romantic love as the determining factor in these novels: "Falling in love with a woman who offers affection, passion, or simply an intimate bond is essential to the protagonist's awakening to his private universe, an essential step in building resistance against the regime" (2001, p. 21). It is true that in some cases—*Nineteen Eighty-Four*, for instance—a genuine and reciprocal love does develop between the recalcitrant pair. But love always follows, rather than precedes, the sexual arousal and political awakening of the lovers. As Paul Robinson (1983) points out, an investment in love as a vehicle for sociopolitical change is personally and ideologically incompatible with Orwell's thinking: "Orwell carefully insists that it is sex, not love, that contains the promise of revolt. He was by temperament, one feels, too tough-minded, too anti-romantic, to propose that love might be the answer" (p. 149).

Indeed, in some projected political fictions, love plays a minimal or even antagonistic role. Though the ongoing relationship between Offred and the Commander is the central concern of *The Handmaid's Tale*, reciprocal love between the two characters is impossible. Rand's Equality 7-2521 is convinced that he has committed the "Transgression of Preference" by yearning for Liberty 5-3000 (1938/2013, p. 41). In *Swastika Night*, despite the intensity of their friendship, Hermann's love for Alfred is unrequited. John the Savage in *Brave New World* is much more troubled by the thought, or to his mind the sin, of wantonly bedding Lenina than by the idea of loving her. Though attracted to Ernest Everhard, London's heroine Avis Cunningham initially hates him for his views on class and politics (1907/1980, p. 28). Likewise, Zamyatin's D-503 loves the Benefactor and hates all that I-330 represents. When he first discovers her seditious intentions, he intends to hand her over to the police. But his hunger for her makes him a coconspirator virtually against his will:

> Her tone was so impudent, so full of mockery [....] I always hated her [....] Suddenly her arm crept round my neck, lips touched lips, went deeper, things got even scarier. I swear, this was a total surprise for me, and maybe that's the only reason why. Because I could not have. I now understand this with absolute clarity. I could not possibly have desired what happened next [....] I became glass. I saw myself, inside [....] I remember I was on the floor hugging her legs, kissing her knees. And I was begging, "Now, right now, this minute..." (1924/1993, pp. 55–57)

D-503's abject, primal obsession with I-330 is based on physical attraction rather than anything as deep and sophisticated as romantic love. But though he feels loyal to his Benefactor and is cognizant of his own guilt throughout the story, atavistic desire quickly undermines years of indoctrination and behavioral conditioning.

Partick Parrinder (2011) approaches my own thinking by citing an illicit love-affair as the catalyst for rebellion in the dystopias of Zamyatin and Orwell, but he exempts Huxley from this paradigm:

> the romantic motifs of danger, passion and suffering must all arise within the society, most often—as in *We* and *Nineteen Eighty-Four*—emerging as the consequence of an illicit love-affair. The novels of both Zamyatin and Orwell employ a somewhat weak protagonist seduced by a fascinating female who may or may not be an *agent provocateur*. (p. 170)

Although there is nothing to suggest that Zamyatin's I-330 is anything other than a committed revolutionary, Parrinder's suggestion that Julia might be a secret agent of the Party is a possibility that I consider in Chap. 7. Nevertheless, even if, for the sake of argument, we assume that Julia is bent on entrapping Winston Smith, the sexual taboos that they break together facilitate his mental emancipation. For Orwell (1946/1968c), all taboos (sexual or otherwise) impede clarity: "Even a single taboo can have an all-round crippling effect upon the mind, because there is always the danger that any thought which is freely followed up may lead to the forbidden thought" (p. 65). Winston's story—like that of D-503, Avis Everhard, John the Savage, Hermann, Equality 7-2521, and Offred—illustrates how the shattering of sexual taboos leads to sociopolitical upheaval because whatever else they can control, governments, no matter how intrusive, can never fully anticipate and regulate the sexual predilections and indiscretions of their citizens.

Gilles Deleuze and Felix Guattari (1972/1983) insist in *Anti-Oedipus* that even a single instance of sensual passion is inherently and pervasively volatile:

> If desire is repressed, it is because every position of desire, no matter how small, is capable of calling into question the established order of a society [....] But it is explosive [....] [D]esire is revolutionary in its essence [....] [N]o society can tolerate a position of real desire without its structures of exploitation, servitude, and hierarchy being compromised [....] [S]exuality and love [...] cause strange flows to circulate that do not let themselves be stocked within an established order. Desire does not want revolution, it is revolutionary in its own right. (p. 116)

Deleuze and Guattari argue that totalitarian institutions are perennially haunted by sexual desire because its volatile wildness threatens social and political entrenchment. Their conception of desire closely parallels what occurs in projected political fiction. The authors of this kind of dystopian literature root insurrections in the potentially liberating instability induced by sexual passion.

In contrast to Deleuze and Guattari, other theorists, such as Michel Foucault, argue that desire can be co-opted and neutralized by the establishment. Extrapolating from the outcome of Winston and Julia's doomed relationship in *Nineteen Eighty-Four*, Booker argues that Orwell shares Foucault's lack of faith in the power of subversive sexuality to effect positive political change: "The dismal failure of the sexual rebellion of Smith and Julia in *1984* casts considerable doubt on the validity of their identification of sex as an inherently subversive activity. In this sense, Orwell's book, though thoroughly informed by the Freudian vision of repression, anticipates Foucault" (1994, p. 77). Foucault (1976/1978), for example, argues that the Sexual Revolution of the 1960s and 1970s was no true revolution, but instead played into the hands of the establishment:

> Power over sex is exercised the same way at all levels [...] whatever the devices or institutions on which it relies, it acts in a uniform and comprehensive manner [....] [F]rom state to family, from prince to father, from the tribunal to the small change of everyday punishments, from the agencies of social domination to the structures that constitute the subject himself, one finds a general form of power, varying in scale alone. (pp. 84–85)

The totalitarian regimes presented in works of projected political fiction endeavor systematically to tame unconventional desire in this way. Booker notes their putative success.

Yet, as Bülent Diken (2011) makes clear, even though Foucault was skeptical of the political efficacy of transgressive sexuality, he did recognize its potential as a foundation for a new ethical system: "After all, what makes sexuality disturbing is not the sexual act itself but the 'mode of life' related to it, which 'can yield a culture and an ethics' (Foucault 2001, pp. 298, 300)" (pp. 163–164). For instance, in considering the larger societal implications of openly acknowledged gay relationships, Foucault (1981/2001) envisions an ethical way of life arising out of sexual practices:

> How can a relational system be reached through sexual practices? Is it possible to create a homosexual mode of life? This notion of a mode of life seems important to me. Will it require the introduction of a diversification different from the ones due to social class, differences in profession and culture, a diversification which would also be a form of relationship and would be a "way of life"? A way of life can be shared among individuals of different age, status and social activity. It can yield intense relations not resembling those that are institutionalized. It seems to me that a way of life can yield a culture and an ethics. (pp. 299–300)

Foucault suggests that this ethical "way of life" allows people to organize in a manner that transcends ethnic, religious, and socioeconomic divisions, creating a basis for entirely new social networks and personal connections:

"The problem is not to discover in oneself the truth of sex but rather to use sexuality to arrive at a multiplicity of relationships" (1981/2001, p. 298). This conception of sexuality as a basis for community is characteristic of projected political fiction, regardless of whether any particular revolution fails or succeeds, again illustrating how facets of this literature prefigure concerns of literary theorists and political philosophers alike.

Since the dystopian literature of the last century was produced primarily by male authors, its treatment of sex often exhibits disturbing tendencies, including a juvenile attitude toward the female body, a reliance on sexist and heteronormative stereotypes, and, occasionally, a troubling link between desire for and violence against women. Nevertheless, exceptions to this norm illustrate the importance of women's sexual independence. For example, as Carlo Pagetti (1990) makes clear, Burdekin, writing under the pseudonym Murray Constantine, challenged this androcentric model during the interwar years:

> Burdekin goes directly against the fundamentally male character of utopian (including dystopian) discourse, especially in regard to its often highly reductive representation of female characters, who are seen as docile interpreters of the system (Lenina in *Brave New World*) or as ambiguous instruments of rebellion (Julia in *1984*). This she does by placing her reflections on the situation of women at the very core of her dystopian representation. (p. 361)

There is no firm evidence to indicate that Margaret Atwood was familiar with *Swastika Night* when she authored *The Handmaid's Tale*, but both writers identify the same logical consequence of sanctifying sexism—the reduction of women to subhuman animals used for breeding, a realization clear to Atwood's narrator:

> We are for breeding purposes: we aren't concubines, geisha girls, courtesans. On the contrary: everything possible has been done to remove us from that category. There is supposed to be nothing entertaining about us, no room is to be permitted for the flowering of secret lusts; no special favors are to be wheedled, by them or us, there are to be no toeholds for love. We are two-legged wombs, that's all. (Atwood 1986, p. 136)

As Sarah LeFanu (1988) indicates, Atwood satirizes a hypermasculine political system that feels like the successor to the fascism witnessed by Burdekin: "As Katharine Burdekin extrapolated from the growth of fascism in the 1930s, so Margaret Atwood in *The Handmaid's Tale* extrapolates from the social and political forces, including the growth of moral conservatism, in the USA in the 1980s" (p. 73). *The Handmaid's Tale* presents female perspectives that are merely implied in *Swastika Night*; yet Burdekin's dystopia, though written nearly half a century before *The Handmaid's Tale*, arguably presents a bolder challenge to the norm by candidly exploring the potential of queer desire, a liberating force on the periphery of most of the other novels in this study.

Whatever form they take, these forbidden sexual relationships do not always end happily. Nevertheless, even when the revolution promised by illicit desire fails, authors of projected political fiction, regardless of where they happen to be on the sociopolitical spectrum, transcend the physical to present sexual desire as a catalyst for a morality apart from organized religion. Rand, for instance, though her materialistic economic notions are admired by many religious conservatives, was a militant atheist. Likewise, as a socialist, Orwell (1940/1968b) in particular believed that humanity needed to move beyond religious faith:

> It was absolutely necessary that the soul should be cut away. Religious belief, in the form in which we had known it, had to be abandoned. By the nineteenth century it was already in essence a lie, a semi-conscious device for keeping the rich rich and the poor poor. (p. 15)

In his analysis of state control of eroticism in *Brave New World* and *Nineteen Eighty-Four*, William Plank (1984) explains why the individual's sexual desire represents a threat to secular and religious authorities alike:

> [E]roticism is more than a private urge, for it involves another: For the tyrant, therefore, every erotic encounter is an implicit plot. It is a secret of two and as such bears the seeds of subversion, of social misbehavior. Two people together in secret, bearing such potential of subversion must be exposed. Christianity, based on an ancient god of War and Power, must control eroticism. (p. 33)

Plank's reasoning reveals why all of the novels discussed in this study are hostile to organized religion: its moralizing about the sexual predilections and practices of consenting individuals veils a desire to eradicate the availability, the expectation, and the perceived threat of privacy. As Booker asserts, the Catholic Sacrament of Confession, through which sins of the body and mind must be revealed for salvation, inspired the emphasis on relentless surveillance central to both Foucault's theories and modern dystopian fiction (1994, p. 74).

While critical of the totalitarian inclinations of religious institutions, writers of projected political fiction nevertheless mourned the loss of the sense of universal ethics that accompanied religious faith. Claeys finds this tendency in *Brave New World*: "There are hints that Huxley thinks the loss of religious belief to be a tragedy for the later moderns" (2017, p. 365). Orwell's nonfiction directly addresses this byproduct of secularism: "The real problem of our time is to restore the sense of absolute right and wrong when the belief that it used to rest on—that is, the belief in personal immortality—has been destroyed. This demands faith, which is a different thing from credulity" (Orwell 1944/2000, p. 100). This is the humanism that Winston confronts his inquisitor with in *Nineteen Eighty-Four*:

> "There is something in the universe—I don't know, some spirit, some principle—that you will never overcome."
> "Do you believe in God, Winston?"
> "No."
> "Then what is it, this principle that will defeat us?"
> "I don't know. The spirit of man."
> "And do you consider yourself a man?"
> "Yes." (Orwell 1949/1977, p. 273)

Under torture, Winston abandons the hope of overthrowing the Party by force or action. But even though he realizes that the humanity will be expunged from his heart, mind, and body, he knows that some intrinsic worth may still remain among the living. In attempting to recreate the idea of this shared dignity, writers of projected political fiction desanctify and appropriate Judeo-Christian religious symbols and pastoral settings. It is this egalitarian human fellowship that sexuality awakens. These writers suggest that because every person has this sense of social responsibility somewhere deep inside themselves waiting to be unlocked by desire, dystopic governments must be committed to the colonization of sexual instinct down to the last individual.

In distinguishing projected political fiction from other speculative literature and in demonstrating how desire works within the genre, I proceed chronologically. Chapter 2 addresses London's complex, somewhat contradictory treatment of both social class and gender in relation to sexual desire in *The Iron Heel*, the first major dystopian novel of the twentieth century. The book enjoyed limited success when first published, but through its foreshadowing of what would later be called fascism it found a new audience a quarter-century after it was written.

While London recognizes the legitimacy of proletarian grievances, he is too sanguine in presenting social class as a fluid characteristic. Class boundaries in *The Iron Heel* are porous: erotic connections allow characters to shed one class identity and assume another. London's treatment of gender is conversely rigid and inconsistent. Women prove to be among the novel's most engaging and successful revolutionaries, yet the text fetishizes stock attributes of conventional masculinity. My analysis explores the queer undertones that inadvertently emerge through the narrator's presentation of Ernest Everhard (the story's idealized hero) and the author's sexualizing of the working class as a collective body.

This chapter also discusses London's dismissal of organized religion—especially Roman Catholicism—as a source of moral wisdom. Initiating a paradigm common to all of these projected political fictions, London argues that the Church is as susceptible to corruption as any other essentially corporate institution. For London, it is sexual desire, not faith, that makes individuals receptive to the wisdom of cooperation and social responsibility.

Conventional turn-of-the-twentieth-century utopian ideas and forecasts form another point of resistance for London. In the seminal late-nineteenth and early-twentieth-century utopias of progressive authors such as H.G. Wells and Edward Bellamy, societies thrive under scientific principles. This valorization of clinical rationalism fostered an interest in regulating sex and pathologizing certain sexual behaviors between consenting adults. Robert S. Baker (1990) points out that Wells believed that sexual relations should be monitored and controlled by medical professionals: "Wells, for example, advocated the state regulation of marriage and sexual experiences. In *Anticipations* he argued that sexual expression should be controlled by the medical doctor and psychologist" (p. 42). Like Zamyatin, Huxley, and Orwell, London was skeptical of utopian notions about the role science should play in both governance and sexuality.

Chapter 3 explores Yevgeny Zamyatin's *We*. Whereas London chronicles the brutal transition from democracy to oligarchy, Zamyatin presents a fully realized totalitarian world in which much of the citizenry, including the narrator, is perfectly at home, suggesting—like Huxley after him—that dystopian regimes can appear utopian, that tyranny can be implemented with good intentions, and that indulgence can be as dehumanizing as oppression.

Among the writers I consider, Zamyatin sees the greatest and broadest potential in sexuality, arguing that human creativity itself depends on it. Darko Suvin (2003) observes that in the face of pervasive cultural uniformity, Zamyatin presents the re-emergence of individuality and personal morality as the product of sexual passion: "Zamyatin uses the political strand of the plot much as I- uses D-: as means to a higher end—the sexual growth into a 'soul' " (p. 70). Here, D-503's "soul" is a figurative representation of his innate moral compass, the product of his "sexual growth."

Building on London's criticism of both *fin de siècle* utopianism and organized religion, *We* also satirizes the intersection of evangelism and colonialism, primarily through inversions of biblical themes and imagery. Other issues considered in this chapter include the author's problematic but thoughtful portrayal of women, and the tense juxtaposition of modernity and primitivism in the text.

Huxley's *Brave New World*, a novel with marked similarities to *We*, is the subject of Chap. 4. The book is the most superficially scientific of these dystopian novels. As one of the World Controllers admits, in OneState, scientific inquiry has been replaced by cookbook science that consistently produces a known result (Huxley 1932/1965, p. 173). Though superficially a satire of the Wellsian utopia, *Brave New World* presciently addresses the consequences of stupefying an entire society with banal amusements. Controlling the sex lives of the citizenry is the largest and most aggressively pursued political concern in Huxley's World State. This is done through satiation, not repression. Like Zamyatin, Huxley foresees a pain-free future in which the government controls people by gratifying rather than criminalizing their desires. Huxley's thinking anticipates a similar point that Herbert Marcuse presents more than thirty years later in *One-Dimensional Man*. Marcuse observes that economic and social totalitarianism are just as insidiously effective as overt repression:

> For "totalitarianism" is not only a terroristic political coordination of society, but also a non-terroristic economic technical coordination which operates through the manipulation of needs by vested interests. It thus precludes the emergence of an effective opposition against the whole. Not only a specific form of government or party rule makes for totalitarianism, but also a specific system of production and distribution (1964/1991, p. 3).

In *Brave New World*, as in *We*, such a system of production and distribution, rather than the will of some despot or group of oppressors, determines the direction of society; and, in both books, sex is similarly commodified. Huxley, as Booker makes clear, viewed this tendency as an outgrowth of unrestrained capitalism: "In the ultracapitalist society of *Brave New World* even human beings are thoroughly commodified. Sexuality is commodified as well. Deprived of any 'use value' through universal contraception, sexuality becomes an area of pure 'exchange value,' with sexual favors being freely traded like any commodity" (1994, p. 53). The political implications of impassioned connections between individuals are prevented by the reduction of sex from the culmination of a desire for one person to a series of routine orgasms with an endless stream of interchangeable partners.

Though the cold, methodical regimes of Zamyatin and Huxley can anticipate simple lust, they are threatened when a fundamentally unpredictable and often illogical attraction to one particular person arises. Conventional sex is freely available in these dystopias, but human dignity is undermined through the diminishment of the individual's irrational, ineffable capacity to desire. In the face of this demeaning policy of satiation, both Zamyatin and Huxley present a revival of sexual longing not just as a means of conceptualizing freedom but as the only way to restore what it means to be human.

The fraught erotic connection between the naturally born John the Savage and the genetically engineered Lenina Crowne forms the moral core of the novel. Lenina's forbidden monogamous tendencies reveal the limits of World State's genetic engineering and social conditioning, highlighting her significance as a social radical. While Lenina, unlike her namesake Vladimir Lenin, lacks a revolutionary ideology, sexual desire focuses her moral intuition. Despite having been insulted, rejected, and physically abused by John, Lenina comes to appreciate the wrong that her society has done to him by driving him to his hermitage and then invading his privacy. The tears that she sheds when she perceives John's misery and the outstretched arms with which she seeks to embrace his suffering body reveal a capacity to empathize, validating the idea that her instinctive passion, unlike John's sententious anger, can catalyze social and ethical renewal. Although circumstance precludes the realization of a monogamous relationship between Lenina and John, Huxley—again anticipating the theories of Marcuse—suggests that the deferral of sexual gratification can be an aspirational and ultimately enlightening force.

Though the differences between *Brave New World* and *Nineteen Eighty-Four* are stark, and the two texts are frequently compared in terms of which has provided a more accurate forecast of the future, Huxley and Orwell both illustrate the harmful effects of control of language on the libido as well as the mind. The authors' common attitude toward organized religion is another crucial similarity. Both Huxley and Orwell suggest that the common Christian attitude toward sexuality impedes individual and communal development. Booker (1994) points out that according to Huxley, "conventional Christian morality" stunts and precludes the development of substantive bonds among people as effectively as the licentious policies of World State: "For Huxley, both the repression of sexuality in conventional Christian morality and the devaluation of sex in his amoral, materialistic dystopia represent obstacles to the achievement of genuine intersubjective attachments" (p. 54). Like its predecessor, this chapter addresses the way the author, though eschewing religious faith, appropriates well-known religious tropes to imbue his story with hope.

Katharine Burdekin's *Swastika Night*, discussed at length in Chap. 5, envisions the long-term effects of Nazi ideology. Providing a dubious challenge to the accepted nexus between Nazism and anti-Semitism, Burdekin alleges that the veneration of masculinity is the cause of both the Third Reich and totalitarianism in general. As Claeys explains, by satirizing a proudly androcentric polity, Burdekin anticipates subsequent developments in speculative literature: "*Swastika Night* (1937) is generally viewed as the most significant English-language anti-Nazi novel. It also marks a milestone in the feminist turn in dystopian criticism, anticipating that treatment of gender themes which would become increasingly common in later dystopian writing" (2017, pp. 349–350).

Building on the various feminist readings of this novel, I argue that Burdekin introduces sociopolitical enlightenment, ethics, and hope via queer desire. While she makes a compelling case for gender equality, her investment in gay desire causes the reader to confront the damaging effects of homophobia as well as misogyny on society. Sargent and Sargisson observe that heteronormative forms of sexual resistance dominate the canon of speculative literature: "sexual relationships in canonical utopias have been overwhelmingly heterosexual" (2014, p. 301). This makes *Swastika Night* doubly remarkable for foregrounding both feminist and queer resistance to social oppression. In the novel, Hermann, a loyal Nazi, becomes enamored of Alfred, a charismatic and disaffected Englishman.

Hermann sacrifices his good name, livelihood, and ultimately his life to protect Alfred and his egalitarian cause.

Hermann's illicit passion for an underling of a subjugated people, an attachment running contrary to decades of social, religious, and psychological conditioning, humanizes and ennobles him. If sexual desire can convert such a privileged loyalist, its efficacy is potentially limitless in scope. By depicting Hermann's desire as a physical attraction, Burdekin presents queerness as organic rather than situational, differentiating herself from a range of mid-century intellectuals who misunderstood homosexuality as a conscious choice, a disorder, or a circumstantial phenomenon. Through Hermann's natural, life-affirming romantic connection to Alfred, Burdekin suggests that acceptance of queerness is as necessary as equality between the sexes for justice and social stability.

While this chapter addresses how *Swastika Night* draws on the utopian fiction of Wells and Bellamy, it also examines the ways in which Burdekin anticipates important facets of both *Nineteen Eighty-Four* and *The Handmaid's Tale*, such as the use of colored clothing to mark class status. Chapter 5 also examines some of *Swastika Night*'s deficiencies, including its failure to acknowledge anti-Semitism and its overly idealistic conception of socialism, in particular its favorable view of Stalin's Soviet Russia. Equally troubling is Burdekin's ambivalence toward English imperialism, which borders at times on apologism and reveals a jingoistic belief in the moral superiority of the English people. Burdekin also shows ableist tendencies by making an insecure disabled man the villain of the story. Nevertheless, *Swastika Night* remains illuminating as an indictment of the artificiality of contemporary gender norms, illustrating how these spurious ideas of self and other can be discredited, and what can be individually and collectively gained through doing so.

In Chap. 6 I analyze Ayn Rand's wildly popular *Anthem*, which—apart from being a vivid, compelling dystopia—succinctly summarizes her so-called philosophy of objectivism. As Susan Love Brown (2006) noted almost ten years ago, *Anthem* is widely read but rarely the subject of serious scholarship: "More than three and a half million copies of *Anthem* are in print, and the book sells more than 100,000 copies each year. Over the past decade, studies of Rand's novels have grown, but there is still very little written about *Anthem*" (p. 71). Like Wells, Rand foresaw social liberation in the technology of the future, yet she rejects Wells's ideal of a socialist world state managed by an elite class of technocrats, advocating instead for a particularly extreme version of Social Darwinism.

Despite the sociopolitical differences between her and the other authors considered in this study, Rand shares their belief in the power of illicit desire to enlighten and ennoble. As it does in the projected political fictions of Huxley and Orwell, sexual desire for a renegade woman alters the narrator's moral perspective. Here, however, the desire is reflexively phallic. Far from possessing stereotypically feminine curves, the object of the narrator's desire is thin and straight as iron; her eyes are hard; and her demeanor is merciless, blending both pain and pleasure into a kind of sexualized sadism. Her body mirrors the "straight and thin and hard and strong" limbs of the protagonist, which he describes as his "beauty" (Rand 1938/2013, p. 36), indicating that it is her severe masculine attributes that make her beautiful to the narrator. Through the protagonist's narcissistic gaze, sexual desire for the putative other emerges as male appreciation of the self, revealing both a distaste for feminism and a distortion of queerness.

Jacques Lacan's theory of the Mirror Stage clarifies the crucial link between the realization of self and the valorization of selfishness in the novel. When Rand's protagonist, like his mythological antecedent, sees his reflection for the first time in a pool of water, his passage through the Mirror Stage readies him for the final part of his mental and spiritual development: the acquisition of previously inaccessible language. Rand's emphasis on the revolutionary power of forbidden words echoes Huxley and prefigures Orwell. Presenting her narrator as a male version of the genius she believed herself to be, Rand concludes her otherwise engaging and graceful story with a lengthy monologue on the merits of individualism, partially undermining *Anthem*'s subtlety and power.

Chapter 6 concludes that at the heart of Rand's philosophy of self-reliance is a masochistic love for masculinity, the very tendency that Burdekin presents in *Swastika Night* as the cause of totalitarianism. Yet Rand shares with Burdekin a troubling investment in both imperialism and the superiority of Western culture. While *Anthem*'s cultural and economic claims are questionable, its socioeconomic values still influence contemporary political discourse and policy.

As I illustrate in Chap. 7, *Nineteen Eighty-Four* is, like the other books in this study, constructed around a sexual relationship between an orthodox and a radical character. Here, however, the emphasis is on social class rather than gender and sexuality (as in *Swastika Night*), economic theory (as in *Anthem* and *The Iron Heel*), or the debasing consequences of immediate gratification coupled with labor-saving technology (as in *We* and *Brave New World*). Unlike many critics who see this novel as bleak, I argue that the hope embedded in the story becomes clear when we consider that the Party's claims about its strength, about the political ineffectualness of the proles, and about the impossibility of revolution are all unverifiable propaganda and probably untrue. Although Winston and Julia are ultimately lost, I maintain that Orwell locates a durable system of ethics in the working class, a system sustained by the workers' incorruptible sexual autonomy. The Party, possibly at considerable risk, takes an arrogantly indifferent attitude toward the working class. As Steven Edelheit (1975/1979) points out, "Whatever the Party does, the proles maintain their sanity and their sensuality [....] Like Julia, the proles possess an unqualified, undistorted sexual instinct" (pp. 175–176). This incorruptible, instinctive sensuality allows the proles to think and behave responsibly, unlike both O'Brien, who will do anything for the Party, and Winston, who will do anything to subvert it.

Finding ethics in eroticism, Orwell indicts religious institutions that, as self-proclaimed arbiters of morality, repress sexuality and promote totalitarian ways of thinking. Orwell found Catholicism's repression and distortion of the sexual instinct terrifying because, as Jonathan Rose (2005) points out, Orwell believed that sexual repression was the root cause of totalitarianism: "The conclusion was inescapable: far ahead of Foucault, without reading Wilhelm Reich, and well before he had read Yevgeny Zamyatin, Orwell grasped that sexual repression was the foundation of totalitarianism, and sexual freedom the key to political liberation" (p. 28). Although I concur with Rose, I argue that Orwell also viewed sexual freedom as the key to ethical liberation and as an antidote to the corrupting influence of religious faith. Despite the claims of organized religion, Orwell understood that belief in the supernatural did not facilitate morality. By conditioning people to accept precepts unsupported by evidence and by fostering a herd mentality, religiosity, in Orwell's view, tends to impede both moral discernment and the ability to reason critically. Rather than turning to scripture, Orwell found morality in the instincts of ordinary people, a point he makes clear in a letter to Humphry House sent in April of 1940:

> In any case the churches no longer have any hold on the working class, except perhaps for the Catholic Irish labourers. On the other hand you can always appeal to common decency, which the vast majority of people believe in without the need to tie it up with any transcendental belief. (1940/1968a, p. 530)

The persistence of such common decency in *Nineteen Eighty-Four* indicates a subtle undercurrent of optimism, even though political change is unrealized. For Orwell, the moral value of sexual desire exceeds its political potential.

Even when consummation seems impossible, sexual desire functions as a self-actualizing force in *Nineteen Eighty-Four*. As Marcuse's theories of erotic cognition make clear, in repressive societies such as Burdekin's German Empire, Orwell's Oceania, and Atwood's Gilead, sexual desire is routinely frustrated. Consequently, libidinal satisfaction becomes a fundamental goal that can serve as an opening to more ambitious dreams and sophisticated objectives. In short, Marcuse argues that sexual frustration is a positive and oddly liberating motivational force (1964/1991, p. 73). For example, in *Nineteen Eighty-Four*, Winston's sexual attraction to the seemingly unobtainable Julia leads him to envision a fecund utopian landscape, which he calls "The Golden Country," where they can love but also *live* freely. The larger aspirations of desire can be sociopolitical, not just physical.

This chapter also addresses the sexual component of Winston's relationship with O'Brien, which manifests itself most clearly during the latter's torture of the former. While Robinson finds little chemistry in Winston and Julia's affair, he emphasizes the eroticism of Winston's bond with O'Brien: "*Nineteen Eighty-Four* does, however, contain scenes of genuine erotic power. They occur not between Winston and Julia but between Winston and O'Brien [....] Winston's relationship with O'Brien takes the literary form of an illicit courtship. Perhaps this is simply because illicit sex and political conspiracy share a similar experiential structure" (1983, p. 155). In developing this line of thought, I address Orwell's somewhat problematic portrayal of gay desire.

By exploring intersections of classism and sexism in *The Handmaid's Tale*, Margaret Atwood incorporates Orwell's subtle analysis of social hierarchies into her work while departing from his less sympathetic treatment of gender and non-heteronormative passion. In Atwood's Gilead, a man's access to women's bodies marks and defines his sociopolitical status, stripping relationships of their companionate nature, while class distinctions, such as those between Wives, Aunts, Marthas, Handmaids and Econowives, are the biggest impediment to female solidarity. Following Orwell's lead, Atwood presents totalitarianism as inherently theocratic, since emulating religious institutions empowers political leaders to revise and reshape history in the interests of the regime. In the spirit of Orwell's socialism, Atwood's dystopia offers a compelling critique of capitalism and privatization. Atwood also reworks an important aspect of Orwellian thought by having her narrator embrace doublethink as a means of preserving, rather than undercutting, sanity.

As with *Swastika Night*, Atwood's dystopia addresses how tyranny affects men and women in different ways and to different degrees. Men in Gilead are subjected to classism and other institutional limitations, even though the regime affords them certain powers and privileges denied to women. By showing that the dehumanization of women depends in part on the reductive idea that men take only a sexual interest in them, Atwood suggests that men have a vested interest in being feminists.

Like the other chapters, this one stresses the importance of a sexual relationship between a conservative character and a renegade. Here again, the radical is a woman, but she tells the story. I argue that it is the bizarre sexual relationship between the narrator and the Commander that awakens her moral sensibilities and inspires her to leave her record. Under the pretense of having illicit fun, the narrator and the Commander vigorously debate social and political issues. The narrator's assignations with the Commander give her the requisite information to tell her tale, including secrets about the government and what motivates those who run it, facts about her ill-fated predecessor, and knowledge of clandestine spaces where she discovers what became of her best friend. The Commander never disavows the tenets of his society, but his sexual transgressions inflame his arrogance, causing him to take unnecessary risks that bring about his eventual trial and execution for treason. Reversing Orwell's gender roles, Atwood casts the Commander as a revolutionary from the waist downward. In discussing the revolutionary and rejuvenating potential of sexual desire in this novel, I use Freud's work to elucidate the ludic perversions that eclipse intercourse when societal mores reduce sex to a dispassionate procreative process.

Atwood's contribution, like Burdekin's before her, defies the traditional androcentric paradigm of projected political fiction. To differing extents, London, Zamyatin, Huxley, Rand, and Orwell present female characters as objects of male desire. As unsettling as this is, it should be remembered that the modern Women's Movement had yet to emerge during the period when most of these books were written, so it is perhaps unfair to condemn these writers for lacking our post-Sexual Revolution sensibilities. In most of these books, even the most sexualized women are presented as freethinking and independent. Characters such as Atwood's

Offred, Orwell's Julia, Rand's Gaea, and Zamyatin's I-330 are insightful enough to become revolutionaries of their own accord despite overwhelming government propaganda, conditioning, and terror tactics. They are sources of wisdom as well as sensuality; their relationships with their lovers are as didactic as they are erotic.

Although the sexual relationships in this literature are frequently, though not always, tragic, the hope that they enable generates a redeeming sense of social responsibility. In *We*, this promise vests in an unborn child. In *The Iron Heel* and *Swastika Night*, it survives in clandestine manuscripts preserved by underground communities. In *Brave New World*, it emerges through the portrayal of John the Savage as a latter-day, secular John-the-Baptist figure. In *Anthem* and *Nineteen Eighty-Four*, it comes about through a renewal and expansion of language. In *The Handmaid's Tale*, it survives via the novel's ambiguous conclusion and the narrator's apparent escape. These novels do not specifically show or explain how the transition to a better world comes about, yet they all imbue individuals and occasionally small communities with a rudimentary moral framework arising out of the revolutionary potential inherent in sexual desire. These dystopian classics illustrate a surprising progression from lust to resistance to virtue.

References

Atwood, M. (1986). *The Handmaid's Tale*. Boston, MA: Houghton Mifflin.
Atwood, M. (2004, May). *The Handmaid's Tale* and *Oryx and Crake* in Context. *PMLA, 119*(3), 513–517.
Baker, R. S. (1990). *Brave New World: History, Science, and Dystopia*. Boston, MA: Twayne Publishers.
Booker, M. K. (1994). *The Dystopian Impulse in Modern Literature: Fiction as Social Criticism*. Westport, CT: Greenwood Press.
Brown, S. L. (2006). Essays on Ayn Rand's Fiction. *The Journal of Ayn Rand Studies, 8*(1), 63–84.
Browning, G. (1970). Toward a Set of Standards for Everlasting Anti-Utopian Fiction. *Cithara, 10*(1), 18–32.
Claeys, G. (2011). The Origins of Dystopia: Wells, Huxley and Orwell. In G. Claeys (Ed.), *The Cambridge Companion to Utopian Literature* (3rd ed., pp. 107–131). Cambridge: Cambridge University Press.
Claeys, G. (2017). *Dystopia: A Natural History*. Oxford: Oxford University Press.
Deleuze, G., & Guattari, F. (1983). *Anti-Oedipus* (R. Hurley, M. Seem, & H. R. Lane, Trans.). Minneapolis, MN: University of Minnesota Press. (Original work published 1972)

Diken, B. (2011). Huxley's *Brave New World*—And Ours. *Journal for Cultural Research*, 15(2), 153–172.
Edelheit, S. (1979). *Dark Prophecies*. New York, NY: Revisionist Press. (Original work published 1975)
Foucault, M. (1978). *The History of Sexuality, Volume 1* (R. Hurley, Trans.). New York, NY: Random House. (Original work published 1976)
Foucault, M. (2001). Friendship as a Way of Life (J. Johnson, Trans.). In C. Kraus & S. Lotringer (Eds.), *Hatred of Capitalism: A Semiotext(e) Reader* (pp. 297–303). Los Angeles: Semiotext(e). (Original work published April 1981)
Goodwin, S. W., & Jones, L. F. (1990). Preface. In S. W. Goodwin & L. F. Jones (Eds.), *Feminism, Utopia, and Narrative* (pp. ix–x). Knoxville, TN: The University of Tennessee Press.
Gottlieb, E. (2001). *Dystopian Fiction East and West*. Montreal: McGill-Queen's University Press.
Huxley, A. (1965). *Brave New World*. New York, NY: Harper & Row. (Original work published 1932)
Lefanu, S. (1988). *In the Chinks of the World Machine: Feminism & Science Fiction*. London: The Women's Press.
London, J. (1980). *The Iron Heel*. Chicago, IL: Lawrence Hill Books. (Original work published 1907)
Marcuse, H. (1991). *One Dimensional Man*. Boston, MA: Beacon Press. (Original work published 1964)
Meckier, J. (2011). *Aldous Huxley, from Poet to Mystic*. Berlin: Lit Verlag.
Ní Dhúill, C. (2010). *Sex in Imagined Spaces: Gender and Utopia from More to Bloch*. London: Legenda.
Orwell, G. (1968a). Letter to Humphry House. In S. Orwell & I. Angus (Eds.), *An Age Like This, 1920–1940: The Collected Essays, Journalism & Letters, Vol. 1* (pp. 529–532). New York, NY: Harcourt Brace Jovanovich. (Original work dated 11 April 1940)
Orwell, G. (1968b). Notes on the Way. In S. Orwell & I. Angus (Eds.), *My Country Right or Left, 1940–1943: The Collected Essays, Journalism & Letters, Vol. 2* (pp. 15–18). New York, NY: Harcourt Brace Jovanovich. (Original work published 6 April 1940)
Orwell, G. (1968c). The Prevention of Literature. In S. Orwell & I. Angus (Eds.), *In Front of Your Nose, 1945–1950: The Collected Essays, Journalism & Letters, Vol. 4* (pp. 59–72). New York, NY: Harcourt Brace Jovanovich. (Original work published 2 January 1946)
Orwell, G. (1968d). Review: We by E. I. Zamyatin. In S. Orwell & I. Angus (Eds.), *In Front of Your Nose, 1945–1950: The Collected Essays, Journalism & Letters, Vol. 4* (pp. 72–76). New York, NY: Harcourt Brace Jovanovich. (Original work published 4 January 1946)

Orwell, G. (1977). *Nineteen Eighty-Four*. New York: Harcourt Brace Jovanovich. (Original work published 1949)

Orwell, G. (2000). The Edge of the Abyss by Alfred Noyes. In S. Orwell & I. Angus (Eds.), *As I Please, 1943–1945: The Collected Essays, Journalism & Letters, Vol. 3* (pp. 99–101). Jaffrey, NH: Nonpareil Books. (Original work published 27 February 1944)

Pagetti, C. (1990). In the Year of Our Lord Hitler 720: Katharine Burdekin's Swastika Night. *Science Fition Studies, 17,* 360–369.

Parrinder, P. (2011). Utopia and Romance. In G. Claeys (Ed.), *The Cambridge Companion to Utopian Literature* (3rd ed., pp. 154–173). Cambridge: Cambridge University Press.

Plank, W. (1984). Orwell and Huxley; Social Control Through Standardized Eroticism. *Recovering Literature, 12,* 29–39.

Rand, A. (2013). *Anthem*. Lexington, KY: Denton & White. (Original work published 1938)

Robinson, P. (1983). For the Love of Big Brother: The Sexual Politics of Nineteen Eighty Four. In P. Stansky (Ed.), *On Nineteen Eighty-Four* (pp. 148–158). New York, NY: W.H. Freeman and Company.

Rose, J. (2005). Abolishing the Orgasm: Orwell and the Politics of Sexual Persecution. In T. Cushman & J. Rodden (Eds.), *George Orwell: Into the Twenty-First Century* (pp. 23–44). Boulder, CO: Paradigm Publishers.

Sargent, L. T., & Sargisson, L. (2014). Sex in Utopia: Eutopian and Dystopian Sexual Relations. *Utopian Studies, 25*(1), 299–320.

Steinhoff, W. (1975). *George Orwell and the Origins of 1984*. Ann Arbor, MI: The University of Michigan Press.

Suvin, D. (2003). Reflections on What Remains of Zamyatin's We After the Change of Leviathans: Must Collectivism Be Against People? In M. S. Barr (Ed.), *Envisioning the Future: Science Fiction and the Next Millenium* (pp. 51–82). Middleton, CT: Wesleyan University Press.

Zamyatin, Y. (1993). *We* (C. Brown, Trans.). New York, NY: Penguin. (Original work published 1924)

CHAPTER 2

The Sexualized Proletariat in Jack London's *The Iron Heel*

Published in 1908, Jack London's *The Iron Heel* comments on familiar trends in contemporary society: the enervation of both workers' rights and labor unions; the collusion of corporate and religious institutions to find moral and philosophical justifications for economic exploitation; the defunding and deterioration of public education; the loss of objectivity in the mass media; and the ossification of class distinctions into a hereditary caste system. Gorman Beauchamp (1981) points out that, taken together, these strategies amount to a comprehensive process of privatization designed to concentrate wealth and power in the fewest hands (p. 96). Jonathan Auerbach (2006) argues that London was among the first to see how easily, subtly, and rapidly various putatively independent social institutions could quickly coalesce into what he terms a "corporatist state" (p. xiv). London presciently recognized that while each class has its own particular needs and priorities, the middle class, at least from a strictly economic standpoint, has more in common with the proletariat than the rich. London's literary reputation rests on his depictions of the struggle for survival in harsh naturalistic environments, but he also merits recognition for satirizing the feral nature of unrestrained capitalism.

H. Bruce Franklin (1980) distinguishes London from other turn-of-the-century socialists by emphasizing the author's belief that electoral victories would be ineffective against the power and influence of the plutocrats (p. v). Beauchamp notes that by emphasizing the idea that meaningful

© The Author(s) 2018
T. Horan, *Desire and Empathy in Twentieth-Century Dystopian Fiction*, Palgrave Studies in Utopianism,
https://doi.org/10.1007/978-3-319-70675-7_2

reform would depend on violent conflict, London breaks with the utopian socialists of the *fin de siècle* and revives an earlier Marxist perspective: "The scientific socialism of Marx had exposed [...] the inevitability of class conflict as the dynamic of all historical change—conflict not willed by individual men, and therefore not amenable to conscious choice, but ordained by the materialist dialectic of history" (1981, p. 93). The zest for violent revolution in *The Iron Heel* echoes the concluding paragraph of Karl Marx and Freidrich Engels's *The Communist Manifesto*: "The Communists disdain to conceal their views and aims. They openly declare that their ends can be attained only by the forcible overthrow of all existing conditions. Let the ruling classes tremble at a communistic revolution" (1848/1998, p. 77).

While subscribing to the Marxist notion that a just, communal society must arise through bloodshed, the novel does present a utopian destiny for humankind. Indeed, for a dystopian book, *The Iron Heel* is surprisingly utopian in tone and structure. Like many utopian novels, and even some dystopian novels with pronounced utopian sentiments, such as Burdekin's *Swastika Night*, much of *The Iron Heel* consists of long didactic conversations and debates between the story's democratic-minded hero and characters who, for different reasons, are invested in the dominant hegemony. Though what he produces is occasionally reductive and crude, London makes a serious and often successful attempt to make Marxist philosophy accessible to everyone through the conventions of the popular novel.

Although London's would-be manifesto influenced *Nineteen Eighty-Four*, Orwell (1946/1968a) was well aware of its deficiencies:

> *The Iron Heel* is not a good book, and on the whole its predictions have not been borne out. Its dates and its geography are ridiculous, and London makes the mistake, which was usual at that time, of assuming that revolution would break out first in the highly industrialized countries. (p. 24)

These shortcomings aside, Orwell, like his contemporaries on the left, recognized that London's dystopian novel offered an early forecast of fascism (1946/1968a, p. 24).

While London was remarkably perceptive in his assessment of the extreme right, he overestimated the appeal of the progressive left. *The Iron Heel* reflects the author's naïve, overly sanguine belief that the urban proletariat would rapidly and overwhelmingly embrace socialism in the near future. For example, it depicts the socialist party winning control of

Congress in 1912 by a landslide (London 1907/1980, p. 129). London shows no awareness of the deep sociopolitical conservatism of the working class and its emotional and psychological investment in the rhetoric of laissez-faire economics, even when the harsh inequities of capitalism differ considerably from the meritocratic rhetoric surrounding it.

Nevertheless, like Orwell, London, through the words of the novel's protagonist Ernest Everhard, presents the workers as fundamentally unconquerable:

> Our strength, the strength of the proletariat, is in our muscles, in our hands to cast ballots, in our fingers to pull triggers. This strength we cannot be stripped of. It is the primitive strength, it is the strength that is to life germane, it is the strength that is stronger than wealth, and that wealth cannot take away. (1907/1980, p. 99)

London likewise finds the lineaments of socialism, the ultimate cooperative endeavor, in humanity's earliest communities, as Ernest explains:

> Combination is stronger than competition. Primitive man was a puny creature hiding in the crevices of the rocks. He combined and made war upon his carnivorous enemies. They were competitive beasts. Primitive man was a combinative beast, and because of it he rose to primacy over all the animals. And man has been achieving greater and greater combinations ever since. It is combination *versus* competition, a thousand centuries long struggle, in which competition has always been worsted. Whoso enlists on the side of competition perishes. (London 1907/1980, p. 85, emphasis in original)

In the spirit of Wells, if not Orwell, London presents democratic socialism as an inevitable consequence of rational human development, but he foresees it coming only in the distant future following much bloodshed. He also differentiates himself from contemporaries such as Frank Norris and Willa Cather, who saw so-called primitive societies as individualistic and competitive rather than cooperative.

The Iron Heel embodies the hope that pervades the start of a new century by presenting a sexual relationship between characters initially at opposite ends of the societal spectrum that triggers what in the long run develops into a successful revolution against the authoritarian state. Like Orwell's *Nineteen Eighty-Four*, *The Iron Heel* was written for an immediate purpose. Although the novel presents a contemporary manuscript that has been edited and annotated by someone living centuries from now, it is not a confident prediction of the distant future like Huxley's *Brave New World* or even Zamyatin's *We*. Francis Shor (1996) points out that London always maintained that he "didn't write [...] [*The Iron Heel*] as a prophecy at all" (p. 75). Moreover, as Orwell (1940/1968b) makes clear, London did not anticipate the fanatical nationalism that partially defined fascism preceding and during World War II: "It is mere a tale of capitalist oppression, and it was written at a time when various things that have made Fascism possible—for instance, the tremendous revival of nationalism—were not easy to foresee" (p. 30).

Instead, London attempted to alert the working class to the danger of reactionary tendencies that would ultimately merge into something virtually indistinguishable from fascism, which Franklin (1980) defines as "the form that the capitalist state assumes when its oligarchy feels that its economic and political power is seriously threatened by working-class revolution" (p. ii). Like Burdekin, London took an expansive view of the roots and long-term implications of right-wing ideologies. Both authors thought that fascism would drag humanity back to a condition resembling feudalism: "The small manufacturer is like the farmer; and small manufacturers and farmers today are reduced, to all intents and purposes, to feudal tenure" (London 1907/1980, p. 100). Further, both *The Iron Heel* and *Swastika Night* serve as enduring reminders that Adolf Hitler's government should not define and limit our conception of fascism. Fascism, whether it is identified by that name or not, remains possible. *The Iron Heel* is prophylactic rather than prophetic in tone.

In London's dystopia, the capitalist elite of the USA seize power and form a hereditary oligarchy, which the socialists call "the Iron Heel." Two failed attempts to overthrow the Iron Heel form the backdrop of this story about the long struggle for democratic socialism. The plot initially centers on the love that develops between Avis Cunningham, a privileged ingénue, and Ernest Everhard, a working-class intellectual and socialist politician. The narrative is presented as an incomplete manuscript authored clandestinely by Avis shortly after her husband's death. The paradigm of the annotated manuscript is useful because it enables the author to indicate that the dystopian regime will fall without obliging them to indicate exactly when and how that fall will come about. According to John Whalen-Bridge (1992), London's use of this literary convention was not entirely well received when *The Iron Heel* was published but ultimately influenced other authors of dystopian fiction:

One 1908 reviewer found "hackneyed" the "prophecy" and "found manuscript" conventions which were praised in recent novels such as Orwell's *Nineteen Eighty-Four* (1949) and Margaret Atwood's *The Handmaid's Tale*. Thus, the late twentieth century predisposition toward the prophetic school tends to obstruct our view of the novel as it would have been read by its original audience. (p. 67)

In keeping with London's paradigm, Orwell's *Nineteen Eighty-Four* concludes with a scholarly appendix discussing the linguistic policies of the Party in the past tense, and Atwood's *The Handmaid's Tale* finishes with a lecture held at an academic conference years after the dystopian period in which the story is set. Because of the thematic and structural similarities between the dystopias of Orwell and London, Beauchamp argues that *The Iron Heel* "reads much like a prologue to *1984*" (1981, p. 92). Like the Inner Party of Orwell's Oceania, the ruling class in *The Iron Heel* sacrifices many of its own privileges to consolidate and perpetuate its power. What London failed to foresee was the extent to which the stigmatization of poverty would shame and demoralize the American proletariat. Few Americans in the early twenty-first century will even identify as working class, much less recognize that the laborer and the large shareholder do not necessarily benefit from the same policies.

Although it looks with some accuracy into the future, *The Iron Heel* is a work of projected political fiction, though, as Alessandro Portelli (1982) notes, this kind of speculative fiction anticipates contemporary science fiction to some extent:

Between the year of the Haymarket Riot, 1886, and that of conservative restauration, 1896, more than 100 works of a utopian character were published in the US alone [....] The mention of H.G. Wells's name in *The Iron Heel* is there to remind us that the imagination of those years was also laying the foundations of contemporary Science Fiction. (pp. 180–181)

While it does not emphasize technological advancement, London's dystopia does look favorably on Wells's faith in the leadership abilities of those with scientific training. Tony Barley (1995) emphasizes that, as an intellectual, London strove to emulate Wells: "Whenever London departs from Marxism in his speculative social fiction, he proves a Wellsian copyist" (p. 154). Wells is explicitly praised by the annotator of the Everhard manuscript, Anthony Meredith. Through him the reader learns that Wells's work is still valued seven centuries after the events presented in Avis's account: "Wells was a sociological seer, sane and normal as well as warm [....] Many fragments of his work have come down to us, while two of his greatest achievements, *Anticipations* and *Mankind in the Making*, have come down intact" (London 1907/1980, p. 159). Clearly, Wells's utopian writings inspired London, which is why most of the revolutionary leaders in *The Iron Heel* have had some type of scientific training.

Yet London understood the limitations of Wells's confidence in the liberating power of science. As Barley recognizes, London did not believe that Wells fully appreciated the determining influence that class warfare would have on the future:

> Wells's rejection of class struggle as the motive force of historical change and his belief in the constancy of a socially-transcendent 'human nature' leads to visions of the future in which alternately benevolent or malevolent castes of the élite instigate or prevent change, and govern by virtue of their superior intellect or sensibility. (1995, p. 154)

In contrast to Wells, London thought that the interests of the elite and the masses were fundamentally irreconcilable and that therefore tension between them arose naturally. When Ernest is asked by Bishop Morehouse why class conflict exists at all, he responds that it is endemic to human nature: "'Why should there be such a conflict?' the Bishop demanded warmly. Ernest shrugged his shoulders. 'Because we are so made, I guess'" (London 1907/1980, p. 22). In London's opinion, a social model (such as Wells's) that underestimates class antipathy is unrealistic.

Even if rational scientific thinking could, as Wells believed, enlighten everyone and unify humanity, both the masses and the plutocrats in *The Iron Heel* are either ignorant or dismissive of the sociological value of science. As Ernest tells Avis, those who thrive in a capitalist society cannot grasp the implications of their behavior due to their ignorance of science:

> The weakness in their position lies in that they are merely business men. They are not philosophers. They are not biologists or sociologists. If they were, of course all would be well. A business man who was also a biologist and a sociologist would know, approximately, the right thing to do for humanity. But, outside the realm of business, these men are stupid. (London 1907/1980, p. 46)

Johan Heje (2002) points out that after World War I, a conflict in which technology was harnessed by both sides for mass destruction, it seemed naïve to argue that scientific training made people rational and good; dystopian literature consequently became more critical of Wells's and London's shared attitude toward the ameliorative nature of scientific progress (pp. 169–172). Furthermore, the lack of scientific training among the privileged that Ernest bemoans is more pronounced among the working class, the very people who must be persuaded to act swiftly and cooperatively for socialism to triumph. Although he appreciates the importance of a scientific education and the political wisdom it imparts, London—through Ernest's failed attempts to enlighten others—suggests that scientists can be crushed as easily as the electorate beneath the iron heel of the plutocrats.

Just as Wells envisioned a scientific vanguard of genuine public servants, the tyrannical oligarchs in *The Iron Heel* are partially driven by delusions of altruism. Clearly they are forthright about their intention to crush the left with brute force. Like O'Brien in *Nineteen Eighty-Four*, the capitalist Wickson is intoxicated by and addicted to power:

> We are in power. Nobody will deny it. By virtue of that power we shall remain in power.... We will grind you revolutionists down under our heel.... There is the word. It is the king of words—Power. Not God, not Mammon, but Power. Pour it over your tongue till it tingles with it. Power. (London 1907/1980, p. 63)

But unlike Orwell's O'Brien, who views power as an end in itself, these plutocrats see the brutal exercise of power as necessary to the preservation of human civilization:

> The oligarchs... as a class... disciplined themselves.... They were taught, and later in turn taught, that... from beneath their feet rose always the subterranean rumbles of revolt... [which] they must dominate if humanity were to persist. They were the saviours of humanity, and they regarded themselves as heroic and sacrificing labourers for the highest good.... This has been the strength of the Iron Heel, and too many of the comrades have been slow or loathe to realize it... ascrib[ing] the strength of the Iron Heel to its system of reward and punishment. This is a mistake.... The great driving force of the oligarchs is the belief that they are doing right. (London 1907/1980, p. 190)

Intriguingly, this realization is lost on the science-minded Ernest Everhard, who ascribes the lowest possible motives to the oligarchs: "In the arid desert of commercialism [...] I found nothing but stupidity [...] monstrous selfishness and heartlessness, and a gross, gluttonous, practised, and practical materialism" (London 1907/1980, p. 55). Ernest believes the oligarchs are simply thugs in tailored suits. That Ernest's wellborn wife, Avis, clearly comprehends the nature of the Iron Heel may simply suggest that as a former member of the upper class she can intuitively grasp its intentions. But her cognizance could also indicate that London believed that women were more politically savvy in certain ways than men.

It is, after all, women who succeeded in preventing war between the USA and Germany through their support of a general strike: "the women proved to be the strongest promoters of the strike. They set their faces against the war" (London 1907/1980, p. 135). Additionally, Barley points out that women were among the most effective fighters in the resistance: "Women revolutionaries such as the 'slender girl' Madeline Provence and 'The Red Virgin' Anna Roylston prove the most dauntless avengers" (1995, p. 165). Little wonder then that Avis proves to be a more effective revolutionary than her husband. Nevertheless, Auerbach discounts the idea that an undercurrent of feminism runs through the text:

> While it might be argued from a feminist slant that the hero's unexpected disappearance from the narrative's climax allows the heroine Avis to come into her own and play a primary role for the first time rather than a supporting one, the fact is that during these scenes of violence she is still accompanied by male revolutionist companions, who act to protect and save her from the rampaging mob. (2006, p. xvi)

Yet having Avis work alongside male colleagues during the uprising in Chicago indicates that London believed that women should and would play an essential role in the revolution, which is why, in Whalen-Bridge's opinion, London chose Avis, rather than Ernest or Anthony Meredith, to tell the story of the nascent socialist movement in his imagined America: "London presents us, word for word, with Avis Everhard's view more than that of any other character [....] London, writing before women had the right to vote, imagined a future in which several women play key roles in the resistance to the absolutely patriarchal Oligarchy" (1992, p. 72). Avis and Ernest play complementary roles in the struggle. That these roles are defined in part by gender is problematic, but when removed from Avis, Ernest's deficiencies—a byproduct of his exaggerated manliness—become apparent.

Though courageous and clever, Ernest is as much a straw man as a hero, and his thinking is somewhat inconsistent. In his debate with Wickson, for instance, Ernest seems as bedazzled by raw power as his imperious adversary:

> Power will be the arbiter, as it always has been the arbiter. It is a struggle of classes [....] It does not matter whether it is in one year, ten, or a thousand—your class will be dragged down. And it shall be done by power. We of the labour hosts have conned that word over till our minds are all a-tingle with it. Power. It is a kingly word. (London 1907/1980, p. 64)

Admitting so freely that he is captivated by power and seeing it in absolute, "kingly" terms reveals that Ernest has no conception of the extent to which power can corrupt those who wield it.

As Auerbach observes, the draconian methods of exercising power employed by the resistance are for the most part indistinguishable from those used by the Iron Heel: "the violence here retains a strange kind of logic whereby revolutionists and state oligarchs effectively mirror one another in their covert operations" (2006, p. xv). Avis readily concedes that many revolutionaries remain loyal out of fear: "In fact, so terrible did we make ourselves, that it became a greater peril to betray us than to remain loyal to us" (London 1907/1980, p. 158). We are told that the insurgents love the cause, but to ensure their loyalty the penalties imposed by the socialists are even harsher than those meted out by the Iron Heel, a regime whose enemies vanish without a trace (London 1907/1980, p. 157). On the one hand, Avis stresses the socialists' unwavering adherence to due process: "No agent of the Iron Heel was executed without a trial. We may have made mistakes, but if so, very rarely" (London 1907/1980, p. 155); yet shortly after making this boast, she proudly tells of the cold-blooded murder of a government agent, who doesn't even receive a hearing, let alone a fair trial:

> He captured the spy, and as to what then happened Carlson gave us a fair idea. "I fixed him," was Carlson's unimaginative way of describing the affair. "I fixed him," he repeated, while a sombre light burnt in his eyes, and his huge, toil-distorted hands opened and closed eloquently. "He made no noise. I hid him, and tonight I will go back and bury him deep." (London 1907/1980, p. 176)

This impromptu killing, despite all of the lip service paid to fair trials, highlights the discrepancy between the idealistic rhetoric of the socialists and their actual behavior; in that sense the revolutionaries are very like the Iron Heel and the propaganda machine justifying its rule. Orwell recognizes that only ideological discrepancies distinguish the two sides in a class war:

> A ruling class has got to have a strict morality, a quasi-religious belief in itself, a mystique [....] They can only maintain their position while they honestly believe that civilization depends on themselves alone, and therefore in a different way they are just as brave, able and devoted as the revolutionaries who oppose them. (1940/1968b, p. 31)

In support of revolution, Ernest employs and endorses tactics worthy of the Iron Heel: Biedenbach, one of Ernest's coconspirators, identifies as a "terrorist" (London 1907/1980, p. 186); Ernest himself is an unabashed "propagandist" (London 1907/1980, p. 118). Whalen-Bridge points out that London referred to the novel in these inflammatory terms, consequently diminishing its value in the eyes of literary critics: "London [...] generally referred to his 1908 dystopian fantasy as 'propaganda.'... [F]or literary critics propaganda is usually a pejorative word, often designating the degraded form of art which follows from the failure to separate artistic from political commitments" (1992, p. 67).

For London, socialist ends justify both savage and manipulative means, but neither the author nor the characters with whom he asks the reader to sympathize feel that they will be adversely affected by routinely resorting to unscrupulous behavior for expediency. According to Orwell, this is because London, although he opposed brutality, was intrinsically brutal himself: "London could foresee Fascism because he had a Fascist streak in himself: or at any rate a marked strain of brutality and an almost unconquerable preference for the strong man as against the weak man" (1946/1968a, p. 25). For London, brutality was not simply a necessary evil; it was, as Barley makes clear, also frequently an appealing one: "London does betray signs of gleeful, extravagant fascination with disguise and terrorism" (1995, p. 169).

Ernest's (and by implication London's) sense of human nature is equally paradoxical. When Bishop Morehouse speaks of the harmony that can exist between capital and labor, Ernest espouses a Hobbesian picture of human nature: "'Are you discussing the ideal man?' Ernest asked, '— unselfish and godlike, and so few in numbers as to be practically nonexistent, or are you discussing the common and ordinary average man [....] Who is weak and fallible, prone to error [....] And petty and selfish?'"

(London 1907/1980, p. 22). Yet Ernest contradicts his own grim assessment of humanity when he relates his experiences among the literate members of the working class:

> Amongst the revolutionists I found, also, warm faith in the human, ardent idealism, sweetness of unselfishness, renunciation, and martyrdom—all the splendid, stinging things of the spirit. Here life was clean, noble, and alive [....] All about me were nobleness of purpose and heroism of effort, and my days and nights were sunshine and starshine. (London 1907/1980, pp. 52–53)

Here again we find a strange incongruity: in spite of human nature, the socialists embrace "unselfishness, renunciation, and martyrdom," living solely to serve others. Yet, through Avis, the novel offers a polemic against charity:

> I did not concern myself with charity. I had become convinced that Ernest was right when he sneered at charity as a poulticing of an ulcer. Remove the ulcer was his remedy; give to the worker his product; pension as soldiers those who grow honourably old in their toil, and there will be no need for charity. (London 1907/1980, p. 123)

The notion that everyone can be self-sufficient under the right circumstances is characteristic of objectivism rather than utopian socialism. In London's critique of capitalism, humanity is naturally corrupt, yet when making his case for socialism, he posits that the exact opposite is true.

Just as he perceives human nature to be mutable, London also believes (unlike Orwell) that an individual's class affiliation can easily change. Ernest tells Berkeley professor John Cunningham that he, like Bishop Morehouse, will soon be a proletarian: "You are travelling the same path that Bishop Morehouse is, and towards a similar smash-up. You'll both be proletarians before you're done with it" (London 1907/1980, p. 69). Social class, of course, is determined by circumstance and lineage over the course of a lifetime. It is, as Orwell asserts in *The Road to Wigan Pier*, akin to a fixed characteristic that fundamentally affects how we see ourselves and the world (1937/1958, pp. 161–162). In presenting a string of characters, such as Avis, Bishop Morehouse, and John Cunningham, who change their social class simply by changing their thinking on specific issues but who do not become fundamentally different people in their new milieus, London—like the dubious hero of his dystopian novel—displays a simplistic understanding of class. For him, class is defined by little more than economics; one can move up or down the social hierarchy as easily as one's financial portfolio rises or falls.

London misunderstood the impediment that classism presents to the realization of democratic socialism, but he was not so naïve as to think that humanity progressed linearly from the ice age to the industrialized world. Like the Commanders of Atwood's Gilead, the Iron Heel is a new political order embracing archaism. This suggests that the ruling class possesses a deep-rooted fear of modernity akin to that found in *Swastika Night*, *Anthem*, *Nineteen Eighty-Four*, and *The Handmaid's Tale*, and distinct from the scientifically oriented, planned communities in *We* and *Brave New World*. In dystopian literature, either the past or the future is glorified at the expense of the present because the present is both the point in time at which oppression is imposed and the moment in which resistance to that oppression is acutely desirable.

Realizing the volatility of the present helps clarify why sex is perceived as such a danger to these totalitarian regimes. The orgasm is, after all, a completely immediate experience. Since controlling sexuality is the focus of governmental power, it comes as no surprise that *The Iron Heel*, like the other novels in this study, is fueled by an illicit relationship between an orthodox and a revolutionary character. Avis Everhard starts out a prominent, content socialite and ends up living and dying as a political fugitive due to her sexual cravings. Her story is as much a romance as an illustration of political theory. Whereas the other books in this study use a sexual relationship between a loyalist and a revolutionary as a mechanism for the underlying purpose of exploring political and ethical themes, here the plot is so lurid that London's socialist philosophy becomes almost a distraction from the tawdry romance. *The Iron Heel* reads like an amateurish piece of fiction by D. H. Lawrence, complete with the strapping, passionate proletarian who rejects the stale existence of the upper classes for "real life" among the common people and is consequently worshipped by the unfulfilled society girl whose mind and libido are stimulated by her working-class hero/lover. To London's thinking, the fascist juggernaut could be repelled only by the working class. He hoped that this book would be a widely read call to arms for the exploited, and it therefore made sense that he would write in a gripping, sensational style.

Like *The Handmaid's Tale*, *The Iron Heel* is set just a few years beyond the present in what was formerly the USA. In both stories, democracy has fallen victim to a rightwing dictatorship, but here, unlike in *The Handmaid's Tale*, the ruling caste, though served by organized religion, is secular:

> London imagines a proletarian revolution breaking out in the United States and being crushed, or partially crushed, by a counter-offensive of the capitalist class; and, following on this, a long period during which society is ruled by a small group of tyrants known as the Oligarchs, who are served by a kind of SS known as the Mercenaries. (Orwell 1946/1968a, p. 24)

Like Offred in *The Handmaid's Tale*, the narrator tells her story in journal form. She hails from what is fast becoming the oligarch class. Her lover, who has the fitting surname Everhard, initially looks like a putative working-class socialist, though closer examination reveals him to be a thinly disguised member of the middle-class intelligentsia.

In this sense, London's novel is somewhat self-contradictory. Its radical protagonist, by provocatively conjuring the image of grinding bodies, argues on the one hand that the middle class is small, powerless, and politically irrelevant: "The middle class is a pygmy between two giants. Don't you see, you poor perishing middle class, you are caught between the upper and nether millstones, and even now has the grinding begun" (London 1907/1980, p. 97). And yet, as Portelli argues, the working class is the segment of the population that appears most aimless and feeble in *The Iron Heel*: "Notwithstanding his revolutionary terminology, London offers a reformist image of social relationships: the working class does not appear as an active force in politics and production, but rather as a suffering, victimized class" (1982, p. 184). Concurring with Portelli, Auerbach notes that the proletariat is essentially absent from the text:

> Up until this final chaos of clashing bodies, in fact, the figure of the proletariat has remained conspicuously missing from the entire novel [....] Everhard earns his living through intellectual work—translating essays and giving speeches—not physical labor. Ernest and his circle of extraordinary comrades thus battle and speak on behalf of the masses but are not of them. (2006, p. xvii)

The novel actually affirms the importance of privilege in generating revolution by giving its firebrand the right pedigree and a cosmopolitan background:

> He had been born in the working class, though he was a descendant of the old line of Everhards that for over two hundred years had lived in America

[....] He was self-educated, had taught himself German and French [....] [H]is earnings were added to by the royalties from the small sales of his own economic and philosophical works. (London 1907/1980, p. 19)

Everhard ostensibly represents the disaffected, downtrodden laborer, but his employment, lineage, and attitude remove him completely from a typical working-class existence. While he speaks for those who toil in sweatshops, Everhard concerns himself with the rarified pursuits of philosophy, economics, and mastery of foreign languages. To Portelli, the irony is overwhelming: "Avis perceives him as a 'natural aristocrat' [...] a member of the closest thing America has to a blood aristocracy, the 'old American stock,' which is contrasted with a working-class identity more suited for recent immigrant stock" (1982, p. 185). Both Portelli and Auerbach are right to place special emphasis on London's idea of the "natural aristocrat," but this term should not be confused with the blue-blooded aristocrats of old. London's irregular use of status language is compelling, yet also peculiar and initially confusing.

The key to understanding London's sense of what it means to be an aristocrat is to focus on the adjective "natural." London believed that true aristocracy was defined by internal moral qualities coupled with roots deeply planted in the American land. Orwell recognizes that for London, intrinsic strength defines what it is to be noble: "He hated exploitation and hereditary privilege [....] [H]is instinct lay towards acceptance of a 'natural aristocracy' of strength, beauty and talent" (1946/1968a, p. 26). Ernest's toughness, his honesty, his perceptiveness, and most of all his loyalty to the socialist cause make him a natural aristocrat and render by comparison characters such as Wickson, Hammerfield, and Colonel Van Gilbert, whom the reader would normally think of as aristocratic in the genteel sense, base and venal.

Class issues are further complicated by the fact that though the story opens with Ernest attacking the "weird" bourgeois study of metaphysics (London 1907/1980, p. 11), he himself reads Immanuel Kant (London 1907/1980, p. 116), author of *Groundwork of the Metaphysic of Morals*, and earns enough through the translation of esoteric treatises to feed, clothe, and house three adults at a time when few can afford bread (London 1907/1980, pp. 118–119). Indeed, Ernest's "command of the field of knowledge" (London 1907/1980, p. 62) is such that he easily rises to the top of the social scale, but he readily rejects the hypocrisy and comfort of elite circles to embrace the authenticity of the hoi polloi:

Ernest went on to rise in society, till at last he came in touch with members of the upper classes and rubbed shoulders with the men who sat in the high places. Then came his disillusionment [....] Fresh from his revolutionists, he was shocked by the intellectual stupidity of the master class. (London 1907/1980, p. 53)

Caught between the corruption of the boss class and the ignorance of the worker, Ernest is nominally a man of the people but in reality a book-trained organizer for the people. Therein lies the paradox: Ernest must be gifted and educated enough to harness and direct the brute power of the so-called "people of the abyss," yet he himself must never succumb to the sort of bestial inclinations which they display during, for example, the Chicago Uprising (London 1907/1980, p. 213). Ernest must also be spared the common ignominy of an overtly violent or treacherous death, and so—like Elijah being whisked away by a whirlwind into heaven—he simply vanishes at the end of the story. Ernest is set apart from those whom he leads by a degree of refinement. Ironically, in attacking one caste system by condemning the middle and upper classes, London merely generates a new type of "natural" hegemony.

Ernest's sexuality must also maintain a complex balance between universal appeal and ultramasculinity. Ernest has to be charismatic and potent enough to attract men to his struggle, yet his overstated manliness cannot be exaggerated to the point of hinting at queerness. Scott Derrick (1996) argues that this unconventional sexualization of the male rather than the female body creates a tension throughout London's fiction whereby an implicit homoeroticism is delimited by the author's explicit homophobia:

> On the one hand [...] the reader of his tales and novels confronts a boundary-violating play of desire between masculinity and femininity and between the homoerotic and heteroerotic, which can make London seem to be a writer of surprising liberatory impulses. The reader also confronts a narrative rigidity [...] which engineers a containment of its own homoerotic impulses. (p. 110)

In keeping with this paradigm, Ernest's physical magnetism draws devotees, yet because Ernest's bodily attractiveness emerges through the narrative constraints of the heteronormative love story, the author disassociates Ernest from anything unconventional.

For all his education and eloquence, Ernest, as Auerbach points out, is politically effective only when viewed as a sexually dangerous creature:

"But his ability to sway others depends more directly on his magnificent sheer presence and his charisma, which in turn depend on his sexualized body that continually captures and compels the attention of Avis. He is, after all, Ernest Everhard—no Viagra needed" (2006, p. x). It is not through word or example that he wins converts, but rather through his appealing physique. Recalling meeting Everhard for the first time, Avis admits that she was moved more by passion than persuasion:

> I liked him; I had to confess it to myself. And my liking for him was founded on things beyond intellect and argument [....] There was something in that clarion-call of his that went to my heart [....] And there were further reaches of vague and indeterminate feelings that stirred in me. I almost loved him then. (London 1907/1980, p. 18)

Blushingly vivid descriptions of Ernest's firm, muscular body make this attraction all the more erotic. From a physical standpoint, Ernest, as his provocative surname would suggest, is little more than a glorified, swollen phallus:

> He wore a ready-made suit [....] [T]he cloth bulged with his muscles [....] His neck was the neck of a prizefighter, thick and strong, those bulging muscles and that bull throat [....] And then, when he shook hands with me! His handshake was firm and strong, but he looked at me boldly with his black eyes—too boldly, I thought. (London 1907/1980, p. 7)

Whereas the prole in the ill-fitting suit is typically a figure of fun or satire, here the tension in the strained formal clothing makes Ernest more tantalizing. London seems unaware of the incongruity of a character who earns his living through white-collar work but looks like a muscled laborer. He molds the perfect man in order, perhaps, to gaze at him safely but adoringly through the eyes of a female narrator. Derrick points out that London frequently develops homosocial relationships in his fiction so that male characters can appropriately admire the bodies of other men: "London's fiction works to distinguish between his homosocial love of men and an eroticism phobically rejected [....] This splitting of desire paradoxically allows an 'innocent' gaze at clean, white male bodies" (1996, p. 111).

This implicitly homosexual perspective is further tempered by removing the final assessment of Ernest from the narrative of his wife to the annotations of the prosaic Anthony Meredith. Whalen-Bridge (1998) tells how "through the corrective lenses of the historian Meredith, we see the shortcomings of Avis Everhard's glorification of her husband. Meredith offers a fuller historical perspective within which to figure the discreet actions of the individual" (p. 47). This final narrative distance keeps *The Iron Heel* from reading like an endorsement of the Great Man Theory, but, more importantly, it obscures the novel's homoerotic undertones. The implication is that though the instinctive and transgressive are necessary catalysts of social change, they must always be contained by the intellect and released only in specific ways and measured doses.

There are, of course, a few characters in *The Iron Heel* more moved by persuasion than passion. The sexuality and danger associated with Ernest do not convert Bishop Morehouse to the socialist cause. Morehouse is the character who seems to listen most attentively to Ernest's rhetoric. But though Ernest changes the Bishop's personal life and behavior drastically, the good cleric remains an apolitical character throughout the book, as his response to Ernest's suggestion that he use some of his money to fund the production of socialist propaganda makes clear: "I do not have much faith in politics. In fact, I am afraid I do not understand politics" (London 1907/1980, p. 128). Ernest has conveyed a sense of social injustice to the Bishop, but without the possibility of a sexual connection he is unable to effect a political epiphany.

The Bishop's inability to grasp socialism also reflects London's belief in the fundamental irreconcilability of progressivism and organized religion, specifically Catholicism. Like London, Ernest is an atheist. When he sees the havoc wrought by the plutocrats, he wishes he could believe in eternal punishment: "I do not believe in hell-fire and brimstone; but in moments like this I regret my unbelief" (London 1907/1980, p. 161). As Claeys (2017) explains, "The socialist cause is represented as a return to pure Christian teaching" (p. 332). London uses Christian imagery to enhance Ernest in the reader's eyes. Ernest meets his future wife and father-in-law when he accepts an invitation to "preacher's night" (London 1907/1980, p. 7). Avis presents him as a "father confessor" (London 1907/1980, p. 38), "apostle of truth" (London 1907/1980, p. 42), and forecasts his martyrdom through the evocation of Christ's passion: "I thought of Ernest. Was he, too, destined for the cross?" (London 1907/1980, p. 42). Like Jesus, Ernest is tried and convicted by the political authorities for a crime he did not commit (the bombing of Congress). His death, like Christ's, remains shrouded in mystery, even after the establishment of the

Brotherhood of Man (London 1907/1980, p. 224). In addition, his followers, the persecuted socialists, find refuge in catacombs like the early Christians did (London 1907/1980, p. 180).

Portraying Ernest in quasireligious terms helps to resolve one of the great paradoxes of *The Iron Heel* and of projected political fiction in general, which is the presentation of the revolutionary cause through the life of the individual despite the fact that the individual life is meaningless in relation to the greater movement. By making Ernest a kind of secular saint, he becomes a person who is as much the embodiment of a larger struggle as a representative member of a group. In this way, London stretches beyond the story's plot to bridge figuratively the gap between the crushed revolution and the realization of socialism under the Brotherhood of Man by locating hope in the tribulations of a prophetic figure, a technique that anticipates Huxley's depiction of John the Savage in *Brave New World*.

Nevertheless, the idea that such comparisons constitute an endorsement of religiosity is belied by pointedly sacrilegious correlations: Ernest's "laughter was Mephistophelian" (London 1907/1980, p. 29), anticipating the positive portrayal of Satan as the primeval revolutionary in Zamyatin's *We*. The death of Ernest's father is represented in terms that parody the Last Supper and the Catholic miracle of transubstantiation: "Think of it. For profit—his life blood transmuted into a wine-supper" (London 1907/1980, p. 71). Moreover, Ernest emphasizes the secular nature of the development and enlightenment of the proletariat: "The proletariat has grown up outside the Church and without the Church" (London 1907/1980, p. 25). Avis refers casually to the deity throughout the text, but her lingering faith, which is disconnected from any religious denomination or specific doctrine, may be a residual consequence of her conventional patrician upbringing. For just as the working class, according to London, has no need of religion, the ruling class depends on it. Ernest asserts to Bishop Morehouse that the teachings of the Church, which are a crude distortion of Christ's collectivist message, are in actuality an unethical mechanism for buttressing class inequity: "That is the meaning of the capitalist system. And that is what your Church is standing for, what you are preaching for every time you get in the pulpit. Pig-ethics! There is no other name for it" (London 1907/1980, p. 24). In *The Iron Heel*, Roman Catholic doctrine epitomizes the so-called "pig-ethics" of contemporary Christianity. Ernest calls the mindset of the oligarchs "Jesuitical" (London 1907/1980, p. 46). Unsurprisingly, the truth about the bombing of Congress, the crime for which Ernest is framed, is concealed within the Vatican Library (London 1907/1980, pp. 164–165).

Organized religion, especially Catholicism, also serves the capitalists as a wedge that divides labor and consequently undermines its solidarity, an observation that somewhat contradicts Ernest's claim that the proletariat has matured without the Church: "It was the Plutocracy, through its secret agents, that raised the cry that socialism was sacrilegious and atheistic; it was the Plutocracy that whipped the churches, and especially the Catholic Church, into line, and robbed us of a portion of the labour vote" (London 1907/1980, p. 132). Unlike Burdekin and Orwell, London views Catholicism as compliant with more than complicit in the oppression of the proletariat. London also takes care to present his criticism of religion as a condemnation of all Christian denominations, not simply Catholicism. When Bishop Morehouse reads a poem to his congregation contrasting the princely wealth of the Holy See with the poverty of Christ, he explicitly states that he is not speaking only of his own church: "It must not be mistaken for an attack upon the Catholic Church. It is an attack upon all churches, upon the pomp and splendour of all churches that have wandered from the Master's path and hedged themselves in from his lambs" (London 1907/1980, p. 74).

Extending the Bishop's critique beyond religious institutions, Ernest contrasts all metaphysics unfavorably with science:

> They declaimed about famine and pestilence as being scourges of God, while the scientists were building granaries and draining cities. They built gods in their own shapes and out of their own desires, while the scientists were building roads and bridges. They were describing the earth as the centre of the universe, while the scientists were discovering America and probing space for the stars and the laws of the stars. In short, the metaphysicians have done nothing, absolutely nothing, for mankind. (London 1907/1980, p. 12)

Here and throughout the novel, as Barley explains, Ernest discounts the utilitarian value of religious thinking: "In successive debates, Ernest presses home the superiority of historical materialism over religious idealism" (1995, p. 162). As David Seed (1980) makes clear, London further alleges that religion does greatest harm when economic times are hardest: "he never loses sight of the fact that religious mania is both a response to economic poverty and a cause of its increase" (p. 10). As the working class steadily loses ground to the Iron Heel, a grassroots religious revival ensues that condemns the abuses of the rich but deflects the proletariat from practical strategies to address inequity:

> And truly the religious revival assumed formidable proportions. The people, what of their wretchedness, and of their disappointment in all things earthly, were ripe and eager for a heaven where industrial tyrants entered no more than camels passed through needle-eyes. Wild-eyed, itinerant preachers swarmed over the land; and despite the prohibition of the civil authorities, and the persecution for disobedience, the flames of religious frenzy were fanned by countless camp-meetings. (London 1907/1980, p. 148)

Whereas Burdekin and Huxley are invested in personal spirituality, London views all permutations of religion as harmful distractions from the truth of socialism. Auerbach therefore aptly characterizes the first third of the novel as a conversion narrative:

> The first third of the novel thus works simultaneously as a love story and a conversion narrative, as Ernest, with his rough, bold mannerisms, talks and charms his way into her life at the same time he convinces her, her father, and family friend Bishop Morehouse to join the socialist movement. (2006, p. x)

While repudiating the substance of religion, London approves of socialism mimicking religion's form to facilitate conversion, which is apparent from Avis's characterization of "the Cause":

> The Revolution took on largely the character of religion. We worshipped at the shrine of the Revolution, which was the shrine of liberty. It was the divine flashing through us. Men and women devoted their lives to the Cause, and newborn babes were sealed to it as of old they had been sealed to the service of God. We were lovers of humanity. (London 1907/1980, p. 158)

Seed asserts that by drawing this correlation, London imbues socialism with the status and solemnity of Christianity, since both are utopian movements: "London is here attempting to give the movement of Socialism the same historical substance and dignity as Christianity once possessed. He implies that the *form* of the earlier movement can be transferred appropriately on to the political organization, since both look forward to ideal future states" (1980, p. 2, emphasis in original). In key ways *The Iron Heel* does resemble a religious scripture; it concludes, as Seed observes, with an "apocalyptic ending" (1980, p. 10), and through Anthony Meredith, London provides a God's-eye-view of the plot: "He is commenting with the benefit of seven centuries' hindsight from 1932, the present of the manuscript. In other words he seems to represent a godlike viewpoint, that of history itself" (Seed 1980, p. 3). These appropriations from Christianity are somewhat contradictory in light of the novel's overall commitment to rationality. Despite his investment in scientific and rational thought, London presents personal investment in socialism as passionate, visceral, and—as Whalen-Bridge points out—surprisingly sentimental (1992, p. 72).

Even when he converts his pliant wife, reason is a secondary consideration. Ernest must indirectly invoke a sexual concern by achieving her enlightenment through an investigation of Jackson's severed arm, a metaphorical representation of a severed penis. In keeping with this "symbolic castration," Auerbach interprets Jackson as a foil to Ernest, emphasizing the latter's sexual and sociopolitical potency: "Jackson has been left with a dismembered, emasculated body in stark contrast to Everhard's own bulging virility" (2006, p. xi). More importantly, through learning Jackson's story, Avis sheds her virginal naïveté and is initiated into full maturity: "There was Jackson, and Jackson's arm, and the blood that stained my gown" (London 1907/1980, p. 45). Indeed, sex and politics are so intertwined in the process of her indoctrination that Avis cannot remember whether she became a revolutionary in response to sedition or seduction: "Whether it was my love for Ernest, or the clear sight he had given me of the society in which I lived, that made me a revolutionist, I know not, but a revolutionist I became" (London 1907/1980, p. 105). As the incendiary story of Jackson's arm unfolds, so too does Ernest's sexual prowess: "For never was there such a lover as Ernest Everhard [....] His arms around me before I knew. His lips were on mine before I could protest or resist. Before his earnestness conventional maiden dignity was ridiculous. He swept me off my feet by the splendid invincible rush of him" (London 1907/1980, p. 48). A link is established between political and sexual passion. Ernest, who is "ever hard," and so has potency to spare, becomes the defender of virility and manhood itself, as well as the sacred guardian of social justice. Desire for Ernest initiates the process through which Avis comes to empathize with and realize her responsibility to Jackson and the other disadvantaged people affected by the injustice done to him. This compassion prepares Avis, a beneficiary of the market system, to stand in solidarity with capitalism's numerous victims.

Avis's role is especially important in making sense of how gender works in the novel. Jackson's arm, as Shor indicates, shows that though many women are disempowered by capitalism, working men such as Jackson—and for that matter all those compelled to testify against him when he seeks justice in court—are rendered impotent:

> London's emphasis on Jackson's being reduced to a peddler and his attendant loss of income suggests not merely symbolic castration but an ironic representation of the loss of manhood in an era when making a decent living was the measure of true masculinity, especially for men of the working class. (1996, p. 81)

Although the Iron Heel oppresses both sexes, London suggests that it poses a particular physical threat to working-class men. Conversely in *Swastika Night* and *The Handmaid's Tale*, though everyone is victimized by the conservative political system to varying degrees, it is women who suffer most.

Since revolution in these novels is always sexual and both men and women must be recruited to the cause, London is obliged to create a female equivalent to Ernest Everhard. He does so through the tantalizing character known as the Red Virgin:

> Anna Roylston [...] known as the Red Virgin [...] became one of the inspired figures of the Revolution.... Furthermore, she was a genius and lovable, and we could never discipline her anyway. She is in a class by herself and not amenable to the ordinary standards of the revolutionists [....] [She] was a fascinating woman. All she had to do was to beckon a man to her. She broke the hearts of scores of our comrades, and scores of others she captured, and by their heart-strings led into our organization. (London 1907/1980, p. 179)

Like Ernest, Anna is "in a class by herself" and thus above the limitations of and restrictions on the average proletarian. By casting her as both erotic and untamable, London suggests that sexuality can never be fully assimilated by any regime or organization.

Indeed, London perceived class barriers and restrictions as flimsy in the face of sexuality. Through her desire for Ernest, Avis is able to transform herself and her family, by means of a "love-adventure," from elites of Mayflower stock (London 1907/1980, p. 113) into genuine proletarians, just as passion for Anna turns wealthy Philip Wickson into a rank-and-file comrade (London 1907/1980, pp. 185–186):

"Now we shall become real proletarians," [Avis'] father said, when we were driven from our home. "I have often envied that young man of yours for his actual knowledge of the proletariat. Now I must see and learn for myself." [...] He embarked upon the adventure with the joy and enthusiasm of a child [....] Even I found some relief in our change of living [....] And the change was to me likewise adventure, and the greatest of all, for it was love-adventure. (London 1907/1980, pp. 115–116)

Following this metamorphosis, the very work from which Ernest seeks to liberate his comrades becomes like play to Avis and her father, and the workers accept them with open arms despite their privileged upbringing and former status:

He [Avis's father] had become enamoured of proletarian life. He looked upon our slum [...] as a great sociological laboratory, and he had embarked upon an apparently endless orgy of investigation. He chummed with the labourers, and was an intimate in scores of homes. Also, he worked at odd jobs, and the work was play as well as learned investigation, for he delighted in it [...] bubbling over with new adventures. (London 1907/1980, p. 150)

This wholly unrealistic description of a tolerant, fulfilled proletariat living in a paradisiacal slum demonstrates a willful naïveté. Yet the sexual language employed in this description of a family's political and social rebirth is striking. John Cunningham becomes "enamoured of" the proletarians who provide him with "an apparently endless orgy" of investigation. He's an "intimate" of the laborers in their homes, "delighting" and "bubbling over" with excitement for these new adventures. His empathy for the poor is, like his daughter's, rooted in sexual desire.

As with London's physical description of Ernest, this degentrification of Cunningham is intensely homoerotic. But it is also an unusual process because it constitutes eroticism without a particular male object. Instead the working class itself is collectively sexualized; consequently, London must maintain a certain distance between the formerly patrician Cunningham and the residents of the slum. As born aristocrats, the Cunninghams can approach the raw, chiefly sexual power of the people, but only on a scientific level, which turns the ghetto into a huge "laboratory." An individual cannot really be part of a community if they see it in clinical terms. Thus, though it appears as though the impoverishment of the Cunninghams is a harbinger of a classless society, in reality their story constitutes an evasion of class integration.

The Cunninghams' fall (or rise as the case may be) also reflects a reluctant, indirect acknowledgment of the importance of the intelligentsia in fomenting revolution. The solution London reaches is to make the working class into a sort of surrogate bourgeoisie engaged in the same pursuits and studies as the oligarchs but besting them at these endeavors: "We found time to laugh and love. There were artists, scientists, scholars, musicians, and poets among us; and in that hole in the ground culture was higher and finer than in the palaces or wonder-cities of the oligarchs" (London 1907/1980, p. 184). London likewise imbues his proletariat with the perspective and erudition normally associated with the intelligentsia. It is as though when the Cunninghams arrive at the slum they bring the entire neighborhood up to their level of refinement rather than sinking down to the poverty, vice, and despondency that they initially encounter. In effect, London unwittingly, and perhaps unwillingly, preserves patrician concerns behind a salt-of-the-earth veneer.

Not only are gulfs between socioeconomic classes readily bridged through socialism, but also communication with future generations is fairly easy, since the oligarchs appear not to have recognized the connection between controlling language and controlling thought. Orwell, through Winston's private meditations in *Nineteen Eighty-Four*, emphasizes the difficulty of conveying information from within dystopias to future generations: "How could you communicate with the future? It was of its nature impossible. Either the future would resemble the present, in which case it would not listen to him, or it would be different from it, and his predicament would be meaningless" (1949/1977, p. 9). Yet Orwell's post-narrative appendix on Newspeak may well have been inspired by the appendix which concludes *The Iron Heel*, suggesting, or at least hinting, that the present evils of totalitarianism can be understood and avoided by future generations. As Erica Briscoe (1998) points out, the leading socialists in London's seminal dystopia all write as relentlessly as they fight, thereby making the struggle for social justice one of pen and ink as well as blood and iron:

> The book that Avis's father, Professor Cunningham, is writing is itself buried by the forces of the Iron Heel because it poses a threat to that regime's ideology [....] Likewise we learn that Everhard himself was in the process of writing a book when he first met Avis, but that this book continued to be printed secretly throughout the three centuries of the Iron Heel [....] [T]his translates to an acknowledgement of the efficacy of texts as weapons in the fight for social change, themselves agents in the power play between reactionary and revolutionary forces. (pp. 28–29)

Not surprisingly, the real-life fascists who eventually governed in Germany, Italy, and Spain felt threatened enough by intellectual opposition that they took the time and trouble to court various artists, most notably Ezra Pound, P. G. Wodehouse, Leni Riefenstahl, and Richard Strauss. Briscoe reminds us that Ernest in his speech to the Philomaths observes that the upper classes enlist literary works such as the Seaside Library novels to brainwash restless commoners (1998, p. 31). In contrast to his vague, idealized depiction of the working class, London accurately assesses the tactics and tenacity of the elite.

Eventually, London questioned whether the working class had the will to liberate itself and consequently resigned from the Socialist Party, claiming, according to Andrew Furer (1996), "that it had lost its revolutionary fire" (p. 171). Jonathan Berliner (2008) notes that as London became less enchanted with political activism, he sought to establish a primal connection to the land: "After tendering his resignation from the Socialist Party in 1916, London told his wife that 'more and more [he] turn[ed] to the land' rather than politics [....] London consistently sought a regeneration through the primitive, embracing just the kind of naturalism that Western Marxists would come to reject" (pp. 63–67). This investment in primitivism is central to *We*, signaling a direct rebuttal of H. G. Wells in contrast to London's muted, respectful critique. London and Zamyatin also differ in their ideas of revolution itself. London, according to Seed, saw "the socialist uprising" as "the revolution to end all revolutions" (1980, p. 2). Zamyatin, as will be shown in the next chapter, suggests that revolution is a naturally recurring process necessary to the human condition.

References

Auerbach, J. (2006). Introduction. In J. London (Ed.), *The Iron Heel* (pp. vii–xxi). New York, NY: Penguin.

Barley, T. (1995). Prediction, Programme and Fantasy in Jack London's *The Iron Heel*. In D. Seed (Ed.), *Anticipations* (pp. 153–172). Liverpool: Syracuse University Press.

Beauchamp, G. (1981). Jack London's Utopian Dystopia and Dystopian Utopia. In K. M. Roemer (Ed.), *America as Utopia* (pp. 91–107). New York, NY: Franklin.

Berliner, J. (2008). Jack London's Socialistic Social Darwinism. *American Literary Realism*, 41(1), 52–78.

Briscoe, E. (1998). *The Iron Heel*: How Not to Write a Popular Novel. *Jack London Journal*, 5, 5–37.

Claeys, G. (2017). *Dystopia: A Natural History.* Oxford: Oxford University Press.
Derrick, S. (1996). Making a Heterosexual Man: Gender, Sexuality, and Narrative in the Fiction of Jack London. In L. Cassuto & J. Campbell Reesman (Eds.), *Rereading Jack London* (pp. 110–129). Stanford, CA: Stanford University Press.
Franklin, H. B. (1980). Introduction. In J. London (Ed.), *The Iron Heel* (pp. i–vi). Chicago, IL: Lawrence Hill Books.
Furer, A. (1996). "Zone-Conquerors" and "White Devils": The Contradictions of Race in the Work of Jack London. In L. Cassuto & J. Campbell Reesman (Eds.), *Rereading Jack London* (pp. 158–171). Stanford, CA: Stanford University Press.
Heje, J. (2002). George Orwell (Eric Arthur Blair). In D. Harris-Fain (Ed.), *Dictionary of Literary Biography, Volume Two Hundred Fifty Five: British Fantasy and Science-Fiction Writers 1918–1960* (pp. 164–174). Detroit, MI: The Gale Group.
London, J. (1980). *The Iron Heel.* Chicago, IL: Lawrence Hill Books. (Original work published 1907)
Marx, K., & Engels, F. (1998). *The Communist Manifesto* (S. Moore, Trans.). London: Verso. (Original work published 1848)
Orwell, G. (1958). *The Road to Wigan Pier.* New York, NY: Harcourt, Brace, Jovanovich. (Original work published 1937)
Orwell, G. (1968a). Introduction to *Love of Life and Other Stories* by Jack London. In S. Orwell & I. Angus (Eds.), *In Front of Your Nose, 1945–1950: The Collected Essays, Journalism & Letters, Vol. 4* (pp. 23–29). New York, NY: Harcourt Brace Jovanovich. (Original work published November 1968)
Orwell, G. (1968b). Prophecies of Fascism. In S. Orwell & I. Angus (Eds.), *My Country Right or Left, 1940–1943: The Collected Essays, Journalism & Letters, Vol. 2* (pp. 30–33). New York, NY: Harcourt Brace Jovanovich. (Original work published 12 July 1940)
Orwell, G. (1977). *Nineteen Eighty-Four.* New York: Harcourt Brace Jovanovich. (Original work published 1949)
Portelli, A. (1982). Jack London's Missing Revolution: Notes on *The Iron Heel*. *Science Fiction Studies, 9*(27), 180–191.
Seed, D. (1980). The Apocalyptic Structure of Jack London's *The Iron Heel*. *Jack London Newsletter, 13*(1), 1–11.
Shor, F. (1996). Power, Gender, and Ideological Discourse in *The Iron Heel*. In L. Cassuto & J. Campbell Reesman (Eds.), *Rereading Jack London* (pp. 75–91). Stanford, CA: Stanford University Press.
Whalen-Bridge, J. (1992). Dual Perspectives in *The Iron Heel*. *Thalia: Studies in Literary Humor, 12*(1–2), 67–76.
Whalen-Bridge, J. (1998). How to Read a Revolutionary Novel: *The Iron Heel*. *Jack London Journal, 5*, 38–63.

CHAPTER 3

Redemptive Atavism in Yevgeny Zamyatin's *We*

Starting with *We*, projected political fictions become truly nightmarish because the characters are internally as well as externally altered by totalitarianism. Yevgeny Zamyatin grasped that the aim of totalitarianism was the negation of individuality. This differentiates *We* from *The Iron Heel* and also makes the oppressions of Rand's *Anthem* and Burdekin's *Swastika Night* appear less encompassing than the despotism found in Zamyatin's OneState. The horror of subjugating the individual from within remains the most compelling political anxiety of our time, which is why *We* is as relevant today as *Brave New World* and *Nineteen Eighty-Four*.

By presenting a primordial world as an alternative to the glittering city, Zamyatin implies that an impulse toward devolution is endemic to human nature. D-503 is troubled by this impulse in others and fears it in himself: "even in our day you can still very occasionally hear coming up from the bottom, from the hairy depths, a wild, ape-like echo" (Zamyatin 1924/1993, p. 15). These primal hungers demand personal gratification, privileging the repressed individual over the community.

Unlike the conventional grim dystopia, Zamyatin's projected world is visually elegant, again anticipating Huxley's World State. Daily life in OneState is precisely choreographed. Action is taken simultaneously by millions of identically clad people who are differentiated only by the assigned numbers that appear on their immaculate blue-gray uniforms. Living and working in identical clear-glass buildings, the OneStaters are merely mass products of the societal machine. The victorious few who triumphed in the 200-Years War, which brought humanity to the brink of extinction, fashioned political, social, and economic models, and then conditioned younger generations to think and behave exactly as they did. The well-adjusted Number sees him- or herself as a proto-machine, striving to emulate a well-maintained mechanical device; a Number is but a cog in the giant automated apparatus of the state.

This frame of mind may seem stifling to readers from democratic societies, yet it is not unusual to hear people talk about wanting to feel part of something larger than themselves, an inclination found even in increasingly diverse communities such as the USA, a nation where individualism is a bedrock principle. D-503 derives great personal satisfaction from his position within the collective: "It cheers you up: You see yourself as part of an immense, powerful, single thing. And such a precise beauty it is: not a wasted gesture, bend turn" (Zamyatin 1924/1993, p. 34). Although Orwell presents this feeling in bleaker terms in *Nineteen Eighty-Four*, D-503's sentiments are much like the sense of immortality O'Brien finds in being part of the Party: "Can you not understand, Winston, that the individual is only a cell? The weariness of the cell is the vigor of the organism. Do you die when you cut your fingernails?" (Orwell 1949/1977, p. 267). Apart from the apparent influence that Zamyatin had on Orwell, these examples suggest that sophisticated, intelligent individuals can be just as susceptible to a herd mentality as average people, if for somewhat different reasons.

Ironically, this line of thought can affirm individuality because it allows one person to appropriate the accomplishments of many:

> I saw again, as though right then for the first time in my life, I saw everything: the unalterably straight streets, the sparkling glass of the sidewalks, the divine parallelepipeds of the transparent dwellings, the squared harmony of our gray-blue ranks. And so I felt that I—not generations of people, but I myself—I had conquered the old God and the old life, I myself had created all this, and I'm like a tower. (Zamyatin 1924/1993, p. 7)

In comparing himself to a tower and presenting collective human achievement as a challenge to divinity, D-503 evokes the biblical story of the Tower of Babel, a myth that showcases the godlike achievements possible through human cooperation. Here, however, the meaning of the original myth is inverted: a story that for the ancient Semites cautioned people to relegate their endeavors to mundane matters and remain firmly on the ground now suggests that people can and should claim the heavens and live as gods: "The gods have become like us—ergo, we've become like gods" (Zamyatin 1924/1993, p. 68). In this reworking of common religious themes, D-503 makes an important distinction between "the old God" of the Bible and the Benefactor, who is, paradoxically, steeped in Judeo-Christian symbolism.

While a human connection to the unseen old God depended largely on the salvation of the individual, here the supreme authority rules visibly and directly over his people, demonstrating his power not through enigmatic miracles but via shows of strength such as public executions. These punitive spectacles have a distinctly erotic overlay. While keeping coitus variegated and available subjugates subversive sexual energy, executions mimic public ceremonial rapes and loosely resemble The Two Minutes Hate in *Nineteen Eighty-Four*, the orgy-porgy at the close of *Brave New World*, and the Salvagings in *The Handmaid's Tale*. The Justice Gala brings vicarious sexual satisfaction to the viewer as the Benefactor's rigid hand presses down on the lever and discharges a penetrating blast into the supine, sacrificial receiver. "The stone hand of the Benefactor, the unbearable blade of light, and up there on the Cube, the spread-eagled body with the head thrown back. I shuddered" (Zamyatin 1924/1993, p. 54). Like a body damp from sex, the Benefactor descends from the platform wet with condensation: "Lined up in front of Him, were ten female Numbers with flushed faces.... According to an old custom, the ten women decorated with flowers the Benefactor's yuny [uniform], which was still damp from the spray" (Zamyatin 1924/1993, p. 48). Public executions in OneState tap into and release sexual aggresion through an alluring celebration of satiation and cruelty.

The need for the killing of deviants in a world so regimented as Zamyatin's OneState suggests that conformity can never be absolute. The narrator himself concedes in the very first entry of his Record that the Numbers are not entirely united: "But I am ready. Like all of us, or nearly all of us" (Zamyatin 1924/1993, p. 4). No matter how thoroughly people seem to be integrated into the dominant paradigm, firebrands will emerge. As Zina Gimpelevich (1997) observes of Zamyatin, "He claims [...] progress in literature and in real life is possible only through eternal revolution or, in other words, the search for eternal freedom. In Zamyatin's philosophy, it is only heretics who are able to achieve this goal of freedom" (p. 16). Heresy manifests itself forcefully when D-503's sexual passion compromises his loyalty and awakens revolutionary impulses.

The object of D-503's subversive desire is the beautiful I-330, leader of the Mephi, an extensive underground movement comprising people living both within and outside the city committed to subverting the Benefactor's reign. In an algebraic comparison, D-503 associates I-330 with the unknown quotient from their very first meeting: "something about her eyes or brows, some kind of odd irritating X that I couldn't get at all, a thing I couldn't express in numbers [...] like the sharp horns of an X, and for some reason I got confused" (Zamyatin 1924/1993, p. 8). The "sharp horns" of the X, subsequently referred to as a "four-pawed X" (Zamyatin 1924/1993, p. 23), along with her "white, sharp teeth" (Zamyatin 1924/1993, p. 8), imbue I-330 with a feral, dangerous mystique. I-330 proselytizes with her body rather than through verbal or written propaganda. R. Mark Preslar (2008) points out that "both the OneState and the rebel Mephi make use of various forms of coercion to guard or influence the worldview of the populace" (p. 47). As in *The Iron Heel*, the ends justify the means for both revolutionaries and loyalists.

In the first moment they share alone, I-330 reiterates the dogma of OneState while changing from her uniform into a tight evening dress. D-503 is thus implicitly offered a choice between orthodoxy and I-330 herself:

> The dress was made of a very thin silk--I could clearly see that the stockings were long and came way above her knees. And the neck was cut very low [....] "It's clear," she broke in, "that to be original means to distinguish yourself from others. It follows that to be original is to violate the principal of equality. And what the ancients called, in their idiotic language, 'being banal' is what we call 'just doing your duty.'" [...] I remember how I was trembling all over. I should have [...] I don't know [...] grabbed her. (Zamyatin 1924/1993, p. 30)

It is D-503's obsession with I-330, an almost stock femme fatale, rather than political consciousness, that binds him to her cause, eventually bringing him to the point where, though he believes that he is doing evil in promoting the revolution, he resigns himself to it for the sake of his passion: "There was no saving me, not any longer. *I did not want to be saved* (Zamyatin 1924/1993, p. 179, emphasis in original). As Ní Dhúill (2010) observes, D-503's sexuality, though irrational, causes him to question pervasive norms and begin to think critically: "Sexual desire works in Zamyatin's *We* to subvert the dominance of rationality: it is the protagonist's desire for E-330 which undermines his acceptance of the mathematically infallible happiness his society has constructed for its members" (p. 39).

Through this process of critical thought, morality emerges: I-330's sensuality does not reduce her to a male-pleasing object of lust; instead, she becomes the first Number to achieve full personhood in D-503's eyes: "I stared at her [...] as something that had dropped out of nowhere. She was no longer a Number, she was simply a person" (Zamyatin 1924/1993, p. 122). Whereas previously everyone was literally a number, D-503 can now recognize and value individuality as well as his responsibility to both himself and at least one other person. Although skeptical of eroticism's power to effect a successful revolution, Booker (1994) recognizes its humanizing effect: "Still, *We* does seem to suggest a positive subversive potential in sexuality in the way the sexual relationship with I-330 leads D-503 to experience a genuinely humanizing emotion" (p. 35). Having been humanized and made morally cognizant, D-503 wants his relationship with I-330 to be a genuine bond. It is the monogamous nature of D-503's desire, like Lenina's in *Brave New World*, that makes it transgressive.

As in *Brave New World*, the government of OneState knows that monogamy can undermine the state by introducing a competing personal loyalty, just as sexual deprivation can induce volatile jealousy. The *Lex Sexualis* states that "any Number has the right of access to any other Number as sexual product" (Zamyatin 1924/1993, p. 22). Furthermore, the number of weekly hours in which a Number can legally have sex corresponds to the individual's physiological appetite:

> They give you a careful going-over in the Sexual Bureau labs and determine the exact content of the sexual hormones in your blood and work out your correct Table of Sex Days. Then you fill out a declaration that on your days you'd like to make use of Number (or Numbers) so-and-so and they hand you the corresponding book of tickets. (Zamyatin 1924/1993, p. 22)

The only real constraint on sexual activity is that a Number whose body chemistry calls for a large number of sex days may have to wait temporarily on the availability of a desired Number with a naturally lower sex drive. However, since the amount of available choices in the densely populated city is large, there is nothing in the story to suggest that such an inconvenience is even perceptible. Because sex is always so freely and readily available at precisely the right time, it is completely desublimated, at once harmless to the government and meaningless to citizens. What makes this state of affairs truly horrifying is that it normalizes rape, as Brett Cooke (2002) makes clear: "One particularly offensive feature of the *Lex Sexualis* is that a citizen may not resist the sexual advances of another, provided the latter has obtained the necessary approvals. This can amount to a form of legalized rape, one that men may practice on women—or women on men" (p. 134).

Nonetheless, this scientific system of sexual gratification proves incapable of containing D-503's forbidden sexual desire. He becomes obsessed with becoming I-330's sole sexual partner. O-90, another lover of D-503, on recognizing D-503's love for I-330, becomes equally obsessed with having a child with D-503, which is, of course, illegal (Zamyatin 1924/1993, pp. 102–103). O-90's desire to reproduce is not derived from lustful impulses, but it does constitute the commission of sexual intercourse for a criminal purpose. O-90's revolution is reproductive; I-330's is political. But the nexus of their distinct revolutions is sexual intercourse. O-90, I-330, and D-503 all ignore their society's repressive moral code and the fear of execution solely for what they can achieve through illicit sex.

C. Moody (1976) notes that this awakening of sexual desire creates in D-503 a compulsion to write, shifting the focus of his journal from a paean to Onestate to an account of personal turmoil and growing self-awareness:

> The true catalysts of revolution in *We* are love (sex) and art, which is allied with genuine intelligence [....] D-503's latent individuality expresses itself first in his sexual relationship with E-330 and O-90 who is also a rebel in her desire to have a child. The Single State, in its turn, seeks to regiment and neutralize sexual relationships to break down true intimacy between individuals. The rebellion of D-503 expresses itself partly in his desire to write. (p. 32)

Cooke argues that this literary transformation is facilitated by D-503's decision to compose a personal narrative, a type of writing that often forces the author to confront the subconscious:

> His chosen genre inclines him to confession, self-reflection, and many digressions. These have the fateful result of calling subconscious aspects of

his psyche, such as memory, instinctual desires, and association patterns, into a more prominent role in shaping his consciousness [....] Although D-503 begins by announcing his intention to send his manuscript to extraterrestrials, he more and more comes to write for himself. (2002, pp. 174–175)

Cooke makes clear that this imperative to assert innate individuality against conditioned uniformity through the process of writing is situationally connected to sex, since both endeavors occur during D-503's personal hours: "Until I-330's machinations relieve him from the official daily schedule, D-503 usually writes during the standard Personal Hours. Significantly, he writes at times otherwise often devoted to sexual intercourse" (2002, p. 171). By the time D-503 appreciates the scope of the plot against the Benefactor, his attachment to I-330 is inextricably conflated with his need to complete his manuscript:

it isn't because I don't have the strength to go against her wishes. That's ridiculous! Of course not [....] I'm afraid that if I lose her, I-330, I might lose the only key to explain all the unknowns [....] And explaining them—I now feel duty-bound to do it, if only because I am the author of these records, to say nothing of the fact that the unknown is in general the enemy of man, and *Homo sapiens* is not fully man until his grammar is absolutely rid of question marks. (Zamyatin 1924/1993, p. 114)

D-503's transparent self-deception lets him assuage his guilt for transferring his allegiance to I-330 and the impending revolution.

When it arrives near the end of the novel, the clash between individuality and groupthink is, necessarily, a violent one. But civil disobedience is largely presented in erotic terms: "In several buildings I could see through the glass walls [...] that men and female Numbers were copulating without the least shame, without even lowering the blinds, without so much as a ticket, in broad daylight" (Zamyatin 1924/1993, p. 212). Alex M. Shane (1968) emphasizes Zamyatin's belief in the centrality of sexuality to human psychology and development; romantic love and sex are distinguished only by the strength of the impulse: "In *My* [Russian for *We*,] love is a strong sexual attraction which, as in 'Ostrovitjane' and 'Lovec celovekov,' symbolizes revolution against an existing philistine order" (p. 146). The government's response to this sexual revolution is a public announcement that the population is suffering from the corrupting influence of a disease called Imagination. The Benefactor is correct in realizing that the human capacity to imagine allows for the link between the organic act of sexual intercourse and the transcendent realm of aspirations. Zamyatin himself says as much in a letter to the artist Yury Annenkov about *We* that Shane quotes in his biography of the author: "there are two priceless fountainheads in man: brains and sex. From the first proceeds all science, from the second—all art. And to cut off all art from yourself or to force it into your brain would mean to cut off... well, yes" (1968, p. 142). Yet in this and other works of projected political fiction, sexual desire does far more than facilitate creativity.

Through his fraught physical relationship with I-330, D-503 is forced to realize that he has a moral responsibility to himself and those around him, in particular O-90, an obligation far more important than allegiance to the state. Despite the fact that his feelings for I-330 might not be reciprocated, D-503's desire, as Jeanne Murray Walker (1987) observes, awakens his natural empathy:

> Ultimately the only satisfying exchange is sexuality. D-503 experiences a violent attraction for I-330 [....] Because he feels this need for interaction and possession, he begins to comprehend O's need for exchange with him. Therefore, he protects her as though she were his "private child" [....] In a state where structure and stasis are the ideal, sexual desire poses a great threat. Not only is it one of the few exchanges which cannot be taken over by the State; it is intense and demanding and leads to distinctions of radical kinds between individuals. (p. 119)

By having D-503's passion for I-330 bring about a sense of parental responsibility toward his former lover, Zamyatin shows how sexual desire engenders ethical bonds beyond those that connect sexual partners.

Ultimately, D-503, like many other Numbers, is subjected to a medical procedure that disables the portion of the brain responsible for imagination, an operation that makes desire impossible, which Elaine Hoffman Baruch (1983) calls a "fantasiectomy" (p. 52). After this surgery, D-503 becomes totally amoral—placidly watching the torture of I-330 through suffocation and even finding it beautiful: "Then they put her under the Bell. Her face got very white, and since she had eyes that were dark and big, this was very beautiful" (Zamyatin 1924/1993, p. 225). In contrasting the Benefactor's brand of doctrinal ethics with the organic morality catalyzed by sexual desire, Zamyatin rejects the supposedly wholesome motive behind religion's condemnation of sexuality and efforts to control it. Through the narrator's orthodox perspective, the author correlates the fantasiectomy with the torture employed by Catholic inquisitors to quash heresy: "there were certain idiots who compared Operations with the ancient Inquisition" (Zamyatin 1924/1993, p. 79). As with London, Zamyatin's critique of Catholicism anticipates Orwell's hostility to Rome.

Like the torture of I-330, the fantasiectomies, which become legally required of all Numbers by a specified day, are justified by patriotism, piety, and the greater good—motives seldom subject to critical scrutiny. The ultimate purpose of the operation is to cure the human race of any tendency to rebel. What once were people emerge from shadowy laboratories as goose-stepping, flesh-and-blood automatons:

> The door of the auditorium at the corner is wide open and out of it is coming a slow, heavy column of about fifty men. Or rather not "men"—that isn't the word. Those weren't feet but some kind of heavy, forged wheels, drawn by some invisible drive mechanism. Not men but some kind of tractors in human form. Above their heads, snapping in the breeze, was a white banner embroidered with a golden sun, in the rays of which was a device: "We are the first! We have already had the Operation! Everyone follow us!" (Zamyatin 1924/1993, p. 182)

In keeping with Zamyatin's suspicion of the Vatican, the "white banner embroidered with a golden sun" visually recalls the yellow and gold flag of the nineteenth- and early twentieth-century papacy. Allowing Catholic ideology, including its restrictive code of sexual behavior, to determine one's thinking is thus indirectly likened to the deactivation of a portion of the brain.

In *Discipline & Punish*, Foucault (1975/1995) argues that the notion of "curing" undesirable behaviors in secret through ostensibly therapeutic procedures instead of punishing in public can be traced back to the loss of torture as a spectacle at the close of the eighteenth century: "[A] whole army of technicians took over from the executioner [...] warders, doctors, chaplains, psychiatrists" (p. 11). Bearing Foucault's assertion in mind, it is revealing that executions, though public, are quick and relatively painless in *We*, while the extended torture of I-330 takes place behind closed doors (Zamyatin 1924/1993, p. 225). Foucault asserts that as this notion of curing bad behavior develops, the highly ordered environment of the penitentiary spreads across the entire social body. As a result, remedies for particular offenses give way to social policies for departures from the prescribed "normal" behavior: "By operating at every level of the social body [...] the carceral lowers the level from which it becomes natural and acceptable to be punished" (1975/1995, p. 303). Thus, those found in government-controlled areas of the city at the end of the novel, including D-503, are forced to undergo the Operation whether loyal to the Benefactor or not. The novel ends with the suggestion that everyone in OneState will be turned into a "human tractor" by this procedure.

Humankind's loss of imagination, one of the attributes that separates it from machinery, would seem to signal the end of human history. But hope is preserved through the implied promise of a messiah, D-503's unborn child, which the pregnant O-90 is carrying when she escapes from the city with I-330's help: "So I [I-330] sent her [O-90] [...] she's there already, on the other side of the Wall. She's going to live" (Zamyatin 1924/1993, p. 194). Whatever happens to D-503, both O-90—who has already demonstrated her revolutionary potential—and the child he conceived with her are beyond the grasp of the Benefactor and are therefore potential opposition leaders of the future.

Like Orwell's depiction of Julia in *Nineteen Eighty-Four*, Zamyatin's almost pre-Enlightenment view of women embodies a stereotypical contrast between the male and female body, with the male representing a controlled, rational, ordered environment while the female reflects a mysterious, ungovernable, potentially dangerous space, offering always the possibility of upheaval and renewal—but in a sometimes crude and dehumanizing way. Nevertheless, I-330's promiscuity, for which she eventually pays with her life, brings her a kind of prophetic insight, as though sexual desire contains the essence of wisdom. Through I-330's heroism, the reader is invited to compare her favorably with the doctrinaire Benefactor.

Through I-330, Zamyatin argues that whenever an apparent utopia becomes rational, ordered, and predictable to the point of stifling individuality, it is a mathematical certainty that revolution will ensue. Just as order must necessarily arise out of chaos for civilization to exist, so must order give way to chaos for social regeneration to occur. Clarence Brown (1993) observes that I-330's political philosophy is the author's: "She is also the philosophical voice of Zamyatin's favorite idea, the central thematic idea of the book" (p. xxii). The two speak of revolution in nearly identical language. In his essay "On Literature, Revolution, Entropy, and Other Matters," Zamyatin presents revolution as a recurring phenomenon necessary to the perpetuation of human community:

Revolution is everywhere, in everything. It is infinite. There is no final revolution, no final number. The social revolution is only one of an infinite number of numbers: the law of revolution is not a social law, but an immeasurably greater one. It is a cosmic, universal law- like the laws of the conservation of energy and of the dissipation of energy. (1923/1970, pp. 107–108)

As Cooke makes clear, this perspective endorses a conception of utopia that is antithetical to the equally static OneState of the Benefactor and the Christian idea of heaven: "The idea of historical development's coming to a halt, when society will reach 'perfection' is also projected in Marxism and in traditional Christianity, both of which are commonly associated with the Single State" (2002, p. 82). For Zamyatin, no paradise can be permanent; revolution comes sooner or later to remedy the deadening stagnation. I-330 expresses the same understanding of revolution to D-503:

I jumped up. "This is unthinkable! It's stupid! Can't you see that what you're plotting is... revolution?" "Yes—revolution! Why is that stupid?" "Stupid— because there can't be a revolution [....] [O]ur revolution was the final one" [....] Her brows make a sharp mocking triangle: "My dear, you are a mathematician [....] Tell me the final number" [....] "But I-330, that's stupid. Since the number of numbers is infinite, how can there be a final one?" "And how can there be a final revolution?" (Zamyatin 1924/1993, p. 168)

The author's hypothesis that revolution inevitably recurs brings hope to the novel's overtly dispiriting conclusion; it also undermines the idea that *We* is a critique of the Russian Revolution in particular or socialism in general.

Orwell claims that Zamyatin "had a strong leaning towards primitivism" and eschewed modern technology (1946/1968, p. 75). Like Orwell, William Hutchings (1981–1982) writes of the "ambivalence toward machinery that is evident in Zamyatin's work" and Zamyatin's "distaste for urbanization" (p. 92). Hutchings concludes that in *We*, "Energy, revolution, and even nature itself exist only in an area beyond the Green Wall that surrounds the city" (1981–1982, p. 92). But I-330's conversation with D-503 about the aims of her revolution call this line of thinking into question. I-330 does not criticize the ideals that brought the Benefactor to power, just the notion that those ideals constitute immutable, infallible, universal laws, precluding any further revolutions:

" 'But, I-330—remember, just remember: That's just what our ancestors did—during the 200-Years War....' 'Oh, and they were right, they were a thousand times right. They made only one mistake: Afterward, they got the notion that they were the final number—something that doesn't exist in nature' " (Zamyatin 1924/1993, p. 169). Moody points out that I-330 and her followers seek to break down the barrier between the novel's two communities rather than foist the ways of one on the other: "E-330 and the Mephis do not seek to destroy the Single State but the Green Wall which surrounds it and thereby to reunite the two sides of the personality of man to form the whole man and the harmonious society" (1976, p. 31). Thus, in writing *We*, Zamyatin's quarrel seems to have been with both those who privileged science over instinct and those who fetishize the premodern world.

Approaching science with an attitude akin to religious faith troubled Zamyatin, who saw this tendency among socialists in both Russia and Britain and consequently satirized it in his dystopia. Zamyatin was not opposed to science. Indeed, he was keenly interested in the link between genetics and revolution. Although the citizens of OneState, and perhaps the Benefactor too, think that their community consists of the whole of humanity, I-330 informs D-503 that refugees from the 200-Years War are thriving in the so-called primitive state of freedom:

> But you didn't know, only very few knew, that a small part of them managed to survive and went on living there, on the other side of the Walls. They were naked and went off into the forest. There they learned from the trees, animals, birds, flowers, sun. They grew coats of fur over their bodies, but beneath the fur they kept their hot red blood. You had it worse. You grew numbers all over your body, numbers crawled about on you like lice. (Zamyatin 1924/1993, p. 158)

Here, scientific thought, represented throughout the text by numbers, is presented as an infestation; previously, D-503 considered it to be infallible: "The ancients' God created ancient—that is, prone to error—man, and so erred himself. The multiplication table is wiser and more absolute than the ancient God. It never—repeat, never—makes a mistake" (Zamyatin 1924/1993, p. 65). Through I-330, D-503 becomes aware of another organic strain of humanity, living in apparent harmony with nature and coated in fur. The "hot red blood" of these forest dwellers suggests their revolutionary zeal, and, while they lack the advanced technology of the OneStaters, they are much better acclimated to the natural environment. D-503 had always assumed that his hairy hands, a source of constant embarrassment to him, were an instance of atavism: "I can't stand people looking at my hands. They're hairy, shaggy, some kind of stupid throwback. I stuck out my hands and said with as steady a voice as I could manage: 'A monkey's hands' " (Zamyatin 1924/1993, p. 9). But he learns from I-330 that the hair on his hands might indicate his mixed lineage:

> "Your hand... You don't know, there are few who do know, that there are women from here, from the city, who have come to love those others over there. You, too, probably have a drop or two of that sunny forest blood. Maybe that's why I..." There was a pause, and strangely enough, the pause, the blank, the nothing, made my heart race. (Zamyatin 1924/1993, p. 157)

Through I-330's physical attraction to D-503, his hirsute hands become symbolic of his interconnected sexual and political awakenings. As Andrew Barratt (1985) rightly asserts,

> These 'shaggy paws', to which the engineer had referred earlier as 'an absurd atavism' [...] have now become the external mark of the powerful instincts which have been aroused in him through contact with I-330. Taken together, these two 'backward looking' images reveal D-503's subliminal awareness that his own sexuality represents a potential threat to the existence of the One State. (p. 662)

The importance ascribed to the look of D-503's hands implies that he is genetically predisposed to rebel and that this can be deduced from his appearance. Since Zamyatin equates revolution with renewal and development, this suggests that the restive people outside the wall are genetically superior to the docile people within it.

The pride I-330 takes in her unlawful association with the people of the wilderness shows her to be the embodiment of evil under the Benefactor's moral code: "Humility is a virtue, pride a vice; *We* comes from God, *I* from the Devil" (Zamyatin 1924/1993, p. 124). Although she comes from the opposite end of the political spectrum, Rand attacks this same quasibiblical conception of evil in *Anthem*. While the Benefactor is likened to the unchanging Elohim, I-330 symbolizes the mercurial Lucifer. As she tells D-503, those who follow her are fallen angels: "'Well, fallen angel. Now you're ruined,' she said, reverting to the formal *you*" (Zamyatin

1924/1993, p. 73). Just as I-330 epitomizes the Satanic, André Reszler (1985) argues that the Benefactor's regime is implicitly equated with a Christian church: "In Zamyatin's *We*, the utopian community appears as a 'powerful organism of millions of cells' organized along the lines of a 'united church' " (p. 204). Thus, *We* is more a satire of organized religion than an indictment of the Soviets.

But though I-330's insurgents are clearly associated with the rebel angels, this loaded imagery should not be misconstrued as Satanic in the biblical sense. Patrick A. McCarthy (1984) makes clear that Zamyatin wanted the Mephi to emulate the constant striving represented by Johann Wolfgang von Goethe's Faust: "For Zamyatin, the true writer must be a heretic and revolutionary constantly in revolt... against the dead alive people who are like machines [...] [having] a Faust's eternal dissatisfaction with the present and the attainable" (p. 122). Zamyatin viewed established religion as a system begetting conformity and subordination to an omnipotent, supreme order and therefore as something to be resisted, even against impossible odds. The Benefactor's speech to D-503 lays bare the underlying purpose and aims of the Church:

> Remember the scene: a blue hill, a cross, a crowd [....] And this same Christian, all-merciful God—the one who slowly roasts in the fires of Hell all those who rebel against him—is he not to be called *executioner*? [...] But, all this notwithstanding, you see, this is still the God who has been worshipped for centuries as the God of love. Absurd? No, on the contrary. It is the patent, signed in blood, of man's indelible good sense. Even then, in his savage, shaggy state, he understood: A true algebraic love of mankind will inevitably be inhuman, and the inevitable sign of the truth is its cruelty [....] [People] want someone to tell them, once and for all, what happiness is— and then bind them to that happiness with a chain [...] angels, the slaves of God. (Zamyatin 1924/1993, pp. 206–207)

Through the voice of the novel's dictator, Zamyatin addresses the problem of how to reconcile God's loving nature with the cruelty of acts such as the damning of sinners and unbelievers, the genocide of the indigenous Canaanites, the immolation of Jephthah's daughter, and so forth. Zamyatin's answer is that a loving god must necessarily be a cruel one because people cannot be trusted to choose happiness; happiness must be chosen for them and then foisted on them without exception.

To Orwell the Benefactor is just another power-hungry despot who takes satisfaction in harming others and imposing his will upon them:

"It is this intuitive grasp of the irrational side of totalitarianism—human sacrifice, cruelty as an end in itself, the worship of a Leader who is credited with divine attributes—that makes Zamyatin's book superior to Huxley's" (1946/1968, p. 75). But James Connors (1975) rightly identifies the inherent subjectivity in Orwell's assessment of the Benefactor. Connors observes that the Benefactor resorts to cruelty for practical, not sadistic, reasons:

> It is worth pointing out that Orwell to some extent was smuggling his own version of totalitarian ruling elites, both in his criticism of Huxley and in his praise of Zamyatin. With respect to the latter it was done at the expense of fidelity to the novel. I cannot find any evidence in *We* indicating that cruelty is practiced as "an end in itself". (1975, p. 123)

Connors also emphasizes the evenhanded way in which the Benefactor metes out punishment, belying Orwell's claim that his rule is "irrational": "There is no evidence indicating that the Well-Doer or the Guardians are either cynical or capricious in their roles as society's protectors: ruthless, logical consistency; complete dedication to achieving maximum happiness are their hallmarks" (1975, pp. 115–116). Connors is neither praising nor defending the Benefactor, but he does suggest that the Benefactor, unlike Orwell's O'Brien, may honestly believe his rule is just or at least have faith in the ideology determining his actions.

I-330, on the other hand, functions as a sort of pagan Christ figure, emblematic not of evil but of rebellion against a seemingly omnipotent force. Her speech to the rebels outside the city wall closely resembles the moment of communion where the blood of Christ is consumed. "She has a cup in her hands, a wooden cup, apparently. She drinks from it with her red lips and hands it to me and I shut my eyes and drink, I drink greedily" (Zamyatin 1924/1993, p. 151). I-330 is also standing on a skull-shaped rock which recalls the passion at Golgotha—the place of the skull: "a naked stone that looked like a human skull" (Zamyatin 1924/1993, p. 149). Just as Christ resisted the temptation to flee to safety when he prayed in the garden in the hours before his arrest, I-330 refuses D-503's offer to escape into the depths of the forest: "'I-330, darling, before it's too late [....] [W]e'll go together, over there, beyond the Wall' [....] She shook her head" (Zamyatin 1924/1993, p. 157). I-330 is also linked to Christ through a dark cross which appears when her brow tenses: "I say nothing but merely look at her face: The dark cross on it is now especially vivid" (Zamyatin 1924/1993, p. 157). Though I-330, like both Jesus and Rand's Transgressor, is apprehended and tortured, she stays silent and spiritually strong:

> They brought in that woman. She was supposed to give testimony in my presence. The woman was stubbornly silent and kept on smiling [....] Then they put her under the Bell [....] When they started pumping the air out of the Bell, she threw her head back, and half closed her eyes and pressed her lips together [....] Then they pulled her out, quickly brought her to with the help of electrodes, and put her back under the Bell. This happened three times, and she still didn't say a word. Others that they brought in with that woman turned out to be more honest. Many of them began talking right after the first time. Tomorrow they'll all go up the steps of the Machine of the Benefactor. (Zamyatin 1924/1993, p. 225)

Torture cannot bring about I-330's submission. Though D-503 tells the story, I-330 is its hero. The idea that the committed self can remain inviolable under torture is one that Orwell will challenge in *Nineteen Eighty-Four*.

We ends on an ambiguous note, but, as Barratt makes clear, hope persists:

> Although I-330 is tortured cruelly at the end of the novel, she has not yet been executed, owing to her stubborn refusal to provide her torturers with information. In this, as in the final uncertainty regarding the outcome of the revolution and the prospect of O-90 rearing her child beyond the Green Wall, there is some room at least for hope. (1985, p. 672)

Indeed, Cooke points out that given the numerous twists and turns of the novel's episodic plot, I-330 may well be rescued by S-4711, her mole within the Bureau of Guardians:

> [I]n a novel that is characterized by so many reversals of plot and fortune, a novel that has run roughshod over various generic expectations, can we really be so sure that the executions will take place? What if S-4711 turns out to be their jailer? By now the reader should be advised to take a wait-and-see attitude. (2002, p. 124)

We provides numerous avenues for hope. In addition to the chance that I-330 will escape, there is a sizable rebellion raging in the city on the novel's final page; O-90 has escaped and also carries a potentially messianic baby to continue her radicalism. The redemptive power of illicit sex is realized in this child, who will learn of the ordered city from his mother and experience freedom in natural surroundings, making him whole in a way that no one has been for generations. Most importantly, the rustic community in the wilderness remains beyond the grasp of the Benefactor.

Moreover, Cooke stresses that the fantasiectomy has rendered D-503 an unreliable narrator and that the procedure may have the unintended consequence of adversely affecting the loyalists' ability to fight effectively:

> Another bone of contention is the fate of the Mephi rebellion. According to many commentators, the Single State crushes it [....] However, this requires acceptance of D-503's words as authoritative, an especially doubtful practice after his Operation. Notably, he is only predicting a victory for the Single State. He mentions continuing strife and chaos, as well as a temporary wall that the forces of the Single State have erected in what seems to be the *middle* of the city. We should consider that the loyalists are fighting within the city limits behind a barricade constructed on the fortieth of at least fifty-nine avenues. Obviously, the battle is still in progress and the issue is left hanging in the balance at the end of the novel. Furthermore, if D-503's new barren prose style and poor perception are any indication of the fighting ability of other lobotomized citizens, the Single State is clearly in trouble. (2002, p. 124, emphasis in original)

In keeping with Zamyatin's perspective on revolution, Moody reminds the reader that even if this uprising fails, there will always be another insurrection: "The next revolution may appear to fail also but it will be followed by another and another. For Zamyatin life can never be static [....] Zamyatin's was a philosophy of optimism" (1976, p. 33). Despite D-503's loss of humanity through medical intervention, Reszler finds hope in the fact that his story of emergence as an individual is just one of many: "In *We*, when D-503 is told that a soul has formed within him, he also learns that individual soul formation has spread like an epidemic. Around the figure of the last man, whole islands of individual resistance are constituted. And on these islands, conspiracy prevails" (1985, p. 212). There is also, as Vasa D. Mihailovich (1974) notes, a lightness of style that tempers the darker overtones of Zamyatin's projected political fiction, distinguishing it from Huxley's and Orwell's: "There are additional differences in style, as well as in optimism and ironic humor exhibited by Zamyatin but not the other two [Huxley and Orwell]" (p. 329). The hope embedded in the novel's conclusion and the occasional levity of Zamyatin's prose indicate that *We* is not an entirely dystopian novel. Beauchamp (1973) sees it as an extrapolation of a typical utopia: "Zamiatin's imagination has projected the ideal of utopian organization to its logical extreme" (p. 289). Beauchamp's concise assessment of *We* applies just as fittingly to Huxley's *Brave New World*.

Utopian tendencies in *We* emerge primarily in bonds of social responsibility rooted in sexual longing: I-330's frequent unavailability engenders D-503's commitment to her well-being; O-90's passion for the preoccupied D-503 inspires her to escape with their unborn child; and the Numbers who reach for sexual freedom by copulating without state approval during the insurrection are ultimately the ones who fight for their human dignity by resisting the fantasiectomy. In *We*, Zamyatin presents sexual longing as a moral accelerant, an idea further developed by Huxley in *Brave New World*.

REFERENCES

Barratt, A. (1985). The X-Factor in Zamyatin's *We*. *The Modern Language Review*, *80*(3), 659–672.

Baruch, E. H. (1983). The Golden Country: Sex and Love in *1984*. In I. Howe (Ed.), *1984 Revisited* (pp. 47–56). New York, NY: Harper & Row.

Beauchamp, G. (1973). Of Man's Last Disobedience: Zamyatin's *We* and Orwell's *1984*. *Comparative Literature Studies*, *10*(4), 285–301.

Booker, M. K. (1994). *The Dystopian Impulse in Modern Literature: Fiction as Social Criticism*. Westport, CT: Greenwood Press.

Brown, C. (1993). Introduction. In Y. Zamyatin (Ed.), *We* (pp. xi–xxvi). New York: Penguin.

Connors, J. (1975). Zamyatin's *We* and the Genesis of *1984*. *Modern Fiction Studies*, *21*(1), 107–124.

Cooke, B. (2002). *Human Nature in Utopia: Zamyatin's We*. Evanston, IL: Northwestern University Press.

Foucault, M. (1995). *Discipline & Punish* (A. Sheridan, Trans.). New York, NY: Random House. (Original work published 1975)

Gimpelevich, Z. (1997). "We" and "I" in Zamyatin's *We* and Rand's *Anthem*. *Germano-Slavica: A Canadian Journal of Germanic and Slavic Comparative Studies*, *10*(1), 13–23.

Hutchings, W. (1981–1982). Structure and Design in a Soviet Dystopia: H.G. Wells, Constructivism, and Yevgeny Zamyatin's *We*. *Journal of Modern Literature*, *9*(1), 81–102.

McCarthy, P. A. (1984). Zamyatin and the Nightmare of Technology. *Science Fiction Studies*, *11*(33), 122–129.
Mihailovich, V. D. (1974). Critics on Evgeny Zamyatin. *Papers on Language & Literature*, *10*(3), 317–334.
Moody, C. (1976). Zamyatin's *We* and English Antiutopian Fiction. *Unisa English Studies*, *14*(1), 24–33.
Ní Dhúill, C. (2010). *Sex in Imagined Spaces: Gender and Utopia from More to Bloch*. London: Legenda.
Orwell, G. (1968). Review: *We* by E. I. Zamyatin. In S. Orwell & I. Angus (Eds.), *In Front of Your Nose, 1945–1950: The Collected Essays, Journalism & Letters, Vol. 4* (pp. 72–76). New York, NY: Harcourt Brace Jovanovich. (Original work published 4 January 1946)
Orwell, G. (1977). *Nineteen Eighty-Four*. New York: Harcourt Brace Jovanovich. (Original work published 1949)
Preslar, R. M. (2008). Yevgeny Zamyatin's *We*: Forbidden Knowledge and Coercion in Utopia. *Soundings: An Interdisciplinary Journal*, *91*(1/2), 33–61.
Reszler, A. (1985). Man as Nostalgia: The Image of the Last Man in Twentieth-Century Postutopian Fiction. In S. Friedlander, G. Holton, L. Marx, & E. Skolnikoff (Eds.), *Visions of Apocalypse* (pp. 196–216). New York, NY: Holmes & Meier.
Shane, A. M. (1968). *The Life and Works of Evgenij Zamjatin*. Berkeley, CA: University of California Press.
Walker, J. M. (1987). Totalitarian and Liminal Societies in Zamyatin's *We*. *Mosaic*, *20*(1), 113–127.
Zamyatin, Y. (1970). On Literature, Revolution, Entropy, and Other Matters. In M. Ginsburg (Ed. & Trans.), *A Soviet Heretic: Essays by Yevgeny Zamyatin* (pp. 107–112). Chicago, IL: The University of Chicago Press. (Original work published 1923)
Zamyatin, Y. (1993). *We* (C. Brown, Trans.). New York, NY: Penguin. (Original work published 1924)

CHAPTER 4

The Sexual Life of the Savage in Aldous Huxley's *Brave New World*

Brave New World presents sexual desire not just as a means of regaining personal liberty but also as the only way to restore what is human. In a review from 1935 of Vilfredo Pareto's *Trattato Di Sociologia Generale*, Huxley approvingly summarizes Pareto's observation that people are primarily motivated by instinct and emotion, with reason merely glossing over our atavistic tendencies:

> But the instincts and emotions do not assert themselves undisguised. Hunger and thirst after rationality are fundamental human traits. The residues put on the fancy dress of derivations and, paying attention only to the fancy dress, men persuade themselves that they are acting in accordance with the dictates of reason. In fact, of course, they are acting in accordance with the dictates of instinct and feeling, and inventing pseudo-logical derivations after the event to justify their actions. To human beings in society, the derivations seem important; but, in fact, they are not important. (1935/2003c, pp. 27–28)

Totalitarian rule depends on the manipulation of instincts and emotions. The valorization of scientific thinking both facilitates and conceals this insidious process. Though well intentioned, faith in science brings about humanity's cultural degradation in Huxley's forecast.

In *The Dialectic of Enlightenment*, Max Horkheimer and Theodor Adorno (1944/1972) explain how the dominant Western culture of decadence, which Huxley parodies in *Brave New World*, erodes memory and imagination by categorizing and narrowing the range of artistic, utilitarian, and recreational experience:

> The man with leisure has to accept what the culture manufacturers offer him [....] While the mechanism is to all appearances planned by those who serve up the data of experience, that is, by the culture industry, it is in fact forced upon the latter by the power of society [....] There is nothing left for the consumer to classify [....] The whole world is made to pass through the filter of the culture industry [...] [leaving] no room for imagination or reflection. (pp. 124–126)

Since scientific and industrial progress have made human labor unnecessary, everyone in Huxley's World State would be considered a person of leisure by Horkheimer and Adorno. Whether Alpha or Epsilon, these citizens do the same work of placidly consuming whatever the culture manufacturer—in this case the state—offers them. The process of filtering all quotidian experience through the machine begins in the hatchery with prenatal care. Then, as the children grow to become adults, drugs, hypnosis, and Pavlovian conditioning acclimate them to their predetermined places in the hierarchy. The machine is so effective at producing and maintaining happiness that society perpetuates itself with limited conscious guidance.

World State has realized a concept of controlled human development, first conceived and rudely implemented by the governments of Europe in the late eighteenth century, which Foucault (1975/1995) calls the manufacture of docile bodies: "it defined how one may have a hold over others' bodies, not only so that they may do what one wishes, but so that they may operate as one wishes, with the techniques, the speed and the efficiency that one determines" (p. 138). The docile body will not simply act on command without hesitation; it will behave as programmed even when unattended. The sexual potential of the docile body is of primary importance to both Zamyatin and Huxley. Both authors ask whether sexuality is the last potentially self-determinant zone of the otherwise docile self. In their projected political fictions, this question is a matter of life and death. Controlling the sex lives of World Staters is the largest and most aggressively pursued government concern. Yet control is achieved through satiation rather than repression. By custom and law, people in *Brave New World* have unlimited access to the bodies of their fellow citizens. Diken (2011) recognizes that this commodification of sex is achieved through making the body public property:

Huxley, a liberal, perceives 'belonging' as a property relation. Correspondingly, sexuality is socialized in the brave new world only in the sense that the body is no longer private property but becomes a public property, a property of the state. As erotic drives are institutionalized, the body is captured by the system and functions as an instrument of regulation and domination. (p. 167)

Giving people all the sex they want defuses the revolutionary danger implicit in sex by removing the volatile element of deferred desire. Instead of actively imagining and pursuing new avenues of sexual excitement, the inhabitants of the World State are gratified by an expansive state-controlled system of sensuality.

As Marcuse observes, by providing a superabundance of sexual satisfaction and pornographic entertainment, governments can rob the sexual act of any greater significance it might carry and thus neutralize it as a threat. Marcuse argues that because of its inspirational component, frustration of sexual desire is, oddly enough, a positive and liberating force:

[T]he technological reality *limits the scope of sublimation.* It also reduces the *need* for sublimation. In the mental apparatus, the tension between that which is desired and that which is permitted seems considerably lowered [....] The organism is thus being preconditioned for the spontaneous acceptance of what is offered. Inasmuch as the greater liberty involves a contraction rather than extension and development of instinctual needs, it works *for* rather than *against* the status quo of general repression—one might speak of "institutionalized desublimation." The latter appears to be a vital factor in the making of the authoritarian personality of our time. (1964/1991, pp. 73-74, emphasis in original)

According to Marcuse, when sexual urges go temporarily or entirely unfulfilled because culture and environment restrain them, these impulses beget dreams and aspirations that transcend the self, encouraging the individual to realize and struggle for something beyond quotidian reality. The individual envisions the realization of these lofty desires as taking place in an ideal landscape, which—even if unachievable—embodies the encouraging dream of a utopia and inculcates the will to work toward establishing it. Unlike the complacent, sated Londoners, John the Savage, who is the product of sexually frustrating circumstances, never stops believing in and searching for a better world, even though he ultimately judges himself to be unworthy of one. In the dystopias of London, Burdekin, Rand, Orwell, and Atwood, sexual passion is largely unsatisfied. It therefore serves as a gateway to ambition because it takes place within a larger framework of libidinal experience. By striving for inaccessible objects of sexual desire, people learn to reach beyond their grasp in every aspect of life. Huxley, like Zamyatin, demonstrates that the subversive power of desire lies not in sex itself but in the longing for bodies that are forbidden.

The urgent awareness of self brought on by deferred desire triggers what Marcuse refers to as erotic cognition: "[E]rotic as well as logical cognition break the hold of the established, contingent reality and strive for a truth incompatible with it [....] In the exigencies of thought and in the madness of love is the destructive refusal of the established ways of life" (1964/1991, p. 127). Though it has all but completely atrophied in *Brave New World*, erotic cognition forcefully emerges in *Nineteen Eighty-Four*. Winston's passion for the seemingly unobtainable Julia leads him to envision an entire utopian landscape, the "Golden Country," where they can love but also live freely. In Atwood's *Handmaid's Tale*, the author's native Canada becomes the elusive sexual and social free state to which Moira, Offred, and other characters seek to escape. Zamyatin and Rand both present a wilderness beyond the collective where characters find refuge.

But in *Brave New World* there is no envisioned space where sexual freedom and political liberty coalesce because when people get a surfeit of sexual activity without any effort, exertion, or chance of disappointment, sexuality itself is thoroughly desublimated. No concept of liberty or individuality can arise from mere lust because the constant gratification of sexual inclinations precludes the greater perspective which arises from the deferment of consummation. As Dominic Baker-Smith (2001) asserts, instant gratification facilitates political predestination: "Immediate passage from desire to gratification leaves little space for the cultivation of a higher self; consequently its value as an instrument of political manipulation is all too evident" (p. 103). By making sex easily and continually available, the government fosters complacency and people become content with a pleasure system that doles out liaisons like meal tickets. The political applications of desire are negated. In short, an erotic compulsion that what was once strong enough to contravene even the most intense sociopolitical conditioning is reduced to the complacent expectation of routine gratification.

To satiate the desire for variety and to truncate any ambitions arising out of the desire for unfamiliar or novel sensations, new forms of deviance are quickly absorbed into the state-controlled pleasure machine.

The turbulence of violent crimes such as kidnapping and rape are tamed when reduced to fetishistic "feely" films such as *Three Weeks in a Helicopter*. And when John the Savage retreats to the lighthouse to engage in self-flagellation, his actions are almost immediately televised, leading to both a pornographic movie about his lifestyle, *The Savage of Surrey*, and an onslaught of imitators descending on his Spartan sanctuary. As Horkheimer and Adorno make clear, "Anyone who resists can only survive by fitting in. Once his particular brand of deviation from the norm has been noted by the industry, he belongs to it" (1944/1972, p. 132). The concern for these theorists—and for Huxley and Zamyatin—is not just that eccentricity so rarely emerges within totalitarian structures but the rapidity with which it is assimilated.

But like other authors of projected political fiction, Huxley employs sexual longing as a safeguard, preventing humanity from becoming a race of automatons. Dissatisfied characters such as Bernard Marx, Helmholtz Watson, and Lenina Crowne are found within the upper echelons of society. Their frustrations shift into open unrest through their interactions with an idealistic visitor to their prefabricated civilization, who is ironically called John the Savage. Raised among Native Americans in Malpais—which, as Baker (1990) points out, means "bad place," "bad country," or "dystopia" in Spanish (p. 113)—John comes to World State predisposed to like it. His Beta mother has regaled him with stories of her civilization and even managed to condition him slightly: "The Indians [...] were so beastly to him and wouldn't let him do all the things the other boys did. Which was a good thing in a way, because it made it easier for me to condition him a little" (Huxley 1932/1965a, p. 93). John is essentially the byproduct of two irreconcilable systems: one that fetishizes modern technology and another that venerates premodern supernaturalism. There is, however, an alternative: through the implications and consequences of the fraught erotic connection between the naturally born John and the genetically engineered Lenina, Huxley offers an enriching and sustainable sexual and social outlook.

In John and Lenina we find yet another instance of a relationship rooted in sexual desire between an orthodox and a revolutionary character. The first name, "Lenina," is obviously a feminine variation of Vladimir Lenin. Lenina's surname highlights her political importance.

Lenina is admittedly an atypical political radical. Deanna Madden (1992) finds her to be nothing more than a chauvinistic projection of a mid-twentieth-century sex symbol (p. 290). Madden accurately reads sexist overtones in the novel, and Huxley's own biases may have hampered the development of Lenina's political insight. But, as June Deery (1992) points out, Huxley's somewhat prejudicial perspective is not deliberate: "In Huxley's works, women have as much opportunity relative to men—at least in theory [....] Only on a few occasions does he suggest that women in *Brave New World* are treated differently or more unfairly than the male citizens. In the era of female rights, one might say that Huxley sins more by omission than intention" (p. 271). Huxley was trying to demonstrate that women would achieve equality in the future, but, because he was both the product of a sexist culture and striving primarily to address other issues in his projected political fiction, his portrayal of women remains inadvertently unbalanced.

Although Huxley imbues Lenina with less conscious political insight than Orwell gives Julia, or Zamyatin gives I-330, her refusal to compromise her feelings for John and her commensurate disenchantment with civilization show that the redemptive power of sexuality is not a masculine construct but a rejuvenative force that arises from both female desire and sexual agency. Lenina is more of a nonconformist than she appears to be. In *Prisms*, Adorno (1967) points out that at bottom she is criminally unhappy in a world where happiness is legally required: "Lenina's overzealous defensiveness betrays insecurity, the suspicion that her kind of happiness is distorted by contradictions, that it is not happiness even by its own definition" (p. 111). Lenina acts on this heretical unhappiness initially by disregarding the obligation to be promiscuous and pursuing a de facto monogamous relationship with Henry Foster, which, as Baker makes clear, is shamefully sinful: "In a society where undiscriminating promiscuity is a virtue, Lenina's preference for long-drawn-out affairs with only one male is regarded as perversely immoral" (1990, p. 93). Baker also notes that Lenina's "monogamous tendencies suggest that the World State's control of its citizens is less than absolute" (1990, p. 101). Through her attraction to John, Lenina ultimately embraces the desire to pair-bond openly: "'In a few minutes,' she had said to herself... 'I shall be seeing him, talking to him, telling him' (for she had come with her mind made up) 'that I like him—more than anybody I've ever known'" (Huxley 1932/1965a, p. 133). Her penchant for John is equivalent to the "great transgression of preference" in Rand's *Anthem*, and—if discovered—would be taken more seriously than a capital offense. As the Director of Hatcheries and Conditioning tells Henry Foster,

"No offense is so heinous as unorthodoxy of behavior. Murder kills only the individual—and, after all, what is an individual? [...] We can make new ones with the greatest ease—as many as we like. Unorthodoxy threatens more than the life of a mere individual; it strikes at Society itself. Yes, at Society itself." (Huxley 1932/1965a, p. 113)

When her desire is enflamed, Lenina is willing to follow a monogamous course that does indeed strike at society itself.

David Leon Higdon (2002) draws attention not only to Lenina's deviant sexual cravings but also to the number of subtle ways in which she displays rebellious predilections, particularly her tendency to buck the caste system by dressing in green—the color reserved for Gammas: "Lenina's sexual rebellion poses as large a challenge to the text's motifs as does her wardrobe; it is just a bit less visible to those around her. Just as she questions the codes of color, she questions the code of sexuality, and in both cases, she escapes punishment" (p. 81). Though Lenina lacks the rhetoric of insurgency, she inspires others to rebel. John's irrepressible passion for her transforms him from an ardent admirer of his ancestral home to a social and political radical. Though he would never have been satisfied with the developed world, he would not have become so passionately seditious had he not fallen for Lenina.

Of course, since Lenina offers no explicit revolutionary credo for John to adopt, he can only withdraw from World State instead of moving to overthrow it. Here is another subtle critique of Wells's esteem for the scientific mind in that John finds himself the unwilling subject of one of Mustapha Mond's experiments. Just as the World Controller found "sufficient scientific interest" to authorize Bernard to bring the Savage to civilization (Huxley 1932/1965a, p. 108), as though he were licensing the importation of an exotic creature to a zoo, Mustapha Mond, in the interest of science, ultimately prevents John from joining his friends on an island:

> "I went to see the Controller this morning," said the Savage at last.
> "What for?"
> "To ask if I mightn't go to the islands with you."
> "And what did he say?" asked Helmholtz eagerly.
> The Savage shook his head. "He wouldn't let me."
> "Why not?"
> "He said he wanted to go on with the experiment." (Huxley 1932/1965a, p. 186)

Although the World Controller prioritizes the collective happiness of his subjects, the individual life is clearly no more valuable to him than the life of a rat in a laboratory, despite the fact that he is aware of John's intelligence, honesty, and volition. Mond's scientific ambitions, global perspective, and extensive knowledge have made him more rather than less inhumane.

John the Savage, on the other hand, has a background in the humanities. Renaissance drama, Native American folklore, and his mother's wistful stories of "the Other Place" (Huxley 1932/1965a, p. 97) comprise his informal education and bring him the happiest moments of his troubled childhood. John's frustrations with Fordian civilization and his eventual decision to live and die as a martyr can be traced back to the lexicon he garners from an old, discarded copy of *The Complete Works of William Shakespeare*. In this respect, *Brave New World* is very like *Nineteen Eighty-Four*, *Anthem*, and *Swastika Night* in that these novels explore the dependency of thought on language. In *Brave New World Revisited*, Huxley (1958/1965b) argues that memory, emotional responses, and behavior all depend on language: "Language gives definition to our memories and [...] converts the immediacy of craving or abhorrence [...] into fixed principles of feeling and conduct" (p. 86). Not surprisingly, limitation of language is used in *Brave New World*—as in *Swastika Night*, *Nineteen Eighty-Four*, and *Anthem*—as a tool for social manipulation.

Since the range of human experience has been so successfully narrowed by A.F. 632, the English language has atrophied and shrunk because there are fewer things, feelings, and situations to contemplate and describe.[1] As Angela C. Holzer (2003) points out, what little language remains is contrived to shore up an orthodox perspective: "Language, having (almost) become devoid of meaning, or better, implying its own ironization and instability of meaning, is (intra-textually) an instrument of indoctrination in *Brave New World*" (p. 8). Eschewing the ham-fisted practice of censorship, the World Controllers have advanced thought control through the debasement of potentially subversive words. By stigmatizing instead of suppressing words such as "mother" and "father," the concept of the nuclear family unit becomes reprehensible to the Brave New Worldians. In *Nineteen Eighty-Four*, allegiance to Goldstein—and the human rights with which he is associated—seems wicked and treasonous largely because Modern English has been reduced to Newspeak. In *Swastika Night*, words that acknowledge the natural equality of women and their fundamental worth as human beings have been eradicated, making their full humanity inconceivable even to open-minded characters such as Alfred and von Hess. Individuality becomes similarly unimaginable in *Anthem* with the loss of the word "I." Depending on whether it expands or contracts, language works as either a liberating or a limiting force.

John's process of linguistic self-discovery turns on erotic experience. From early childhood, he passively accepts his mother's prostitution and the anguish it causes, responding with confusion. When the local women punish Linda for her promiscuity, John lacks the necessary vocabulary to contextualize what happened:

> "Why did they hurt you Linda?"
> "I don't know. How should I know?... They say those men are *their* men." (Huxley 1932/1965a, p. 96, emphasis in original)

But as he begins absorbing the language of Shakespeare, John is able to contextualize both his burgeoning desire and his latent rage. One day, when his mother neglects to close her bedroom door while engaging in sexual intercourse with her boyfriend Popé, John's jealousy ignites a political epiphany and he rebels:

> It was as though he [John] had never really hated Popé before; never really hated him because he had never been able to say how much he hated him. But now he had these words [....] [T]he door of the inner room was open, and he saw them lying together on the bed [....] [T]he words [Shakespeare] repeated and repeated themselves in his head [....] The knife for the meat was lying on the floor near the fireplace [....] He ran across the room and stabbed. (Huxley 1932/1965a, pp. 101–102)

At this moment, John comes to understand both the tragic characters of Shakespeare and the personal tragedy of his family life. His passion for revenge transforms literature into a way of engaging the world around him.

When he eventually comes to London, it is likewise through the thought-provoking power of Shakespeare's language that John is able to engender dangerous new impulses in Helmholtz Watson:

> The Savage shook his head [....] [U]nlocking the drawer in which he kept his mouse-eaten book, he opened and read [....] Helmholtz listened with growing excitement [....] [H]e turned pale and trembled with an unprecedented emotion [....] "Why was that old fellow such a marvelous propaganda tech-

nician? Because he had so many insane, excruciating things to get excited about [....] We need some other kind of madness and violence." (Huxley 1932/1965a, p. 142)

Although Helmholtz can appreciate Shakespeare's genius, taken out of the proper cultural context, the great playwright is reduced to a marvelous "propaganda technician," whose writings instigate the vain "madness and violence" of John and Helmholtz defenestrating soma rations. Following arrest, Helmholtz's conditioning enables his peaceful acceptance of state-imposed exile, but the volatile mixture of Native American, World State, and Shakespearean discourses makes matters more complicated for him. Donald Watt (2001) convincingly suggests that the rhetoric of Shakespeare coupled with John's early childhood experiences have blurred the distinction in his mind between his mother and his love interest, derailing his sexual, emotional, and ethical development:

> Is John conflating Linda and Lenina as he chastizes himself? He wants to remember his mother's last seconds at the hospital, not be distracted by images of the voluptuous Lenina. Yet as he cries out to Linda for forgiveness it could be that along with Shakespearean passion John has also picked up some Freudian repressions from his young observations of Linda with Popé. (p. 50)

The language in John's heart and mind irrevocably separates him from his friends, who in being relocated to islands are finally receiving the happiness they wanted from the state, just as it alienates him from Lenina.

Booker (1994) shrewdly suggests that Huxley illustrates the perils of confusing fiction with reality through John's internalization of Shakespeare's writings: "Literature for Huxley can be a powerful humanizing force, but it can be a negative one as well, especially if its readers lose the ability properly to distinguish between fiction and reality" (p. 59). John's Renaissance vocabulary allows him to recognize his attraction to Lenina, yet it also causes him to misinterpret her conditioned sexual advances as deliberate licentiousness and to condemn her under an Elizabethan moral code extinct for nearly a thousand years: "Bound by strong vows that had never been pronounced, obedient to laws that had long since ceased to run" (Huxley 1932/1965a, p. 130). When Lenina initially tries to seduce him, he responds with violent and inappropriate disapprobation: "'Damned whore!' [...] The Savage pushed her away with such force that she staggered and fell [....] '[G]et out of my sight or I'll kill you.' [...] The noise of that prodigious slap by which her departure was accelerated was like a pistol shot" (Huxley 1932/1965a, p. 149).

Nevertheless, though Lenina has no ideology of subversion to offer John in place of Shakespeare, his passion for her carries him to the brink of violent insurrection. Huxley's novel suggests that even where there is no explicit revolutionary rhetoric to follow, sexual arousal still breeds resistance to political subjugation. Not surprisingly, sexual desire is also the means by which John's spiritual renewal takes hold. At the end of the novel, John chooses God over comfort, withdrawing from World State to the lighthouse, but he is only able to make this choice after realizing his sexual desire for Lenina and the promise of fulfillment her body brings.

Huxley's evocation of God in *Brave New World* should not be misunderstood as an endorsement of Christianity. In his essay "Christ and the Present Crisis," written the same year that *Brave New World* was published, Huxley imagines what would transpire if Jesus returned in our time. According to Huxley, one serious problem that the Messiah would face is that modern science precludes rational belief in the existence of Yahweh:

> Jesus would be faced with the problem of finding adequate metaphysical reasons for his teachings. This he did in the past by invoking the will of a personal God. Modern science makes it impossible to believe in a personal God. In the last resort, the only adequate reason for a transcendental ethic is to be found in the human psyche [....] I believe that a second Jesus would have to justify his preaching in terms of a fundamentally humanistic philosophy. (1932/2003b, p. 23)

Given his unstable and ultimately suicidal frame of mind, John's belief in a divine superintendent is not an endorsement of religious faith by the author. Huxley understood the human aspiration for higher consciousness but, as Wilhelm Halbfass (2001) points out, this understanding was rooted in the physical rather than the metaphysical: "According to Huxley, mysticism, which he describes as 'the systematic cultivation of mental quietness' and 'a rule of health,' has nothing to do with a 'union with God'. Atheists and epileptics, too, have received similar inspirations, and they have not ascribed them to a divine source" (p. 225). Huxley believed that individual people could benefit from drawing on and combining the best teachings and practices of Eastern and Western spirituality into a sustaining personal way of life.

Taking Jesus as an example once more, Huxley maintains that religion cannot facilitate productive societal cooperation. Hence Jesus's emphasis on personal rather than communal salvation: "Jesus was concerned with individual souls. Even when he seemed to be talking about politics or economics, he was always really talking about souls. Consistently, he left to Caesar the things that were Caesar's" (Huxley 1932/2003b, p. 21). While Huxley takes the personal struggles of characters such as John, Lenina, Helmholtz, and Bernard seriously, his anti-utopia satirizes the Church of England and, by implication, other organized religious systems: the Archbishop of Canterbury has become the Arch-Community-Songster of Canterbury; soma is revered as holy, which is why the Deltas view the act of throwing it out of a window as "wanton sacrilege" (Huxley 1932/1965a, p. 163); and the Sacrament of Holy Communion has been reduced to a drug- and sex-fueled, biweekly Solidarity Service. Its fluid adaptation to an increasingly trivial society reveals the plasticity of organized religion.

But *Brave New World*, though sympathetic to personal growth, is also not an endorsement of John's chosen ascetic lifestyle. Citing the inapplicability of Jesus's asceticism to modernity, Huxley argues that a policy of renunciation cannot address the problem of overproduction in the post-industrial world:

> Let us frankly admit that, if he were now to return, Jesus could do little to solve our political and economic problems. Spiritual intuitions are no substitute for blue prints [....] The pre-industrial age was an age of under-production. A religion which preached under-consumption was therefore economically admirable. Ours is an age of over-production, and the first duty of the good citizen (at any rate in normal times) is over-consumption. Abnegation is spiritually wholesome and Jesus, if he returned, would certainly preach it. Would his preaching prevail against the economic forces encouraging unlimited acquisitiveness? (1932/2003b, p. 22)

In Huxley's view, just as Jesus would be incapable of reversing the over-consumption and commercialism endemic to the celebration of his own putative birthday, John cannot reasonably hope to foster an appreciation for nonmaterial values among the citizens of World State, a reality to which he resigns himself when he tries to emigrate.

John's rigid views of sexual purity, though adopted from Shakespeare, are, of course, rooted in Christianity and outdated to the point of being counterproductive. Huxley points out that the chastity associated with Jesus and his ministry is incompatible with modernity:

Turn now to the similar problem of chastity. Like voluntary poverty, it is spiritually bracing. Jesus would preach it—preach it to a world that reads Freud and uses contraceptives. In an age when license led to illegitimate children and social disgrace, chastity was good policy as well as good spirituality. Contraceptives have completely altered the circumstances. For how long can an ethic survive in circumstances which have robbed it of its material (though not, of course, its spiritual) significance? (1932/2003b, pp. 22–23)

Adorno rightly interprets John's denial of sexual desire and the physical harm he does to himself as products of the Christian misconception that there is nobility in suffering for the sake of suffering: "When [...] the Savage declares, 'What you need is something with tears for a change,' his deliberately insolent exaltation of suffering is not merely a characteristic of the obdurate individualist. It evokes Christian metaphysics, which promises future salvation solely by virtue of suffering" (1967, p. 107). By becoming a suffering recluse who attempts to spend the remainder of his life punishing himself for circumstances and feelings largely beyond his control, John contravenes the moral philosophy which Huxley puts forth in the first few lines of the 1946 foreword to a reprint of the novel: "Chronic remorse, as all the moralists are agreed, is a most undesirable sentiment. If you have behaved badly, repent, make what amends you can and address yourself to the task of behaving better next time. On no account brood over your wrongdoing. Rolling in the muck is not the best way of getting clean" (1946/1965c, p. xiii). Huxley has shown the reader two unhealthy societies in *Brave New World*: the soulless conglomerate of the many, and the masochistic, monastic madhouse of the one.

Even though desiring Lenina has radicalized him, John cannot inspire others because their programming has made it impossible for Huxley's Londoners to comprehend fully his anti-establishment discourse. Unlike other major works of projected political fiction, *Brave New World* suggests that our mass-produced descendants may not be able even to grasp the concept of political freedom. The escape of Equality 7-2521 and Liberty 5-3000 in *Anthem* indicates a new beginning for humankind; the footnotes to *The Iron Heel* guarantee a forthcoming successful revolution; revolutionaries have infiltrated the regime and are actively at work in both *We* and *The Handmaid's Tale*; the preservation of von Hess's manuscript in *Swastika Night* safeguards the truth for future generations; and *Nineteen Eighty-Four*—even without the subtle implications of the appendix on Newspeak—concludes with the assumption that, though they may be sought out and destroyed by the Party, recalcitrant characters such as Winston Smith will continue to emerge. Though *Nineteen Eighty-Four* is often misconstrued as the darker of the two most famous dystopias, Orwell, in his column "As I Please," for the December 24, 1943 issue of *Tribune*, chided Huxley for his "neo-pessimistic" outlook: "The thing that is common to all these people, whether [...] Pétain [...] Sorel [...] Berdyaev [...] or Huxley, is their refusal to believe that human society can be fundamentally improved. Man is non-perfectible, merely political changes can effect nothing, progress is an illusion" (1943/2000, p. 63). Adorno saw the same paradox in *Brave New World*: "The monolithic trend and the linear concept of progress, as handled in the novel, derive from the restricted form in which the productive forces developed in 'pre-history' [....] In prophesying the entropy of history, Huxley succumbs to an illusion which is necessarily propagated by the society against which he so zealously protests" (1967, p. 114).

The sexual desire that awakens John proceeds from romantic devotion, to frustration, to a failed rebellion, to an act of desperate penance. Just as Rand presents her dystopia as the "city of the damned," Robert M. Adams (1993) argues that the pointless repetitiveness of life in World State recalls the agonies of Dante's *Inferno*: "For in Hell the sinners are doomed to repeat forever an act that was at least originally their own. But here in 'utopia' the choice is already made for them" (p. 134). Acknowledging that the key to regeneration lies in our instinctual desires, Baker chides Huxley for satirizing the Wellsian utopia while offering no viable way out: "In *Brave New World*, the Wellsian scientific utopia is conceived as an oppressive utopia, yet no possibility of a restoration of instinctual or natural values is permitted" (1990, p. 137).

Faint signs of hope do, however, emerge in the text. Huxley, as Meckier (2003) observes, casts John the Savage as a John the Baptist figure, an outcast who lives and dies in frustration but suggests the promise of future deliverance (p. 191). Both the John of the New Testament and the John of *Brave New World* are unexpected children; both emerge from the wilderness pointing the way to salvation; both openly and notoriously challenge the political systems they encounter; both ultimately make their stand on metaphysical grounds; and both die prematurely for their beliefs under sexualized circumstances: John the Baptist is executed after Herod makes a rash promise to his stepdaughter following her seductive dance, and John the Savage kills himself after succumbing to his lust in the heather. Meckier argues that just as the biblical John was the harbinger of

Jesus of Nazareth, the life and death of John the Savage hint at the possibility of an eventual Messiah, someone who can awaken the somnambulists of A.F. 632 (2003, p. 193). John the Savage, like his biblical counterpart, is a pariah who dies tragically. The close correlation between the two suggests that just as John the Baptist left an enduring legacy, so too the end of John the Savage's life does not signify the end of his impact on humanity.

What makes Huxley's anti-utopia frightening is that when the Messiah arrives, we might not want to be freed from our prison of gratification. Huxley himself acknowledges that his fictional world of sexual access, lasting youth, and narcotic ecstasy feels enticingly like a utopian ideal:

> We know what ought to be done; but [...] do we really wish to act upon our knowledge? [...] In the United States [...] an actual majority of young people [...] would be perfectly content, if they can continue to live in the style to which the boom has accustomed them, to be ruled, from above, by an oligarchy of assorted experts. (1958/1965b, pp. 95–96)

But Huxley also thought that no matter how organized and efficient the social system becomes, the human spirit can by nature never be totally assimilated. Even in a society based on the satiation of all desire, there is still a space within each person outside of the system's grasp. The citizens of the Brave New World are encouraged to fill this void with *soma*. Yet for characters such as Lenina, *soma* isn't enough. Through Lenina's yearning for John, the promise embedded in the novel emerges.

Unlike John's ludicrous attempt to "free the slaves" by throwing *soma* rations out of a window, Lenina's expression of love for John presents a genuine threat to the status quo. Bradley W. Buchanan (2008) explains why romantically loving only one person is such a volatile taboo in *Brave New World*: "An 'only love' is an incestuous love, in Huxley's futuristic world, because it tends to work against the social solidarity, which is the key to peaceful life" (p. 29). Lenina's love for John threatens the principles of "community, identity, stability" (Huxley 1932/1965a, p. 1) on which the World State depends. Peter Edgerly Firchow (1999) notes that Lenina moves beyond critical thought to decisive action "in defiance of what she knows to be the properly promiscuous code of sexual behavior" (p. 147). Sean A. Witters (2008) asserts that through Lenina, Huxley suggests that the inclination to be monogamous is instinctive and so deeply ingrained that it resists both genetic manipulation and relentless conditioning:

In Huxley's schema, this is a way of naturalizing monogamy, or rather, indulging the notion that the desire for long-term individual commitment is innate. For Lenina, it seems an instinctual behavior that emerges against her will. It denies her conditioning and the state's power to undo what nature has built. (p. 82)

Witters makes clear that Lenina's monogamous ways are not simply shocking but also a challenge to state authority:

> Monogamy is not just considered distasteful and gauche; it is viewed as absurdly antisocial to even entertain the notion [....] Any form of allegiance that bypasses the state as an intermediary is contrary to its model of stability [....] We are led to see monogamy as a subversive act of unmediated free will, and, ultimately, as a natural behavior [...] that undermines artificial state authority. (2008, p. 82)

Of course, Lenina's subversive desires do not effect change in World State. They do, however, enable her to transcend her incomprehension of John's behavior and genuinely commiserate with him when she finds him in anguish at his hermitage:

> The young woman pressed both hands to her left side, and on that peach-bright, doll-beautiful face of hers appeared a strangely incongruous expression of yearning distress. Her blue eyes seemed to grow larger, brighter; and suddenly two tears rolled down her cheeks. Inaudibly, she spoke again; then, with a quick, impassioned gesture stretched out her arms towards the Savage, stepped forward. (Huxley 1932/1965a, p. 1197)

Desire causes Lenina to empathize with someone whose speech, manner, and motives are largely foreign to her. More importantly, this attraction compels her to the affirmative moral act of reaching out to help John in his distress while everyone else at the lighthouse revels in the spectacle of his suffering. Though he has wrongfully and cruelly judged her, Lenina demonstrates forgiveness and compassion through an affirmative act of nonconformity. In the midst of crowd psychology so infectious that even John succumbs, Lenina alone demonstrates full humanity.

Huxley subsequently sought to emphasize Lenina's substance and complexity. Laura Frost (2006) notes that in *Brave New World: A Musical Comedy*, a planned musical adaptation of the novel from 1956, Huxley transformed Lenina into a free-thinking radical who ultimately becomes John's willing accomplice: "She joins John in reading *The Complete Works of Shakespeare*, and in the conclusion of the musical—where Huxley takes the 'third alternative' he mentions in his 1946 foreword to *Brave New World*—Lenina and John depart to join a community of like-minded exiles in Tahiti" [p. 465]. Frost neglects to mention that the community is in the midst of a civil war (2003a, p. 103), but her assessment of Huxley's portrayal of Lenina in the musical is accurate, if understated.

In Act I Scene i, Lenina is introduced as the story's "heroine" (2003a, p. 40), putting her on par with John. As in the novel, Lenina is a monogamist. When she criticizes Bernard for enjoying the female attention he has been receiving on account of his connection to John, he replies: "You've got nothing to complain of. They run after you too. LENINA: *They* do. But they don't happen to interest me" (2003a, p. 79, emphasis in original). Through a conversation between government officials, the musical forcefully emphasizes that monogamy is a criminal offense, thereby highlighting the depth of Lenina's defiance: "GROMYKA: Rather an unpleasant case, I'm afraid. A Beta Plus male from Emotional Engineering and a female Alpha Pediatrician. It's been discovered that they've been going steady for seven months. DIRECTOR: Seven months? How disgusting! Downgrade the male and have the female transferred to Madrid. GROMYKA: Very good, sir" (2003a, p. 72). While John does not break the law until his epiphany at Park Lane Hospital, Lenina is in quiet but persistent violation from the beginning.

While her appearance is her most striking trait in the novel, Lenina's depth of character defines her in the musical. Before meeting John, she values Bernard for his intelligence and unconventional behavior. Unlike in the novel, their attraction in the musical is presented as mutual: "LENINA (*with dignity*) Bernard Marx is an Alpha Plus Psychologist, and as such he has a perfect right to think for himself. And anyhow, I like him. FANNY: No, You don't. LENINA: I do" (2003a, p. 43, emphasis in original). She looks forward to their visit to the Savage Reservation, telling Fanny: "You and your three-week cuddling parties with nice conventional Alpha Minuses! Who's ever going to take *you* to a Savage Reservation?" (2003a, p. 43, emphasis in original). She is critical of the regime from the beginning, but cunningly feigns happiness in order to blend in, like Orwell's Winston Smith: "Or if you *do* mind, you can easily pretend you don't. Just look as though you're enjoying yourself—that's all they want" (2003a, p. 54, emphasis in original). She finds the *Complete*

Works of Shakespeare absorbing even before she meets John, remaining on the reservation to read it while Bernard returns to their quarters:

> (*She resumes her reading.*)
> BERNARD: Are you coming along?
> LENINA (*without looking up from her book*): No. I'm staying here.
> BERNARD: Okay. Have it your way.... (*Lit by a ray of sunset light, Lenina remains alone, intently reading*). (2003a, p. 67, emphasis in original)

When Bernard begins to exploit his relationship with John for personal gain, Lenina responds with sarcastic contempt:

> LENINA (*ironically*): Think of it! Little Bernard going to dine with the Arch-Uplifter.
> BERNARD (*with dignity*): I suppose you think you're being funny. (2003a, p. 79, emphasis in original)

And when John begins to throw the soma rations out of the window at the hospital, Lenina joins in alongside Bernard:

> JOHN: Good old Helmholtz! I knew you'd be on my side. (*He knocks down another assailant and tosses away another handful of pillboxes.*) And there's Lenina too. (LENINA *by this time has become involved in the fight.*)
> JOHN: Darling! (*He blows her a kiss, and knocks down another* DELTA.)
> LENINA: I'm with you, John. (*She administers a resounding smack on the behind of a* DELTA *female who is attacking* JOHN *from the rear. The* DELTA *female turns on* LENINA, *rushes at her, is tripped and falls flat*). (2003a, p. 98, emphasis in original)

While her gender shields her from full responsibility for her role in John's thwarted rebellion, she willingly chooses John, exile, and freedom in the final scene:

> CONTROLLER: And now, LENINA, what about you?
> LENINA: I'm going where John's going.
> CONTROLLER: You don't *have* to.
> LENINA: I want to.
> CONTROLLER: Monogamy's pretty strenuous, my dear, and there won't be any soma to relieve the tensions.
> LENINA: I don't care [....]

JOHN: You're free, Lenina, You're absolutely free. (*Lenina stands hesitant for a moment. Then throws her arms around his neck and kisses him. It is a long embrace.* (2003a, p. 102, emphasis in original)

Had this musical been produced, critical appreciation for Lenina would be widespread and the latent hope in Huxley's vision of the future would be more apparent.

Aside from fueling her revolutionary impulses, Lenina's sexual desire resets her moral compass. Despite having been insulted, rejected, and physically abused by John, Lenina alone comes to appreciate the wrong that society has done to him when her fellow citizens drive him to his hermitage and then invade his privacy. John Coughlin (2008) argues that by approaching the Savage with a look of yearning, outstretched arms, and tears in her eyes in the novel's penultimate scene, Lenina shows not only love but pathos: "The fact that Lenina had the emotion of pathos was her greatest assertion of individual humanity and compassion, with compassion heretofore an unknown element" (p. 93). Through her desire for John, Lenina, ironically, transforms from sex symbol to Pietà.

While tragedy usually entails the death of the hero, Firchow maintains that Lenina's survival, as opposed to John's suicide, is what makes the story of their love so tragic and allows her to emerge as the story's unexpected heroine:

> For him, the end is swift and tragic. For Lenina, however, there is no end; her tragedy—and for all the comedy and irony in which her love for the Savage is immersed, the word *tragedy* is not entirely inappropriate—her tragedy is that is that she has felt an emotion that she can never express or communicate or realize again. (1999, p. 148, emphasis in original)

There is sexism in this presentation of the tragic heroine, who fulfills the stereotypical role of the woman willing to bear the suffering of others, particularly her man.

Nevertheless, Lenina's erotic desires, unlike John's sententious anger, can catalyze social and ethical renewal. Krishan Kumar (1987) points out that this chance for regeneration flows directly from Lenina's desire for happiness through a sexually gratifying relationship with John:

> The very suggestion of a development in Lenina, following the impulse to pursue her happiness, is an indication that the stuff of a very different sort

of happiness—and the possibility of tragedy—is a potentiality of even so debased a culture as Brave New World. It would be entirely in the spirit of Huxley's ironic fable if, though unintended by him, the immaculately awful society that he created were to be undermined by happiness, its most sacred value and primary rationale. There is a sort of poetic justice in this, that the way both into and out of Brave New World might lie through Lenina's arms. (p. 287)

Thus the sexual pleasure that the founders of World State believed would perpetually subordinate people to the societal machine can awaken self-awareness, political dissent, empathy, and ultimately moral responsibility. Lenina's development shows how sexual desire can inspire liberation within the most docile of bodies.

Although circumstance precludes the realization of a monogamous relationship between Lenina and John, Huxley—anticipating the theories of Marcuse—suggests that the deferral of sexual gratification can be an aspirational and enlightening force. Ultimately, as the author himself points out, the aims of World State can never be fully realized:

> The termitary has come to seem a realizable and even, in some eyes, a desirable ideal. Needless to say, the ideal will never in fact be realized. A great gulf separates the social insect from the not too gregarious, big-brained mammal; and even though the mammal should do his best to imitate the insect, the gulf would remain. (Huxley 1958/1965b, p. 19)

Mustapha Mond confirms this idea of the gulf between mammalian individuality and the collectivism of insects when he admits to himself that happiness is not the purpose of life: "That the purpose of life was not the maintenance of well-being, but some intensification and refining of consciousness, some enlargement of knowledge [...] was, the Controller reflected, quite possibly true" (Huxley 1932/1965a, p. 136). Taking the Controller's words at face value, through her sexual attraction to John, Lenina has come closer than any other character to realizing this expansion of consciousness and knowledge.

This assessment of life's meaning applies just as well to Burdekin's *Swastika Night*. However, unlike *Brave New World* and the other novels previously considered in this study, Burdekin will use the ungovernable potential of sexual desire to challenge the harm caused by hypermasculinity rather than the damage done through overinvestment in political, socioeconomic or scientific ideologies.

Note

1. The World State calendar dates back to the year when Henry Ford introduced his Model T automobile (Deery, p. 259).

References

Adams, R. M. (1993). The Relevance of Brave New World. In N. Karolides, L. Burgess, & J. M. Kean (Eds.), *Censored Books: Critical Viewpoints* (pp. 130–135). Metuchen, NJ: Scarecrow Press.
Adorno, T. W. (1967). *Prisms* (S. and S. Weber, Trans.). London: Neville Spearman Ltd.
Baker, R. S. (1990). *Brave New World: History, Science, and Dystopia*. Boston, MA: Twayne Publishers.
Baker-Smith, D. (2001). The World to Come: Aldous Huxley and the Utopian Parable. In C. C. Barfoot (Ed.), *Aldous Huxley: Between East and West* (pp. 101–112). New York, NY: Rodopi.
Booker, M. K. (1994). *The Dystopian Impulse in Modern Literature: Fiction as Social Criticism*. Westport, CT: Greenwood Press.
Buchanan, B. W. (2008). Oedipus Against Freud: Humanism and the Problem of Desire in Brave New World. In D. G. Izzo & K. Kirkpatrick (Eds.), *Huxley's Brave New World: Essays* (pp. 26–45). Jefferson, NC: McFarland & Company, Inc.
Coughlin, J. (2008). *Brave New World* and Ralph Ellison's *Invisible Man*. In D. G. Izzo & K. Kirkpatrick (Eds.), *Huxley's Brave New World: Essays* (pp. 88–95). Jefferson, NC: McFarland & Company, Inc.
Deery, J. (1992). Technology and Gender in Aldous Huxley's Alternative (?) Worlds. *Extrapolation, 33*(3), 258–273.
Diken, B. (2011). Huxley's *Brave New World*—And Ours. *Journal for Cultural Research, 15*(2), 153–172.
Firchow, P. E. (1999). Huxley's Characters Are Appropriate for the Novel. In K. de Koster (Ed.), *Readings on Brave New World* (pp. 139–149). San Diego, CA: Greenhaven Press, Inc.
Foucault, M. (1995). *Discipline & Punish* (A. Sheridan, Trans.). New York, NY: Random House. (Original work published 1975)
Frost, L. (2006). Huxley's Feelies: The Cinema of Sensation in *Brave New World*. *Twentieth-Century Literature, 52*(4), 443–473.
Halbfass, W. (2001). Mescaline and Indian Philosophy: Aldous Huxley and the Mythology of Experience. In C. C. Barfoot (Ed.), *Aldous Huxley Between East and West* (pp. 221–236). New York, NY: Rodopi.
Higdon, D. L. (2002). The Provocations of Lenina in Huxley's Brave New World. *International Fiction Review, 29*(1–2), 78–83.

Holzer, A.C. (2003). Science, Sexuality, and the Novels of Huxley and Houellebecq. *Comparative Literature and Culture: A WWWeb Journal*, 5(2). Retrieved from http://docs.lib.purdue.edu/clcweb/vol5/iss2/

Horkheimer, M., & Adorno, T. W. (1972). *The Dialectic of Enlightenment* (J. Cumming, Trans.). New York, NY: Continuum. (Original work published 1944)

Huxley, A. (1965a). *Brave New World*. New York, NY: Harper & Row. (Original work published 1932)

Huxley, A. (1965b). *Brave New World Revisited*. New York, NY: Harper & Row. (Original work published 1958)

Huxley, A. (1965c). Foreword. In *Brave New World* (pp. xiii–xxi). New York, NY: Harper & Row. (Original work published 1946)

Huxley, A. (2003a). *Brave New World: A Musical Comedy* (B. Nugel, Ed.). *Aldous Huxley Annual*, 3, 39–103.

Huxley, A. (2003b). Christ and the Present Crisis. *Aldous Huxley Annual*, 3, 21–23. (Original work published 1932)

Huxley, A. (2003c). Pareto's Museum of Human Stupidity. *Aldous Huxley Annual*, 3, 24–32. (Original work published 1935)

Kumar, K. (1987). *Utopia & Anti-Utopia in Modern Times*. New York, NY: Basil Blackwell.

Madden, D. (1992). Women in Dystopia. In K. A. Ackley (Ed.), *Misogyny in Literature* (pp. 289–314). New York, NY: Garden Publishing.

Marcuse, H. (1991). *One Dimensional Man*. Boston, MA: Beacon Press. (Original work published 1964)

Meckier, J. (2003). Onomastic Satire: Names and Naming in Brave New World. *Aldous Huxley Annual*, 3, 155–198.

Orwell, G. (2000). As I Please. In S. Orwell & I. Angus (Eds.), *As I Please, 1943–1945: The Collected Essays, Journalism & Letters, Vol. 3* (pp. 63–65). Jaffrey, NH: Nonpareil Books. (Original work published 24 December 1943)

Watt, D. (2001). A Modest Proposal: *Brave New World* as Contemporary Film. *Aldous Huxley Annual*, 1, 43–64.

Witters, S. A. (2008). Words Have to Mean Something More: Folkloric Reading in *Brave New World*. In D. G. Izzo & K. Kirkpatrick (Eds.), *Huxley's Brave New World: Essays* (pp. 73–87). Jefferson, NC: McFarland & Company, Inc.

CHAPTER 5

Katharine Burdekin's *Swastika Night*, a Gay Romance

Katharine Burdekin's *Swastika Night*, initially published in 1937 under the pseudonym Murray Constantine, was the first major dystopia to identify male supremacy as the source of modern totalitarianism. For Burdekin, Nazism is best understood as an extreme iteration of hypermasculinity, ultimately resulting in a world where women are caged, exploited, and regarded merely as animals for breeding. Though superficially a novel of its time, *Swastika Night*—by identifying sexism as the catalyst of political oppression—presents gender equality as both a remedy for totalitarian tendencies everywhere and a preventative measure to secure democracy.

Although anti-Semitism was undoubtedly the most notorious and destructive prejudice of Hitler and his supporters, Daphne Patai (1985), in her introduction to the Feminist Press's reprint of the novel, addresses the virulent strain of misogyny that Burdekin saw at the core of fascism: "In 1932, a year before the Nazis destroyed all branches of the women's movement, the Reichskomitee of Working Women made an appeal to Germany's working-class women [....] Hitler's view of the proper role of women was originally set forth in *Mein Kampf* (1924): they were to reproduce the race" (p. x). Kate Holden (1999) believes that Burdekin's thesis about the origin of fascist ideology was more perceptive still, since even feelings of hatred toward Jews flow from the cult of masculinity (p. 148). Pagetti (1990) goes further, praising Burdekin for demonstrating that totalitarianism itself results from an ethos of male superiority: "[*Swastika Night*] brings out a deep connection, in the larger perspective of the narration, between totalitarianism and male chauvinism, between the establishment of a strong state based on theocratic principles and the inevitable reduction of the female component to a totally subordinate role" (p. 361). Building on these feminist readings of this novel, I argue that Burdekin introduces hope for ethical renewal via queer desire. This investment in gay desire causes the reader to confront the damaging effects of homophobia, as well as misogyny, on contemporary society.

Although it portrays a dystopia, *Swastika Night* has, as Robert Crossley (1987) recognizes, utopian underpinnings: "For its importance to the tradition of twentieth-century utopian thought, *Swastika Night* is a rediscovery to rank with Charlotte Perkins Gilman's *Herland*" (p. 96). Citing the hope that the novel invests in women, Christians, and its protagonist (an Englishman aptly named Alfred), Crossley thinks that *Swastika Night* is a fundamentally sanguine novel "about a light that manages to burn in the long dark dystopian night of the Nazi terror" (1987, p. 97). Andy Croft (1984) correctly asserts that hope inevitably persists because Burdekin viewed fascism in the same way that Marx regarded capitalism, as a system that would finally implode as a result of its own contradictions:

> *Swastika Night* is a powerful and unique critique of fascism, an argument that it was originally mysoginist [*sic*] and ultimately self-destructive, and that its racial theories had roots in sexual hysteria. *Swastika Night* remains undoubtedly the most sophisticated and original of all the many anti-fascist dystopias of the late 1930s and 1940s. (p. 209)

Yet hope is also apparent in the way the novel exemplifies Wells's faith in the leadership of those with scientific training.

While it is one of the earliest feminist dystopias, *Swastika Night* is arguably the last major Wellsian utopia, placing hope for the future in a class of selfless, charismatic technocrats. Significantly, Alfred is a highly skilled airplane technician capable of servicing and flying different types of aircraft. As Chris Hopkins (2006) makes clear, Alfred's ability to read and write gives him an advantage over most of his German betters: "the technicians' ability to read distinguishes them from most Nazis who, though superior in the hierarchy, do not need to read and are therefore not taught to do so" (p. 149). Like Wells (1933/2005), who in *The Shape of Things to Come* establishes utopia through the "benevolent grip" of an "Air

Dictatorship" comprised of pilots and flight technicians (p. 361), Burdekin implicitly conflates critical thinking and intellectual honesty with the ability to fly. As Hopkins points out,

> [I]ndependence of mind is also associated with flying [....] Indeed, a link is made between flight and "liberty of judgment" (p. 47), the thing which Alfred openly tells the Knight the German state lacks: flight becomes a type of self-determination, "under his own personal will". Flight is also associated with truth-telling about gender roles [....] Alfred's natural flying ability and desire for liberty convinces the Knight that he must inherit guardianship of the Book, the instrument which may one day help to rewrite history. (2006, pp. 150–151)

Alfred's technical training positions him for egalitarian political leadership, for in the Wellsian utopia, as Kumar (1987) observes, "The scientists rule, but in the course of time virtually everyone comes to belong to this class" (p. 214). Like Wells's utopias, the structure of the story also mimics late nineteenth- and early twentieth-century utopian fiction in that it chiefly consists of long, didactic conversations between informed, reliable characters.

The chance for these science-minded saviors to bring the world out of a fascist dark age came seven centuries after Hitler's lifetime. Following a destructive, mid-twentieth-century global war, détente between the fascist superstates of Germany and Japan persists for centuries, but now cultural stagnation and declining birthrates have left both empires on the verge of internal collapse, and a vanguard of scientifically trained men is poised to usher in a new golden age defined by equality between the sexes and among all people. Like Wells, Burdekin, perhaps naïvely, believed that social class could be overcome without a proletarian revolution or other form of class warfare. Unlike Wells, Burdekin presented both Christianity and democracy as essential components of social renewal, reconciling both—as Edward Bellamy did in *Looking Backward*—with socialism.

One of the more controversial ideas put forth in *Swastika Night* is the importance of pacifism. Any kind of resistance by force appears to be incompatible with Burdekin's commitment to nonviolence. As Alfred says, "It is *physical* power that's rotting. It all comes back to that. The rebellion must be unarmed, and the power behind the rebellion must be spiritual, out of the soul. The same place where Bach got his music from. From God, perhaps" (Burdekin 1937/1985, p. 100, emphasis in original). Given the brutality and aggression of Hitler's government, Elizabeth Russell (1992) questions whether the novel advances this claim earnestly or satirically: "What, however, is meant by spiritual power which comes out of the soul? And whose voice is this? Alfred's? Burdekin's? Or is it one more lie?" (p. 42). The 1940 reprint of the novel includes a note from the publisher stating that the author supports armed opposition to the Axis:

> While the author has not in the least changed his opinion that the Nazi idea is evil, and that we must fight the Nazis on land, at sea, in the air and in ourselves, he has changed his mind about the Nazi *power* to make the *world* evil. He feels that, while the material destruction and misery they can and have brought about are immense, they cannot do spiritual harm even in the short run; for they can communicate the disease only to anyone who has a tendency to take it. (cited in Russell 1992, p. 37, emphasis in original)

Nevertheless, since this claim is not directly advanced by Burdekin, its validity cannot be confidently affirmed. Given the close correlation throughout the novel between violence and the cult of masculinity, it is reasonable to conclude that Alfred's pacifism is synonymous with Burdekin's.

Unlike her unconventional support for pacifism, Burdekin's take on sexuality mirrors that found in other works of projected political fiction. Consistent with the other foundational dystopias of the twentieth century, sexual desire draws a complacent character into political awareness and revolution, here—as with Zamyatin's D-503—against his better judgment. However, in this novel the passion is overtly homoerotic. In her survey of Burdekin's speculative fiction, Elizabeth English (2013) notes the connection Burdekin makes between lesbian desire and political consciousness: "It is evident that Burdekin perceived a link between political consciousness and female-centered sexuality" (p. 104). English associates Burdekin with the canonical lesbian modernists through their portrayal of sexual desire as the key to political renewal:

> Thus, what Burdekin and canonical lesbian modernists arguably have in common is not only their interest in popular sexual discourse, but also their celebration of lesbian desire and identity as potentially subversive forces. Burdekin and her canonical peers are united by a shared utopian intent: the desire to disrupt the heteronormative status quo and to promote alternative, and better, ways of living and loving. (2013, p. 108)

English's analysis is convincing yet limited; Burdekin presents queer desire generally—not just lesbian passion—as a liberating force.

In *Swastika Night*, Hermann, a patriotic German youth, is, though he is not fully cognizant of it, gay. Alfred, the older Englishman whom he loves and pines for romantically, is a disaffected radical who becomes the caretaker of a clandestine manuscript and photograph that together refute the mythical claims of the totalitarian regime. The photograph shows an authentic image of Adolph Hitler, who is regarded by the Germans of the early twenty-seventh century as a blonde God of superhuman size, posing with an attractive young woman. Patai (1984b) lays bare the snapshot's volatile potential: "The photograph at one stroke undoes the two central tenets of Hiterlism: that Hitler was never in the defiling presence of a woman, and that women have always been the loathsome creatures that they are in the seventh century of Hiterlism" (p. 86). The manuscript, which was secretly and illegally written centuries earlier by a disgraced member of the hereditary ruling class, provides a fairly accurate (if incomplete) thumbnail history of the Western world that contradicts the spurious, self-serving official record. Hermann allows himself to be publically dishonored, leaves his homeland, and ultimately gives his life to protect Alfred and these revelatory artifacts.

Although Alfred's heterosexuality precludes the physical consummation of his and Hermann's relationship, the text figuratively alludes to it. The two men share a room with one bed removed from the rest of the household: "[Hermann's] pleasure at finding Alfred in his own room, lying on his own bed, had given his face a temporary charming radiance" (Burdekin 1937/1985, p. 58). And when, at the end of the novel, Alfred and Hermann are on the verge of being captured in their hideaway, Fred, Alfred's eldest son, recommends that they lead the authorities to believe that they met for a gay rendezvous: " 'Make them think you and Hermann are here because you wouldn't like to be with him where anyone might find you,' whispered Fred very rapidly, but quite unflustered" (Burdekin 1937/1985, p. 190). George McKay (1994) goes so far as to describe Hermann as "Alfred's lover" (p. 306).

Alfred and Hermann need not conceal the bond they share, for, as Patai indicates, love between men and women is impossible in a society where women have been completely dehumanized and degraded:

> The women are kept in cages in segregated quarters, their Reduction complemented by the exaltation of men. This situation has led to homosexual

attachments among males (Burdekin suggesting that male homosexuality may involve embracing, not rejecting, the male gender role), though procreation is a civic duty for German men [....] Power over women, not sexual pleasure, is the issue—for only boys are considered beautiful, desirable, lovable. (1985, pp. iv–v)

While love between men is understandable in a society where women are reduced to articulate livestock, from the first page the reader sees that Hermann's desire is innately queer as he ogles a chorister during a religious service:

> Not once had he been able to catch the eye of the new solo singer, who with the face of a young Hero-Angel, so innocent, so smooth-skinned and rosy, combined a voice of unearthly purity and tone [....] What hair! Down to his waist nearly. Hermann wanted to wind his hand in it and give a good tug, pulling the boy's head backwards. Not to hurt him much, just to make him mind. (Burdekin 1937/1985, pp. 5–8)

Hermann's indulgence in a rape fantasy is deeply troubling though characteristic of an indoctrinated Nazi. When he later discovers the chorister attempting unlawfully to rape an adolescent Christian girl, he brutalizes him. As Holden explains, "Germans are forbidden to have intercourse with Christians because, Hitler's final solution having successfully exterminated all Jews, Christians subsequently occupy the pariah position" (1999, p. 149). Revealingly, however, Hermann acts not because of the boy's misfeasance but due to an overwhelming feeling of sexual jealousy: "He loathed the boy for being even interested in girls—with his lovely face, his unmasculine immaturity—Hermann was physically jealous" (Burdekin 1937/1985, p. 33). By characterizing Hermann's jealousy as physical, Burdekin presents his homosexuality as instinctive rather than situational, showing that queerness is not the result of an androcentric environment that promotes intimate male bonding.

Patai, though she recognizes that Burdekin was not homophobic, misunderstands gay desire in the novel, viewing it simply as a byproduct of the degradation of women rather than something occurring naturally: "Burdekin is not homophobic. She depicts Hermann's love of Alfred with considerable sympathy and views such attachments as a logical companion of the Reduction of Women" (1984b, pp. 92–93). In fact, Burdekin's awareness extends far beyond sympathy. She herself, as Patai's own research indicates, was probably lesbian. Although Burdekin briefly married, she did so for expediency: "She told her parents that she wished, like her brothers, to attend Oxford, but they did not consent. Since a university education was not a possibility, she married instead [....] Family legend has it that she married simply for lack of other options" (2002, p. 4). Following her marriage, Burdekin's life partner was a woman:

> In 1926 Burdekin met the woman who became her lifelong friend and companion and who, though she wished to remain unnamed, has been the source of much of the biographical information about Burdekin. The two women lived together from 1926 until Burdekin's death [....] Although Burdekin and her companion did not avoid social functions, they maintained quiet, private lives. (Patai 2002, p. 5)

The circumstantial evidence overwhelmingly suggests that Burdekin's companion was her lover. Thus it is not surprising that Burdekin took a personal interest in gay relationships and explored them in her fiction:

> Burdekin's second novel, *The Reasonable Hope* (1924), is a realistic exploration of a young man who is shell-shocked in World War I and of the bohemian artistic circle into which he is drawn. As in some of Burdekin's subsequent works, an important, if unnamed, theme of the novel is homosexuality [....] Her novels, as early as *The Reasonable Hope*, often include same-sex partners whose souls join together harmoniously. (Patai 2002, pp. 5–6)

In *Swastika Night*, Burdekin portrays Hermann's romantic attachment to Alfred as natural and redeeming, suggesting that acceptance of queerness is as necessary for justice and social stability as equality between the sexes. Like sexism, homophobia is yet another symptom of hypermasculinity.

Critics such as Loretta Stec (2001) emphasize that *Swastika Night* is as much a satire of the sexism endemic to traditional European culture as it is a critique of Nazi ideology: "Unlike other dystopian fiction of this era, Burdekin incorporates a devastating critique of gender relations in the Hitlerian future, and in an only slightly veiled fashion, of both Germany and England during the time she was writing" (p. 181). But Burdekin was also directly attacking her own society's treatment of homosexuals and indirectly condemning intolerance toward any minority. Raffaella Baccolini (2000) correctly argues that *Swastika Night* exposes the societal damage that the institutional diminution of any group can cause: "For Budekin, in fact, no society can prosper due to the submission of one of its groups" (p. 19).

Surprisingly, in its attitude toward sexual difference, Burdekin's Holy German Empire is more rational and tolerant than many nations are today, as Alfred's attitude toward his gay son demonstrates:

> Thomas had gone out somewhere. He never went to the Women's Quarters. His whole sexual and emotional life was lived among men. No stigma attached to it, and the German government had nothing to say against a whole-time homosexuality for Englishmen. If they had no children to bear it was their own look out. Alfred, who was as normal as it was possible for a man to be in such a society, had never blamed or envied Thomas for his way of living. (Burdekin 1937/1985, p. 166)

Remarkably, rather than depicting queerness through the lens of the isolated individual, Burdekin envisions gay communities in which Thomas and men like him can enjoy full sexual and emotional lives within a larger world free from anti-gay policies. As Christopher Nealon (2001) observes, "Indeed, the texts of the Anglo-European canon seem allergic to anything like the contemporary model of community" (p. 9). This utopian idea in *Swastika Night* of a communal life without the closet is a marvelous rarity, anticipating an affirming contemporary model of queerness. In the novel, the German government's policy of encouraging heterosexuality among German men comes not from homophobia but from a desire to raise a declining population of ethnic Germans. In contrast to the genocidal policies of Hitler's Third Reich, the state's indifference to non-heterosexual tendencies among both foreigners and Germans who have produced issue reveals the novel's belief that homophobia, unlike racism and anti-Semitism, would atrophy over time because it poses no threat to the blood purity of the Aryans. The conspicuous lack of pink triangles in Burdekin's dystopia is arguably another utopian aspect of the novel.

Nevertheless, the benefit of this cultural tolerance is offset by the enforcement of compulsory sex for procreation among pure-blooded Germans, echoing Hitler's policy of allowing Germans suspected of homosexuality to redeem themselves by producing legitimate offspring. Through a discussion of the penalty that Hermann will face if he does not father children, Burdekin emphasizes his physical revulsion at the idea of vaginal intercourse:

> "Hermann, have you any sons?"
> This was such an unexpected question that Hermann gaped. Then he said, "No."

"I have three now, Alfred said.... Have you had bad luck and had girls?"
"No. I can't stick women."
"But as you are a Nazi, if you haven't any children at all by the time you're thirty you'll be punished [....] Don't leave it too long, Hermann. You might find yourself in difficulties."
"I can't stand them!" said Hermann violently. "Oh, for Hitler's sake don't let's talk about women."
"All right. But I'm glad I'm a normal man. I've got a use for my sons. Women are neither here nor there."
"They're too much here," said Hermann, misunderstanding the English idiom. (Burdekin 1937/1985, pp. 22–23)

Here Burdekin demonstrates how unappealing heterosexual sex is to a person who is gay. Hermann's willingness to risk a criminal charge rather than have sex with a woman emphasizes the horror of cultural and legal dictates that compel gay people to conform to the straight norm.

Hermann, however, is no advocate for gay rights. He is a deeply conservative character, as can be seen through his reaction to the beautiful young woman posing beside Adolf Hitler in the photograph shown to him and Alfred by Friedrich von Hess, who was both a knight and Hermann's feudal master:

"A girl!" Alfred breathed softly. A girl as lovely as a boy, with a boy's hair and a boy's noble carriage, and a boy's direct and fearless gaze. He and Hermann gazed and gazed, wholly ignoring the other people in the photograph. Alfred grew pale and Hermann very red. (Burdekin 1937/1985, p. 68)

Whereas Alfred is dazzled by the girl's physical beauty, Hermann is embarrassed by the transgressive spectacle of a lovely girl presenting as a beautiful boy. While Alfred cannot bear to take his eyes away from the girl in the picture and asks later on to see her again, Hermann says nothing, focusing instead on the discrepancy between Hitler's actual appearance and the Olympian body posthumously conferred on him by government propaganda (Burdekin 1937/1985, pp. 68–69).

Apart from his sexual orientation, Hermann is a conventional Nazi. Through an analysis of Hermann's feelings for Alfred, Alexis Lothian (2016) argues that in *Swastika Night*, gay desire serves as a vehicle for enforcing traditional gender roles:

> The Nazi Hermann abandons his fatherland and eventually dies for the love of the Englishman Alfred, whom he is expected to despise according to the hierarchies of Nazi ideology. But male love is also, through the erotics of the uniform and the idealization of a virility that abhors the feminine, the vector along which fascist power is transmitted [....] In *Swastika Night*, male love reproduces the Nazi future, while motherhood and biological reproduction become sites of abjection. (p. 463)

Lothian is right that the Nazi state endorses certain types of desire between men to shore up the patriarchy to the detriment of women. German men are free, even encouraged, to dominate boys and non-Germans sexually. Yet this state-sanctioned desire, far from being illicit, is permitted only within fixed racial, cultural, and hierarchical norms, just as heteronormative sex is encouraged only within precise, clearly defined parameters in all of the novels considered in this study. There remains an illegal and subversive component to gay desire in *Swastika Night*. Queer desire is transgressive and liberating because it promotes feelings of respect and equality that undermine the fascist society's rigid pecking order. Although he cannot intellectually grasp Alfred's revolutionary aims, Hermann comes to regard him not just as an equal but ultimately as a leader more deserving of faithful service than the state. I find more nuance than Lothian does in Burdekin's presentation of a gay desire that pulls Hermann away from the dominant cultural paradigm into Alfred's just conspiracy.

Sexual passion for Alfred initiates Hermann's reluctant transformation into a rebel with a worthy cause, one that aligns him with the disadvantaged. As Maroula Joannou (1995) realizes, gay relationships in the novel foster moral responsibility and subvert the prejudices undergirding Nazism:

> In *Swastika Night* homosexual relationships, or to use Eve Kosofsky Sedgwick's term, "homo-social" relationships, are detonators of moral responsibility. Such relationships are distinguished from sexual couplings between men and heterosexual couplings. Raising intimate questions about personal identity, "homo-social" relationships destabilise the established boundaries of race and class. We have seen that it is not Hermann's sexual impulses but his strongest emotions which are brought into play by a relationship with another man. (p. 182)

However, Joannou's analysis underestimates the importance of sexual desire to Hermann's moral redemption. While his attraction to Alfred does mature into love, when Hermann unexpectedly sees him again after a five-year separation, he perceives him in erotic terms as a substitute for the choir boy of the novel's opening scene: "Hermann was overcome by a wave of emotion in which love, irritation, fear and a wild sort of spiritual excitement all mingled. He felt as if anything might happen at this moment. He had forgotten the interesting chorister as if he had never existed" (Burdekin 1937/1985, pp. 21–22). The fact that Alfred so readily eclipses the chorister reveals that he is a far more compelling object of sexual desire to Hermann. Hermann's sexual attraction to an Englishman subverts the fascist conventions of male beauty represented by the German boy, thereby eroding, however slightly, the destructive cultural norms of the regime. On seeing Alfred, Hermann experiences a "wave of emotion" so "wild" and primal that it cannot be named. After carefully cataloging each part of Alfred's physical appearance with his gaze, Hermann longs to embrace him as a lover:

> Hermann's heart bounded with a shock of joy. Brown curly hair, brown beard, grey eyes, standing on the grass, hands in pocket, quiet, aloof—it must be he! "Alfred!" he cried [....]
> "Hullo, Hermann!" he said. "Is this your village, then? What luck!"
> "Ja, ja!" said Hermann, longing to throw his arms around the older man's shoulders [....] In the army he had often pined for the land, and it was the more surprising that for Alfred's sake he had so often pined for the army in Germany [....] There had never been any German to take Alfred's place [....] Hermann [...] muttered in broken German, "I never thought I should—see you again. It's only now I realize how lonely I've been—since." (Burdekin 1937/1985, pp. 17–19)

That Hermann could feel such hunger for a person who deviates so from the societal paradigm of beauty epitomized by the choir boy again lays bare the unpredictable and uncontrollable nature of sexual attraction, as well as its ethical potential. Sexual desire pulls Hermann away from a culturally normalized pedophilic interest in a boy to a healthy passion for a grown man, whose beard highlights his maturity, differentiating him from the chorister's girlishly flowing hair.

Hermann's inability to act lawfully and, to his thinking, morally by killing Alfred when he learns of Alfred's treasonous intentions shows the power of sexual desire to counteract ingrained depravity and catalyze socially responsible behavior:

A dreadful idea took shape in his mind. Alfred was a self-confessed traitor, an infidel, a blasphemer, an enemy more vicious and inveterate than any Japanese. And more dangerous [....] [B]ut he could not, he *could not* make his arm obey him to strike downwards into Alfred's body. Personal love did still exist, and Alfred even sleeping had still a stranglehold on Hermann's will. So he was a traitor, a bad German; he was *soft*. Hermann put his knife away and sat in a trance of shame. (Burdekin 1937/1985, pp. 31–32, emphasis in original)

Under Alfred's influence, Hermann's shame quickly gives way to a new and wholesome ethical framework, one that Hermann—like D-503 in *We*—resists intellectually, as is clear from his reaction to the information provided by the manuscript and the photograph: " 'I don't understand,' said Hermann, almost in despair. 'Why should we have to be told things and then helped? Why can't he let us alone? Why did you say *I* was to be told?' " (Burdekin 1937/1985, p. 62). Nevertheless, though his intellect proves impenetrable, Hermann is able to apprehend Alfred's purpose on an instinctive level:

"Hermann, you love me, don't you? You trust me?"
"Yes," said Hermann in a low voice.
"In spite of my being an Englishman?"
"Yes."
"Then, if you can love and trust an Englishman, can you grasp the idea that there might be something important, some knowledge, some wisdom, that's for *all* of us, for all men alike?"
"Yes, I think I see." (Burdekin 1937/1985, p. 63, emphasis in original)

Desire for Alfred allows Hermann to transcend racism, nationalism, and classism, replacing them with an appreciation for a shared human heritage, a heritage that Hermann accesses through subversive lust.

Hermann's commitment to Alfred's cause does, however, have its limits. Patai offers a revealing comparison of Hermann and Julia in *Nineteen Eighty-Four*, emphasizing how both characters sleep rather than listen to their respective paramours read from covert books:

Winston Smith and Alfred each attempt to teach a lover/friend (Julia; Hermann) about the past by reading from the secret book, but meet with resistance or indifference. In both cases a curious detail occurs: Julia and Hermann sleep while the book is read aloud, a mark of their lack of both interest and intellectual development. (1985, pp. xii–xiii)

Hermann, like Julia, is a "revolutionary from the waist downwards" (Orwell 1949/1977, p. 157). He does not fully apprehend the rationale behind or the value of Alfred's rebellion, but his desire for Alfred makes him sympathetic to the cause on a gut level and brings purpose and fulfillment to his life. Whereas Friedrich von Hess wonders why Hermann is always "so gloomy" (Burdekin 1937/1985, p. 46), by the end of the story Hermann has found some measure of happiness:

> [S]ometimes it was hard to believe that he was not really what he seemed to be, a Permanent Exile in red uniform, or shortly, a Red. But on one night in every three he was happy, as whenever he woke from a doze he could see Alfred's dark head and Fred's fair one bent over the book, and hear the mumble of German and English in Alfred's voice. (Burdekin 1937/1985, p. 171)

Hermann's illicit desire for an underling of a subjugated race, a passion running contrary to decades of social, religious, and psychological conditioning, has humanized and ennobled him. If physical desire can convert such a privileged loyalist, its efficacy is potentially universal in scope.

The treatment of sexual desire in the text and Hermann's similarities to Julia suggest that Orwell might have read *Swastika Night* prior to writing *Nineteen Eighty-Four*. Baccolini (1995) believes *Swastika Night* is "a likely antecedent of Orwell's more famous book" (p. 305, fn 9). Croft points to "the abasement of sex and the outlawing of love" found in both dystopias and concludes that "*Swastika Night* clearly anticipates Orwell's *Nineteen Eighty-Four* by several years" (1984, pp. 209–210). McKay sees an important similarity in the names of the would-be heroes of these dystopias: "Both Alfred and Winston have the names of famous and heroic English leaders. The connection of a sense of history and self developed by reading history books is highlighted by their names" (1994, p. 305).

The use of colored clothing to convey class status in both novels may also indicate Burdekin's influence on Orwell. In *Swastika Night*, exiles and Christians wear red, while Knights wear blue and black (perhaps anticipating the black overalls of Inner Party members in Orwell's dystopia). The use of color-coded clothing to delineate societal hierarchy is also found in Atwood's *The Handmaid's Tale*, an overtly Orwellian text. In addition to deeming *Swastika Night* superior to *Nineteen Eighty-Four*, which he regards as merely a retread of *We*, Crossley rightly asserts that *Swastika Night* is an important precursor of *The Handmaid's Tale*:

"*Swastika Night* is a vision of great originality and terror—arguably more profound, and certainly fresher, than Orwell's derivative reworking of Zamyatin's *We*. It anticipates the subtler horrors of Margaret Atwood's near-future narrative of the degradation of women by fundamentalist gynophobes in *The Handmaid's Tale*" (1987, p. 98).

Nonetheless, Crossley does not say whether he believes Atwood knew of Burdekin's work before writing *The Handmaid's Tale*, and Patai concedes that there is no hard evidence indicating that Orwell was familiar with *Swastika Night*:

> There is no direct evidence that Orwell was acquainted with *Swastika Night*, published twelve years before his novel, only the internal similarities suggest that Orwell, an inveterate borrower, borrowed also from Burdekin. As it happens, Victor Gollancz, publisher of *Swastike Night*, was also Orwell's first publisher, and Orwell's *Road to Wigan Pier* was itself a Left Book Club selection, in 1937, just as *Swastika Night* was in 1940. (1985, p. xii)

Orwell was only as much "an inveterate borrower" as any other writer, but the connection to Burdekin through Gollancz and the Left Book Club makes the assertion that he borrowed from her somewhat plausible. Gilbert Bonifas (1987) concurs, believing that because *Swastika Night* was favorably reviewed by a friend of Orwell's in a magazine to which Orwell occasionally contributed, Orwell probably read it:

> For one thing the book was reviewed in *Time and Tide* on 26 June 1937 [....] A few days later Orwell was back in England and might easily have got hold of a copy of the magazine (with which he was about to resume his episodic collaboration); so that it is possible to imagine that the review led him on to read the book. But more interestingly there is the fact that on 12 February 1938 Geoffrey Gorer wrote to the editor of *Time and Tide* to praise *Swastika Night*, which, so far, had apparently attracted little notice [....] As it seems that at the time Orwell read *Time and Tide* regularly (besides his occasional contributions to it), his attention was probably drawn to Murray Constantine's dystopia by what a fairly close friend of his was writing about it. More significant still is Gorer's own opinion, imparted to me in a letter dated 26 January 1984. Gorer had by then no recollection of *Swastika Night*, but went on to say that "if I thought highly of it in February 1938, and if 'George Orwell' was in England and well enough to read, I would very probably have given or lent a copy to him [....] If he was still in hospital then I think you can assume that I did give/lend him a copy." As a matter of

fact Orwell was only to go into a Kent sanatorium a few weeks later, in March, but this in no way invalidates the suggestion of Gorer with whom he kept in touch and who may very well have called on him (according to Bernard Crick, his biographer, he had a lot of visitors). (p. 59)

While we cannot know for certain if Orwell read *Swastika Night*, Patai finds more evidence that he did through a close comparison of the texts, pointing to their thematic commonalities:

> Both *Nineteen Eighty-Four* and *Swastika Night* depict totalitarian regimes in which individual thought has been all but eliminated and towards this end all information about the past, and even memory itself, has been destroyed—much more thoroughly in Burdekin's novel than in Orwell's. In both books the world is divided into distinct empires in perpetual and static competition. There is a similar hierarchy in each novel, and the most despised groups (proles; women) are regarded as brute animals. The hierarchical extremes alone are to some extent free of domination. The knights and the Christians are not subject to constant search in *Swastika Night*—the knights because of their important position, the Christians because they are Untouchable. Similarly, in *Nineteen Eighty-Four*, Inner Party members can turn off their telescreens, and the proles are not obliged to have them installed, for the proles simply do not matter. And in keeping with the very concept of hierarchy, in both societies the upper echelons have material privileges denied to others. (1985, p. xii)

The correlation that Patai draws between the proles in *Nineteen Eighty-Four* and the Christians in *Swastika Night* is partially misleading because the Oceanian proles are disregarded rather than "despised." In *Swastika Night*, women are treated like animals because they are loathed, but in *Nineteen Eighty-Four* the proles are called animals because the Inner Party takes no more notice of them than most contemporary city dwellers take of squirrels; the authorities believe that so long as their basic needs are met, the proles pose no danger to the status quo. The Christians in *Swastika Night*, however, though illiterate and dependent on a dubious oral tradition, are entrusted with von Hess's book at the end of the story, positioning them to be a real, if passive, threat to the fascist establishment.

Patai's argument for Burdekin's influence on Orwell becomes more interesting through her analysis of thought control via the reduction and manipulation of language in these texts:

"Newspeak" is Orwell's term for the reduction of language that is designed to inhibit thought. In *Swastika Night*, too, concepts and words have been lost. "Marriage" and "socialism" are such items, and the idea of women as proud and valuable human beings. "Doublethink" is Orwell's term for the ability to hold contradictory thoughts in one's mind simultaneously without experiencing the contradiction, and by extension it refers to the ability to censor one's own thoughts and memories—as the women do in *Swastika Night* when they negate the evidence of their own senses in favor of the official ideology they have absorbed. (1985, p. xiii)

As Patai notes, in both dystopias the inhibition of thought and corruption of history are achieved through the eradication of language, specifically censorship, book purging, the rewriting of literature and historical records, and the excising of words—along with the thoughts underlying them—from the lexicon. However, this is carried out in a far more systematic and draconian way in *Nineteen Eighty-Four*. Newspeak differs radically from twentieth-century English, and it entails a profound simplification of grammar and syntax, linguistic changes not found in *Swastika Night*. The people in Burdekin's distant vision of the future speak and reason, for the most part, as we do today. Moreover, Newspeak, a language used exclusively by Party members in *Nineteen Eighty-Four*, divides the middle and working classes in Oceania. In *Swastika Night*, linguistic changes apply uniformly. If Orwell did, as Patai thinks, borrow the idea of limiting language from Burdekin, he developed it much more thoroughly and creatively.

Patai does identify an intriguing example of a phenomenon related to Orwellian doublethink in the women's reaction to the Knight's verbal faux pas during his sermon (1985, p. xiii). In the Holy German Empire, spiritual authority and secular power are vested in the same hereditary ruling class. Rather than encourage them to bear sons, as the state religion requires, Friedrich von Hess misspeaks while presiding over the Women's Worship. Before he realizes what he is saying, he urges his female congregation to bear daughters. The women exemplify a thought process akin to doublethink by automatically deciding that they must have misheard von Hess's exhortation:

> They had actually thought, with appalling and yet quite typical feminine stupidity, that he had told them to bear strong daughters. It was all a dreadful blasphemous mistake. He had, of course, said "Sons". "*Sohnen.*" The word was like the deep tolling of an enormous bell. The Knight was thinking it hard, vigorously, like the man pulling the bell-rope. The women felt so deeply guilty that they even blushed. (Burdekin 1937/1985, p. 15, emphasis in original)

Strictly speaking, this is a simple revision of history, not doublethink. In *Nineteen Eighty-Four*, the narrator defines doublethink as "The power of holding two contradictory beliefs in one's mind simultaneously, and accepting both of them" (Orwell 1949/1977, p. 215). Thus, for these women to be engaging in doublethink, they would have to believe simultaneously that the Knight entreated them to produce sons exclusively *and* to produce only daughters.

Orwell gives a familiar example of doublethink and its sociopolitical ramifications in "In Front of Your Nose":

> This is [...] a habit of mind which is extremely widespread, and perhaps always has been. Bernard Shaw, in the preface to *Androcles and the Lion*, cites as another example the first chapter of the Gospel of Matthew, which starts off by establishing the descent of Joseph, father of Jesus, from Abraham. In the first verse, Jesus is described as "the son of David, the son of Abraham", and the genealogy is then followed up through fifteen verses: then, in the next verse but one, it is explained that as a matter of fact Jesus was *not* descended from Abraham, since he was not the son of Joseph. This, says Shaw, presents no difficulty to a religious believer [....] Medically, I believe, this manner of thinking is called schizophrenia: at any rate, it is the power of holding simultaneously two beliefs which cancel out. Closely allied to it is the power of ignoring facts which are obvious and unalterable, and which will have to be faced sooner or later. It is especially in our political thinking that these vices flourish. (1946/1968a, pp. 122–123)

Both Orwell's example from the Gospel of Matthew and Burdekin's portrayal of state appropriation of spirituality illustrate the unsettling point that religious dogma can train people to practice doublethink unwittingly, initially for liturgical purposes but ultimately in other areas of life, such as politics. As an atheist, Orwell's opinion of religion and its effect on the mind differs considerably from Burdekin's. Evocative endorsements of personal faith in God are peppered throughout *Swastika Night*. Kenneth Payne (2005) points out that what Burdekin desired was not an end to religion but an end to churches:

> As Burdekin predicted it, the Christian institutions of church and priesthood would disappear (for Burdekin, this was as much a hope as a forecast), while Christianity as religious philosophy and human community would endure without the Church, although "debased and impure", but with some shreds of its spiritual and humane doctrine still nearly intact. (pp. 8–9)

Stec notes that finding hope in even a nonhierarchical, atomistic Christianity is problematic for a feminist such as Burdekin due to the sexism embedded in certain New Testament scriptures:

> While the novel presents a pessimistic vision of the future joined with a hint that the society can awaken from this Hitlerian nightmare, its potential solution is paradoxical, particularly with regard to Christianity [....] [T]he Nazi hierarchy models itself partly on institutional Christianity. The text indexes St. Paul, whose teachings suggest woman is "nothing", and "nothing she must become" (*SN*, p. 175), beliefs indistinguishable from Nazi ideology. (2001, pp. 183–184)

Burdekin does not acknowledge some of the sexism in the New Testament and fails to recognize that prejudice as a point of commonality with fascism. But apart from their divergent opinions on religious faith and Christianity in particular, Orwell and Burdekin were, like London, united in their condemnation of the Roman Catholic Church.

In his conversation with Friedrich von Hess about the papal power of excommunication, Alfred goes so far as to say that the people who believed in the spiritual authority of Catholic priests were even stupider and less civilized than the people who currently pray to Hitler: "That's crazier still, because it would mean that God deliberately resigned and gave away His freedom of judgment to a lot of priests. Why if these people believed all that they were in a way less civilized than you are. Dumber, anyway" (Burdekin 1937/1985, pp. 135–136). Burdekin's hostility to this putative priestly authority most likely stemmed from the Church's support of Franco and Mussolini rather than a logical critique of Catholic doctrine. After all, religious faith of any kind depends on belief without objective evidence, so there is no reason for Burdekin to have singled out Catholic religious teachings. While Burdekin viewed Catholicism with especial animus, Payne argues that her critique extended to the various churches throughout Germany that offered little if any resistance to Hitler's policies: "Burdekin forecasts the potential intersection and overlapping of the Christian and Nazi categories—a prediction to be borne out by events in Nazi Germany a few years later when the 'official' persecution of German Jewry began in earnest and the Church, with some exceptions, would remain silent" (2005, p. 9).

Orwell's anti-Catholicism was likewise connected to the Church's political policies. In a letter initially published in *Tribune* on January 17,

1947, he asserts that "before the war [...] the Catholic Church was sympathetic to Fascism" (1947/1968b, p. 193), and—as will be seen in Chap. 7— Orwell modeled the Oceanian Inner Party partially on the upper echelons of the Catholic Church. In his analysis of *Nineteen Eighty-Four*, Kumar (1987) affirms that for Orwell the theocratic political views of the Holy See were as restrictive as those of fascism and communism: "The totalitarian ideologies—whether Fascist, Communist or Catholic—claimed possession of the absolute truth about the world. The Party of the Church was the sole repository of that truth. Its actions, however mysterious or even perverse they may at times seem to the member, were not to be questioned" (p. 306).

While she was more sympathetic to communism than Orwell, for Burdekin, fascism and Catholicism as political systems were functional equivalents. The Christians, who remain an ostracized, insular minority in the Holy German Empire, cite Latin phrases such as *Laus Deo* as holy words from the language that they believe was spoken by Christ (Burdekin 1937/1985, p. 182), suggesting that their cultural ancestors used the Vulgate and were Catholic. In making this link, Burdekin implies that the Church's backward attitude and policies toward women in her own time helped lay the foundation for the systematic degradation of women. Von Hess tells Alfred:

> [W]hen the Reduction of Women started the Christian men acquiesced in it, probably because there always had been in the heart of the religion a hatred of the beauty of women and a horror of the sexual power beautiful women with the right of choice and rejection have over men. And when women were reduced to the condition of speaking animals, they probably found it impossible to go on believing they had souls. (Burdekin 1937/1985, p. 73)

While, as possessors of von Hess's book at the end of the novel, the Christians are poised to play a critical role in the decline and fall of fascism, Burdekin, as Payne makes clear, gives no indication of how they will overcome the sexism that permeates their spiritual beliefs: "Christianity *may* endure the Nazi catastrophe, then, although Burdekin does not say if or *how* the Christians of the post-Nazi future will overcome their ancient and ingrained anti-feminism" (2005, p. 10, emphasis in original). While Orwell sees the methodologies of organized religion reproduced in repressive governments, Burdekin focuses more narrowly on the undercurrent of sexism common to most if not all institutional religions. Of course, even if he had read *Swastika Night*, there is no reason to think that Orwell's suspicion of the Catholic Church had anything to do with Burdekin's critique of organized Christianity's latent misogyny. Their quarrels with Catholicism differ, but both Burdekin and Orwell certainly note the dangerous nexus between it and fascism.

In addition to the thematic similarities between *Swastika Night* and *Nineteen Eighty-Four*, Patai identifies some curious parallels in terms of the novels' respective plots and characters:

> As in *Swastika Night*, in *Nineteen Eighty-Four* the secret opposition is called a Brotherhood. Despite the apolitical inclinations of Hermann and Julia, each is drawn into the protagonist's rebellion and ultimately destroyed by it. In both novels, too, there are official enemies to be hated: Goldstein in *Nineteen Eighty-Four*; the four arch-friends, enemies of Hitler, in *Swastika Night*; and the eternal mythical leaders, Big Brother and Hitler, to be adored. Finally, as if in enactment of the theories of William Reich, in both novels a distortion of sexuality occurs: in *Swastika Night* by the degradation and Reduction of women which has made love and sexual attraction a prerogative of men. And in both novels sex is encouraged for the sake of procreation, but only with certain people. (1985, p. xiii)

It is on account of the state's distortion of sexuality that Hermann in *Swastika Night* and Julia in *Nineteen Eighty-Four* come to rebel, and both Hermann and Julia join the resistance movement only at the insistence of their respective love interests. Patai finds a final point of congruence in the process by which both pairs join the opposition:

> Furthermore, in each novel there is a rebellious protagonist who is approached by a man in a position of power (O'Brien, the Inner Party member; von Hess, the knight). This powerful man becomes the mediator through whom the protagonist's tendency to rebel is initially channeled, and in each case he gives the protagonist a secret book and hence knowledge. In both novels, also, a photograph provides a key piece of evidence about the past. (1985, p. xii)

The secret books to which Patai refers were produced by members of the ruling establishment, though the author of one foresees the collapse of the superstate (von Hess in *Swastika Night*) and the other claims it is invincible (O'Brien in *Nineteen Eighty-Four*). Like Orwell, who presents the *book* attributed to Goldstein as both a document of political heresy and a tool for imposing orthodoxy, Burdekin's treatment of von Hess's book, as Pagetti notes, is ambivalent: "Von Hess's book is a partial reconstruction, filled with lacunae, whose content Alfred can grasp only in part (because of his imperfect understanding of German). Besides, von Hess's explanations do not fully satisfy Alfred, who immediately has doubts, for instance, about the theory of the biological inferiority of women" (1990, p. 364). By debunking the myths and ideologies of the cult of Hitler, von Hess's book facilitates the emergence of truth and hope for meaningful change. But as a document rife with sexism, it conditions the reader to assume the same bias that led to the hypermasculinity underlying fascism. As Alfred tells Friedrich von Hess, "your thinking has been conditioned by von Hess [his ancestor who authored the book]. The only hope probably for impersonal thinking is having to think by yourself. *Any* kind of tradition must rot you up" (Burdekin 1937/1985, p. 111, emphasis in original). Whereas Winston Smith in *Nineteen Eighty-Four* struggles to retrieve the traditions of individual liberty that he believes are embedded in history, Alfred feels that tradition impedes critical thinking by subtly inculcating regressive rather than progressive thinking; so by erasing history, and with it nearly all traditions, the fascists have inadvertently created a forum for individualism.

A corresponding duality surrounds the contraband photographs in both dystopias. The photographs are beneficial in that they reveal suppressed facts about the prominent state officials pictured in them. The snapshot of Hitler posing with a young woman belies the popular conception of this revered demigod, disclosing his non-Aryan features, small stature, and underwhelming physique. Baccolini astutely argues that the Aryanizing of Hitler's physical appearance in *Swastika Night* mimics the whitening of Jesus of Nazareth by European Christians, indicating the anti-Semitism underwriting both ideologies: "Burdekin's irony here is double and exposes the social constructions of Jesus's and Hitler's identity. Just as Jesus's 'Aryanness' has been socially constructed by antisemitism, Hitler's has been created out of German theories of the pure race—which thrived on and exhalted [sic] antisemitism, as well" (1995, p. 299). Just as the photograph of Hitler forces Alfred and Hermann to confront startling truths about the belief system in which they were raised, its larger implications beg a reassessment of the prejudice inherent in Christian iconography. The newspaper photograph of Jones, Aaronson, and Rutherford that Winston Smith chances on in *Nineteen Eighty-Four* proves that these founding members of the Party were innocent of some (and presumably all) of the crimes to which they publically confessed:

> It was a half-page torn out of the *Times* of about ten years earlier—the top half of the page, so that it included the date—and it contained a photograph of the delegates at some Party function in New York. Prominent in the middle of the group were Jones, Aaronson, and Rutherford. There was no mistaking them; in any case their names were in the caption at the bottom. The point was that at both trials all three men had confessed that on that date they had been on Eurasian soil. They had flown from a secret airfield in Canada to a rendezvous somewhere in Siberia, and had conferred with members of the Eurasian General Staff, to whom they had betrayed important military secrets [....] There was only one possible conclusion: the confessions were lies. (Orwell 1949/1977, p. 78)

Both images broaden the viewer's sociopolitical perspective and affirm the revolutionary impulse.

Yet these photographs also carry negative connotations. The girl posing beside Hitler is remarkable merely for her physical beauty, and with her smile she tacitly endorses a political system that will ultimately reduce women to domesticated animals. With regard to the photograph in *Nineteen Eighty-Four*, Patai posits that—like *the book*—it may have been manufactured by the Party to entrap Winston in thoughtcrime: "Even the clipping that Winston had accidentally received eleven years earlier, which provided him with the first concrete proof that the Party was falsifying history, may well have been planted by the Party" (1984a, p. 226). In Burdekin's dystopia, the telltale photograph is assiduously preserved; in Orwell's, Winston himself, after surreptitiously viewing it, is compelled to destroy it for the preservation of his life, wondering shortly thereafter if he, unlike those around him who can seemingly rewrite the past with ease, is "a lunatic" (Orwell 1949/1977, p. 80). After being tortured by O'Brien, Winston must, for the preservation of his "sanity" (Orwell 1949/1977, p. 261), convince himself that the photograph was a figment of his imagination all along, which is part of the reason why Patai concludes—though her interpretation disregards the implied hope in the novel's appendix—that *Nineteen Eighty-Four*, unlike *Swastika Night*, ends in "despair" (1985, p. xiv).

Certainly the tone of *Swastika Night* is lighter than that of *Nineteen Eighty-Four*, and not simply because Burdekin's dystopia comes with an unspecified yet foreseeable expiration date. National Socialism has retained its efficiency for centuries, and the ruling class of the Holy German Empire, motivated to a certain degree by collectivist principles, provides well for its people:

> There was no incentive for Nazis or subject races to save money. They would be kept by the State when they were ill or too old to work, their sons were kept by the State, and women were kept by the State too, fairly well kept while immature and at child-bearing age. After that they were on a very narrow margin. (Burdekin 1937/1985, p. 59)

Far from the notion that only the lure of profit can compel people to work, men in *Swastika Night* are both productive and free from economic concerns. Though Burdekin acknowledges the regressive nature of fascism by portraying a feudal structure in which all land and resources are owned by the upper class, Pagetti observes that the Knights are little more than overprivileged bureaucrats: "Furthermore, however aberrant the Germanic 'order' imposed on half the future world may be, the Teutonic knights descending from Nazi leaders are gloomy and contemptuous administrators, not the war criminals tried and sentenced at Nuremberg" (1990, p. 363). The Knights may well be "gloomy and contemptuous," but they are also capable overseers who cooperate with each other and, for the most part, take adequate care of their dependents. Even though socialism was nominally eradicated centuries earlier, its lingering influence permeates Germany's empire. To survive as long as it has, fascism has of necessity taken on some of the characteristics of socialism. While Orwell is interested in how socialism (a potentially utopian system) can swiftly morph into fascism (a distinctly dystopian system), Burdekin asserts that the reverse can occur to some degree.

Burdekin equates socialism with common sense, so any functional community is bound to exhibit some socialist tendencies. Friedrich von Hess goes as far as to present socialism favorably to Alfred, and Alfred immediately identifies as a socialist:

> "Socialism, for instance, was absolutely smashed, practically, but the idea was still there, in men's minds [....] But if *you* were a Socialist you would think the Knights had no right to own all the land and factories and ships and houses of the Empire, you would think the people who actually do the work on the land or in the factories ought to own them."

"Then I am a Socialist." (Burdekin 1937/1985, pp. 78–79, emphasis in original)

This is an idealistic understanding of socialism, and—unlike Orwell—Burdekin has an equally uncomplicated view of the USSR. While giving a brief history lesson to Alfred, Friedrich von Hess presents Soviet Russia as the home of socialism:

> It was really what amounted to the religion of Russia, from the Polish border to Vladivostok, and there were lots of them in every other country. But Russia, after the most tremendous struggle in history (or so says von Hess), was finally beaten, by the combined attacks of Germany and Japan. The home of Socialism was shattered. (Burdekin 1937/1985, p. 79)

Here, Burdekin presciently anticipates World War II, though the Molotov–Ribbentrop Pact would undoubtedly have taken her by surprise. But by presenting Russia as a genuinely socialist nation, Burdekin ignores the historical reality that under the auspices of socialism the Bolsheviks ultimately imposed totalitarian rule by force and that Stalin was as much a dictatorial tyrant as Hitler. As Patai makes clear, Burdekin was careful to condemn spurious ideologies as opposed to the people who foolishly embraced them: "She did not hold the Germans responsible for Hitler, and she did not see Germany as a unique case. The real target of her criticism was the political values that he saw as linked to patriarchy" (2002, p. 10). This tendency accounts for the forbearance Burdekin shows the Germans, yet it also explains her reluctance to condemn the abuses of those who nominally subscribe to egalitarian political philosophies—namely, the Soviets.

Orwell's writings from about the same time that Burdekin published *Swastika Night* evince no such naïvety, in large part because of his experience of fighting in Spain. Under Russian influence, Orwell witnessed government policies that reversed the advancement of workers' rights and created a society almost indistinguishable from fascism. In his essay "Spilling the Spanish Beans," published in the same year as *Swastika Night*, he addressed the foreseeable result of the Spanish government's acquiescence to Stalin's wishes:

> The logical end is a régime in which every opposition party and newspaper is suppressed and every dissentient of any importance is in jail. Of course

such a régime will be Fascism. It will not be the same as the Fascism Franco would impose, it will even be better than Franco's Fascism to the extent of being worth fighting for, but it will be Fascism. Only, being operated by Communists and Liberals, it will be called something different. (1937/1968d, p. 275)

While Burdekin couched war between Germany and Russia as a struggle between fascism and socialism, Orwell realized that it would amount to no more than a fight between two totalitarian governments. A letter from Orwell to Jack Common written in May of 1938 shows his realization that the distinction between fascism under Hitler and socialism under Stalin is a nominal one with little meaningful difference: "I had been thinking that what with Hitler, Stalin & the rest of them the day of novel-writing was over. As it is if I start it in August I daresay I'll have to finish it in the concentration camp" (1938/1968c, p. 330). In keeping with Orwell's thinking, McKay, in his comparison of *Swastika Night* and *Nineteen Eighty-Four*, describes the late 1930s as a moment of confluence between the ideologies of the extreme right and left wings of the political spectrum: "It's worth noting that both texts I am looking at are products of a particular European moment, the conjuncture of Fascism and Stalinism" (1994, p. 303). Contrastingly, Burdekin's conception of the USSR was willfully euphemistic, but—as Orwell observed in his review of *Assignment in Utopia* by Eugene Lyons, which was published on June 9, 1938—such representations of Soviet Russia were characteristic of the left-leaning British intelligentsia of that time, who feared that criticism of Stalin would undermine the general validity of socialism: "It is an unfortunate fact that any hostile criticism of the present Russian régime is liable to be taken as propaganda against *Socialism*; all Socialists are aware of this, and it does not make for honest discussion" (1938/1968e, p. 333, emphasis in original). Furthermore, given the anti-imperialistic sentiments expressed in *Swastika Night*, it is strange that Burdekin did not acknowledge that Soviet Russia was itself an empire that conquered Georgia, Armenia, Azerbaijan, Belarus, and much of the Ukraine by military force. Burdekin's lack of objectivity in this regard dates what is, in its treatment of both sex and sexual orientation, still a progressive and important novel.

As Patai observes, Burdekin appears to take the English to task for their empire:

"Lest it be thought that she is making a specifically anti-German attack, Burdekin includes the detail that jealousy of British imperialism was one of the main motives of German imperialism" (1984b, p. 90). This occurs when Friedrich von Hess chastises Alfred for being proud that his people once enjoyed global dominance:

> You're proud of having had an Empire, are you? Proud of being an Englishman for *that* reason? Look at that poor clod Hermann there—he daren't face anything, believe anything, he hardly dares to *hear* anything, he's a shrinking, shaking *coward*, not so much because he believes in Hitler, not so much because he's a *German*, but because he's got an Empire! You ought to be ashamed of your race, Alfred, even though your Empire vanished seven hundred years ago. It isn't long enough to get rid of that taint [....] [I]t was *you* who taught *us*. Jealousy of the British Empire was one of the motive forces of German imperialism. (Burdekin 1937/1985, p. 78, emphasis in original)

Yet even though Burdekin in this passage singles out England's empire for condemnation and correctly perceives imperialism as a degrading and ultimately debilitating endeavor, she presents its rise in disingenuous terms, claiming that it was a peaceful, relatively egalitarian undertaking:

> It wasn't a conquest empire really. It was made by restlessness. The English and Irish and Scotch and Welsh just roved about on the sea and took places before other Europeans got there, or places the others didn't want, and suppressed the practically unarmed native inhabitants and just stayed there. (Burdekin 1937/1985, p. 113)

In a manner of thinking equivalent to the American idea of Manifest Destiny, Burdekin blithely glosses over England's brutal conquest of the British Isles, fraudulently suggesting that the English, Irish, Scots, and Welsh cooperated and benefited equally in the supposedly benign advancement of England's empire. This sleight of hand is necessitated by her categorical disavowal of conquest, expressed by Alfred as follows: "It is hard to tell which comes first. Whether dull, stupid, soulless nations make the best conquerors, or whether conquest makes nations dull, stupid and soulless" (Burdekin 1937/1985, p. 113). Since conquest degrades and the English in *Swastika Night* retain their integrity and vitality, Burdekin asks us to believe that England's empire was not one of conquest, though certain native inhabitants of foreign territories had to be "suppressed." This assessment of English imperialism is, at best, self-contradictory: by modeling imperialism for Germany, England is partially to blame for the rise of fascism, and the "taint" of empire still remains on Alfred and his countrymen, yet the acquisition of this empire amounted to settling a global frontier rather than conquering indigenous peoples and stealing their land, resources, and labor. Despite her socialist leanings, Burdekin could find no profit motive in this venture; instead, according to her, British imperialism was merely the product of "restlessness." While Orwell, unlike Burdekin, underappreciated the dangerous political implications of sexism, Burdekin, in contrast to Orwell, was unaware of her own susceptibility to nationalism.

A jingoistic belief in the moral superiority of the English people undergirds Burdekin's inconsistent treatment of empire. In reading to Alfred from his ancestor's manuscript, Friedrich von Hess claims that the English were revered for their moral superiority:

[T]he English have one claim to real greatness, which lies in a toughness of moral fibre, an immovable attachment to what they believe, often in the face of large majorities, to be right, that von Hess finds admirable [....] If they get a notion that a certain thing is right they will hold to it with the utmost stubbornness" (Burdekin 1937/1985, p. 114).

The sole example that Burdekin puts forward to support this dubious, self-congratulatory claim is that the Society of Friends emerged in England and remained steadfastly pacifist even during World War I (Burdekin 1937/1985, pp. 114–115). Apart from the fact that the views of a small minority cannot reliably represent the character of an entire nationality, imperialists often misrepresent their crimes as acts of altruism, producing and encouraging a range of cultural propaganda to that effect. Rudyard Kipling's "The White Man's Burden" tells us more about English ideas of morality than the preachings of Quakers. Yet many of those who disseminate such propaganda come to be seduced by it and, losing track of their original motives, subsequently internalize a false sense of moral superiority. When it comes to her view of England's empire, Burdekin, like Kipling, exhibits this tendency.

Because she could not bring herself to condemn imperialism completely and made special allowances for the English, Burdekin somewhat undermines her case against fascism. She even goes so far as to suggest that the Third Reich might constitute a necessary if painful step toward the full development of humanity. At any rate, this is what Friedrich von Hess tells Alfred near the end of their final conversation, and Alfred does not disagree:

> I think that the past civilizations with all their unimaginable complexity and richness—for von Hess says he cannot tell a millionth part of their wonder—sometimes I think that perhaps even they were only the childhood of the race; that this gulf, this dreary blankness, is like the dullness that comes on boys sometimes at adolescence, and that our manhood is yet to be. That perhaps God allowed men to commit this crime against truth through his handy instruments, the Germans and the Japanese, to make a break between childhood and manhood, to give us a rest, to enable us to overcome regret for what cannot come again. If we knew the marvels of our childhood we might want to get back into it *again*; so long as we do not know, but only know that it was *there*, we can go forward with good heart. (Burdekin 1937/1985, p. 131, emphasis in original)

The idea that the fascists, the most blatant of imperialists, might be God's "handy instruments" is particularly appalling from the vantage point of the present day. Rather than insisting that the rise of the Nazis could and should have been prevented, Burdekin implies that the horrors of fascism will purge and improve humanity, a troubling sentiment echoed in the publishers' note to the 1940 reprint: "He [the author] further feels that Nazism is too bad to be permanent, and that the appalling upheaval through which the world is passing is a symbol of birth, and that out of it will emerge a higher stage of humanity" (cited in Russell 1992, p. 37). The note itself constitutes a kind of fascist thinking by suggesting that violence is necessary for the purification of humanity.

Surprisingly, deliberate anti-Semitism is not part of von Hess's historical record. In reply to Alfred's question about the fate of the Jews, von Hess replies,

> They don't exist. They were either absorbed into other nations or wiped out. There were a few left in von Hess's time. The Palestine Jews were killed, massacred to the last man and the last child, when the Imperial German Army took Jerusalem. The German Jews were killed in various pogroms both during and after the Twenty Years' War. (Burdekin 1937/1985, p. 148)

Burdekin does not completely absolve the Germans of the role they played in the annihilation of the Jews. Yet since she published *Swastika Night* two years after the Nuremberg Laws went into effect and at a time when concentration camps were in use, it is puzzling that Burdekin makes no mention of how German anti-Semitism shaped the country's recent history.

In addition to this ambivalent treatment of fascism and the genocide it produced, Burdekin shows ableist tendencies by having a disabled man, Rupprecht von Wied, be the villain of the story. Von Wied authored the myth that Hitler was a god and that human civilization began with his leadership of the German people. To promulgate this fiction and make it appear true, he called for the destruction of all literature, art, philosophy, history, theology, and images that contradicted his ludicrous claim: "This was a typical scholar-knight called von Wied, a bookish person, says von Hess, a complete nervous hysteric, who, though bloodthirsty, had owing to physical disability to content himself with floods of ink" (Burdekin 1937/1985, p. 79). Like Hitler, von Wied came to power with the support of the people, implying a Wellsian critique of democracy. But Burdekin, through von Hess's commentary, explicitly and inappropriately links his sophistry to his disability:

> [T]he enthusiasm for von Wied in the country at large was getting quite hysterical [....] And above this storm, riding it like God on a whirlwind, was the little mean figure of von Wied, a small dark cripple (so says von Hess) without manhood, stability, or even physical courage. Von Wied outside, being hailed as the Prophet, the Apostle, the Deliverer, the Voice of Hitler, even the Voice of God. (Burdekin 1937/1985, p. 83)

Burdekin's use of the word "dark" to describe von Wied's appearance carries unsettling racial undertones. Lothian emphasizes that in *Swastika Night* the future is exclusively for white people: [I]t is worth remarking that the devastated future Europe of *Swastika Night* is wholly white [....] Asians and Africans do apparently exist, but all are safely outside Europe (2016, p. 466). Friedrich von Hess's repeated derogatory and stereotypical remarks to Alfred about the Japanese are another example of the novel's racism: "[T]he Japanese, however slavishly imitative they are, could probably never manage to be as thorough and patient in destruction as our people [....] The Japanese are quite incapable of originating anything at all, or creating anything except yellow-faced babies" (Burdekin 1937/1985, p. 112). Just as Burdekin emphasized von Wied's dark complexion, here we find the supposed deficiencies of the Japanese linked to their skin color. Alfred raises only a mild objection to Friedrich von Hess's comments: "'You are a little prejudiced against them perhaps,' Alfred suggested" (Burdekin 1937/1985, p. 112). While sensitive to the long-term perils of sexism, Burdekin displays limited understanding of other prejudices.

One could also argue that Burdekin's presentation of human history, like von Wied's, is fraught with bias. At first blush, it seems reductive to dismiss the period of human advancement from the Stone Age to Modernity as the "childhood of the race." Yet, as a feminist, Burdekin realized that in European cultures throughout most of that long period, women were regarded as little more than chattel. Burdekin, through Alfred's assessment of gender inequity, traces the cult of masculinity, fully realized in fascism, to the dawn of European civilization:

> "Everything that is something must want to be itself before every other form of life. Women are something—female, they must want to be that, they must think it the most superior, the highest possible form of human life. But of course we must not think it too. Otherwise the crime is committed again, and *we* shall be a mess. Women must be proud of having daughters, we must be proud of having sons. Could a woman, ever in the world, have been as proud of having ten daughters and no son as a man could be of having ten sons and no daughters?"
> "No!" gasped the Knight. "Of course not. As far as I know."
> "Then the crime was committed in the real tribal darkness before history began, and there you are," said Alfred, satisfied.
> "Where are we?" demanded the Knight.
> "There's the explanation why women always live according to an imposed pattern, because they are not women at all, and never have been. They are not *themselves*. Nothing can be, unless it *knows* it is superior to everything else. No man could believe God was She. No *woman* could believe God was He. It would be making God inferior." (Burdekin 1937/1985, p. 107, emphasis in original)

In their reduction of women, the Nazis were simply amplifying what Burdekin terms a prehistoric prejudice for which both sexes bear some, albeit unequal, responsibility. Nevertheless, by suggesting that it is natural for women to feel superior to men and for men to feel superior to women, Burdekin validates a tendency not far removed from the sexism of the Nazis.

Bearing in mind Burdekin's notion that women bear some responsibility for their social degradation, Stec argues that the novel is as much a warning to women as it is a response to fascism: "Burdekin is warning her female readers not to submit to patriarchal or fascist tyranny" (2001, p. 182). Here again, as Pagetti makes clear, *Swastika Night* anticipates *The Handmaid's Tale*: "Burdekin's novel seems to foreshadow not only *1984*, but also Margaret Atwood's feminist dystopia *The Handmaid's Tale*, whose heroine seems to participate in some way in her own reduction to sexual object imposed by a kind of totalitarian revolution which takes place in a futuristic US" (1990, p. 365). What Pagetti fails to realize is that the narrator's construction of herself as a sexual object in *The Handmaid's Tale* is both liberating and a feminist response to the unimaginably limiting circumstance in which she finds herself. Atwood's protagonist subverts her state-imposed identity as a purely reproductive object through her sexuality. The regime's goal in *The Handmaid's Tale* is to divorce sexual intimacy from reproduction and cast women into mutually exclusive roles. The narrator conflates these categories through eroticism and thereby makes a moral stand.

Still, while condemning male oppression, both Burdekin and Atwood place some responsibility for institutional sexism on particular women, such as those who responded favorably to Hitler and the Aunts and Wives who support the Republic of Gilead in *The Handmaid's Tale*. Burdekin makes us wonder what women confident in their own superiority and therefore capable of interacting with men on truly equal terms would be like and what kind of world they would produce. *Swastika Night* intrigues and inspires because it suggests the idea and promise of the whole woman, though the society it depicts cannot yet produce one, which is why, paradoxically, women have no voice in Burdekin's feminist dystopia.

In contrast to the sharp distinction between straight and gay in *Swastika Night*, the line between masculine and feminine is porous because women have always, to differing extents, been what men thought they should be rather than themselves. Thus when Alfred sees that Hermann's vigor has been shaken by von Hess's revelations, Hermann seems to him to be like a woman: "Is he perhaps not so much childish but rather like a *woman*, when women were different? But he's not going to kill anyone, and that's a good thing" (Burdekin 1937/1985, p. 93, emphasis in original). By making Hermann less violent and more sympathetic, this feminization could be construed as a positive development, but it also belies the notion that gender, instead of existing on a continuum, can be split into binary roles. Fortunately, because it is wholly unnatural, the reduction of women is reversible. Even at the beginning of the novel, this process of renewal is under way, as Alfred's unprompted questioning of the status quo suggests.

The long Nazi occupation also eradicated Britain's ancient class hierarchy, which, as Alfred tells Friedrich von Hess, was the only impediment to a durable democracy:

"Has a democracy ever started in a community, a nation, where the men all really considered themselves equal, no one fundamentally and *unalterably* superior to any other?"

"I should think it most unlikely. Democracies rose on decayed aristocracies."

"But you see *we'll* start fair from the bottom. In Germany there'll be numbers of discontented Knights, disgusted at the loss or sharing of their privileges. But not among *us* once the Empire has broken up. All Englishmen are so low in your eyes that they're equal, and we feel equal in our own estimation too. There is no *class*, as there is in Germany. There are only men who can read and men who can't. *That* doesn't really matter". (Burdekin 1937/1985, pp. 147–148, emphasis in original)

Burdekin separates English imperialism and ethnic pride from the traditional British investment in the hereditary class structure. Yet this is not as anomalous as it appears, since the empire allowed working- and lower-middle-class Britons to achieve socioeconomic advancements unavailable in Britain. Indeed, it allowed these common people to feel more British because it gave them the opportunity to define themselves against colonized peoples.

Unlike *the book* in *Nineteen Eighty-Four*, which asserts that people cannot form communities without grouping themselves into a hierarchy of high, middle, and low, Burdekin sees the brutal leveling of British society under fascism along with the mass illiteracy caused by von Wied's purges as essential precursors to a functional democracy. Like capitalists allegedly fulfilling the Marxist prophecy that their system will collapse from its own contradictions, the fascists have unwittingly enabled the type of world they sought to prevent. But this suggests that without fascism, the coming utopia would not have been possible, which is why Burdekin, though writing in opposition to fascist beliefs, surprisingly treated fascism as a necessary evil.

Burdekin makes it clear that just as social class will play no role in her post-fascist utopia, though she idealizes Alfred, no messianic or special individual is necessary to the process of regeneration. Decisively rejecting the Great Man Theory of history, Burdekin suggests that even without Alfred, his sons, and the book and photograph that they risk their lives to protect, the truth—and with it hope for deliverance—will endure. Friedrich von Hess reaches this conclusion as he contemplates his duty to kill Alfred for treason:

Suppose he did give way to the old savage desire to sweep away what *opposed*, what was alien, what dared to criticize; suppose he had Alfred beaten or tortured or murdered, the truth would still be where it was before, in his own mind. "If no one knows it at all," he thought, "if he is dead and I am dead, it will still be there. If there were no men at all, still certain things about men's behavior would be *true*". (Burdekin 1937/1985, p. 47, emphasis in original)

Through this conception of the immortality of truth, the utopian impulse in *Swastika Night* comes across with an inevitability reminiscent of Marxist theory and the utopian fiction of the turn of the century. Although Burdekin's dystopia satirizes fascism, it embodies the optimistic zeitgeist of the late nineteenth century while also emphasizing the danger that sexism and the valorization of so-called manliness pose to any society's political well-being. *Swastika Night* boldly questions the artificiality of pervasive gender norms, indicating how these spurious ideas of self and other can be discredited, and what can be individually and collectively gained through doing so.

REFERENCES

Baccolini, R. (1995). It's Not in the Womb the Damage is Done: Memory, Desire and the Construction of Gender in Katharine Burdekin's *Swastika Night*. In E. Siciliani (Ed.), *Le trasformazioni del narrare: atti del XVI Convegno Nazionale, Ostuni (Brindisi), 14–16 ottobre 1993* (pp. 293–310). Fasano di Brindisi: Schena Editore.

Baccolini, R. (2000). Gender and Genre in the Feminist Critical Dystopias of Katharine Burdekin, Margaret Atwood, and Octavia Butler. In M. S. Barr (Ed.), *Future Females, The Next Generation: New Voices and Velocities in Feminist Science Fiction Criticism* (pp. 13–34). Lanham, MD: Rowman & Littlefield.

Bonifas, G. (1987). Nineteen Eighty-Four and Swastika Night. *Notes and Queries, 34*(1), 59.

Burdekin, K. (1985). *Swastika Night*. New York, NY: The Feminist Press at the City University of New York. (Original work published 1937)

Croft, A. (1984). Worlds Without End Foisted Upon the Future—Some Antecedents of Nineteen Eighty-Four. In C. Norris (Ed.), *Inside the Myth* (pp. 183–216). London: Lawrence & Wishart Ltd.

Crossley, R. (1987). Dystopian Nights. *Science Fiction Studies, 14*, 93–98.

English, E. (2013). Lesbian Modernism and Utopia: Sexology and the Invert in Katharine Burdekin's Fiction. In A. Reeve-Tucker & N. Waddell (Eds.), *Utopianism, Modernism, and Literature in the Twentieth Century* (pp. 93–110). New York, NY: Palgrave Macmillan.

Holden, K. (1999). Formations of Discipline and Manliness: Culture, Politics and 1930s Women's Writing. *Journal of Gender Studies, 8*(2), 141–157.

Hopkins, C. (2006). *English Fiction in the 1930s: Language, Genre, History.* London: Continuum.

Joannou, M. (1995). *"Ladies, Please Don't Smash These Windows": Women's Writing, Feminist Consciousness, and Social Change, 1918–38.* Providence, RI: Berg.

Kumar, K. (1987). *Utopia & Anti-Utopia in Modern Times.* New York, NY: Basil Blackwell.

Lothian, A. (2016). A Speculative History of No Future: Feminist Negativity and the Queer Dystopian Impulses of Katharine Burdekin's *Swastika Night*. *Poetics Today, 37*(3), 443–472.

McKay, G. (1994). Metapropaganda: Self-Reading Dystopian Fiction: Burdekin's *Swastika Night* and Orwell's *Nineteen Eighty-Four*. *Science-Fiction Studies, 21,* 302–314.

Nealon, C. (2001). *Foundlings: Lesbian and Gay Historical Emotion Before Stonewall.* Durham, NC: Duke University Press.

Orwell, G. (1968a). In Front of Your Nose. In S. Orwell & I. Angus (Eds.), *In Front of Your Nose, 1945–1950: The Collected Essays, Journalism & Letters, Vol. 4* (pp. 122–125). New York, NY: Harcourt Brace Jovanovich. (Original work published 22 March 1946)

Orwell, G. (1968b). Letter to the Editor of Tribune. In S. Orwell & I. Angus (Eds.), *In Front of Your Nose, 1945–1950: The Collected Essays, Journalism & Letters, Vol. 4* (pp. 192–194). New York, NY: Harcourt Brace Jovanovich. (Original work published 17 January 1947)

Orwell, G. (1968c). Letter to Jack Common. In S. Orwell & I. Angus (Eds.), *An Age Like This, 1920–1940: The Collected Essays, Journalism & Letters, Vol. 1* (pp. 329–330). New York, NY: Harcourt Brace Jovanovich. (Original work dated May 1938)

Orwell, G. (1968d). Spilling the Spanish Beans. In S. Orwell & I. Angus (Eds.), *An Age Like This, 1920–1940: The Collected Essays, Journalism & Letters, Vol. 1* (pp. 269–278). New York, NY: Harcourt Brace Jovanovich. (Original work published 29 July & 2 September 1937)

Orwell, G. (1968e). Review: *Assignment in Utopia* by Eugene Lyons. In S. Orwell & I. Angus (Eds.), *An Age Like This, 1920–1940: The Collected Essays, Journalism & Letters, Vol. 1* (pp. 332–334). New York, NY: Harcourt Brace Jovanovich. (Original work published 9 June 1938)

Orwell, G. (1977). *Nineteen Eighty-Four.* New York: Harcourt Brace Jovanovich. (Original work published 1949)

Pagetti, C. (1990). In the Year of Our Lord Hitler 720: Katharine Burdekin's *Swastika Night*. *Science Fition Studies, 17,* 360–369.

Patai, D. (1984a). *The Orwell Mystique: A Study in Male Ideology.* Amherst, MA: The University of Massachusetts Press.

Patai, D. (1984b). Orwell's Despair, Burdekin's Hope: Gender and Power in Dystopia. *Women's Studies International Forum, 7*(2), 85–95.

Patai, D. (1985). Introduction. In K. Burdekin (Ed.), *Swastika Night* (pp. iii–ixv). New York: The Feminist Press at the City University of New York.

Patai, D. (2002). Katharine Burdekin (Murray Constantine). In D. H. Fain (Ed.), *Dictionary of Literary Biography, Volume 255: British Fantasy and Science-Fiction Writers, 1918–1960* (pp. 3–14). Detroit: Gale Group.

Payne, K. (2005). Debased and Impure: Christianity and Christian Resistance in Katharine Burdekin's *Swastika Night*. *Notes on Contemporary Literature, 35*(1), 8–10.

Russell, E. (1992). Katharine Burdekin's *Swastika Night*: The Search for Truths and Texts. *Foundation, 55,* 36–43.

Stec, L. (2001). Dystopian Modernism v. Utopian Feminism: Burdekin, Woolf, and West Respond to the Rise of Fascism. In M. M. Pawlowski (Ed.), *Virginia Woolf and Fascism* (pp. 178–193). New York, NY: Palgrave.

Wells, H. G. (2005). *The Shape of Things to Come.* London: Penguin. (Original work published 1933)

CHAPTER 6

Distortions of Queer Desire in Ayn Rand's *Anthem*

Like Zamyatin's *We*, *Anthem* was written by a Russian who suffered under the Bolsheviks. Both novels address nearly identical philosophical concerns—albeit from different ideological perspectives—about the relationship between the individual and the community. Foremost among these is a link between eroticism and utopian thought, which Naomi Jacobs (2007) identifies in these novels and other politically informed works of speculative fiction:

> In dystopian and anti-utopian fiction, this conflation of erotic and Utopian energy is clearly present in works such as Zamyatin's *We*, where D-503's love for I-330 leads him to question the social order, or Ayn Rand's *Anthem*, where love similarly leads the protagonist to break with a collectivist society that restricts erotic connection. (p. 4)

Jacobs emphasizes the love that develops between the characters, yet in both *We* and *Anthem*, sexual attraction is love's point of origin.

While *Anthem* is Rand's shortest novel, Shoshana Milgram (2005) argues that in many ways it is her quintessential work: "She conceived of *Anthem* in Russia, before she wrote any of her novels. She wrote *Anthem* in 1937, while she was planning *The Fountainhead*; she revised *Anthem* for American publication in 1946, while she was planning *Atlas Shrugged*. Small in size, it is nonetheless large in scope" (p. 163).[1] Claeys (2017) characterizes *Anthem* as "the classic statement of the hyperindividualistic

© The Author(s) 2018
T. Horan, *Desire and Empathy in Twentieth-Century Dystopian Fiction*, Palgrave Studies in Utopianism,
https://doi.org/10.1007/978-3-319-70675-7_6

argument," observing that "the philosophy of extreme egoism has appealed to the libertarian right in the United States to this day" (p. 346). *Anthem*'s success as a popular novel is beyond question. In his introduction to the fiftieth-anniversary printing of the novel, Leonard Peikoff (1995) notes that nearly two-and-a half million copies of *Anthem* have been sold worldwide (p. x).

Although her political philosophy is diametrically opposed to the socialism espoused by Wells, Rand saw no downside to technological development. In typical Wellsian fashion, she describes the hero of her story, a character positioned for effective political leadership by the novel's conclusion, as someone with "the adventurous courage of a scientist" (1979/1998, p. 122). Yet Rand perceived a threat to science in left-wing ideologies. This was a radical position for her time, since, as Orwell (1941/1968) points out, Wells popularized the erroneous idea that science and socialism necessarily went hand in hand:

> There survives somewhere or other an interesting controversy which took place between Wells and Churchill at the time of the Russian Revolution. Wells accuses Churchill of not really believing his own propaganda about the Bolsheviks being monsters dripping with blood etc, but of merely fearing that they were going to introduce an era of common sense and scientific control, in which flag-wavers like Churchill himself would have no place. Churchill's estimate of the Bolsheviks, however, was nearer the mark than Wells's. (p. 142)

Rand believed that the idea of working for the public welfare rather than personal advancement would eliminate first the incentive and then the ability of people to both make new scientific discoveries and exploit existing ones. But the plot of *Anthem* belies the idea that innovation cannot emerge within a collectivized society. After all, Equality 7-2521 rediscovers electricity while still believing that the will of his brothers is holy and that his ambition is evil.

The city governed by her World Council feels more like a backwater hamlet during the darkest period of the early medieval era than a futuristic metropolis. Work is done manually with primitive tools during daylight hours marked by sundials. Common knowledge, meanwhile, has shrunk to a miserable pile of premodern inaccuracies:

> We learned that the earth is flat and that the sun revolves around it, which causes the day and night. We learned the names of all the winds which blow

over the seas and push the sails of our great ships. We learned how to bleed men to cure them of all ailments. (Rand 1938/2013, p. 8)

Beneath the burden of harsh conditions, misinformation, and counterproductive medical treatments, the human race itself has sunk into simian dullness. The average life expectancy is a mere forty years (Rand 1938/2013, p. 10). At six feet, the narrator of the story is regarded as freakishly tall. Along with Orwell, who compares the physical characteristics of Oceanians to insects, Rand believed that the long-term effect of poor social policies would be the literal degeneration of the human species (Rand 1938/2013, p. 18).

In her portrayal of both the ruined human body and the ruined body politic, Rand explores the potential perils of Marxist philosophy through a strange nostalgia for our earliest beginnings. The fallen world of contrived communalism must eventually crumble to dust, and a new primal culture of natural discovery will replace it. Rand tells Equality 7-2521's story to create a founding mythology for a self-oriented, future culture, which is why her prose recalls the lyricism of Bible passages and Greek fables. *Anthem* shifts from the tragedy of paradise lost to the hope of paradise regained, equating paradise with modernity.

On the surface, Equality 7-2521's story is an account of the rediscovery of electricity through scientific experimentation. From an objectivist perspective, the eventual rejection of that practical innovation by the World Council of Scholars illustrates the ineptitude of a command economy and the tyranny of insisting on absolute consensus. One member of the Council explains to Equality 7-2521:

> [I]t would bring ruin to the Department of Candles. The Candle is a great boon to mankind, as approved by all men. Therefore it cannot be destroyed by the whim of one [....] It took fifty years to secure the approval of all the Councils for the Candle, and to decide upon the number needed, and to re-fit the Plans so as to make candles instead of torches. This touched upon thousands and thousands of men working in scores of States. We cannot alter the Plans again so soon [....] And if this should lighten the toil of men... then it is a great evil, for men have no cause to exist save in toiling for other men. (Rand 1938/2013, p. 33)

The Council's fear of reducing its citizenry's workload and allowing leisure is characteristic of despotic thought. But while Zamyatin found the veneration of science stifling, for Rand, science promotes individualism because it streamlines production, giving people the time, energy, and opportunity for individual pursuits.

For all the pride Rand takes in technology, the ultimate source of individualism in *Anthem* is not science but language. Like Orwell, Rand believes that meaningful thought and the ability to dissent are dependent on having the requisite words and grammatical structures. In her dystopia, the singular has been cut out of the English language. Noun and verb forms are uniformly plural, ensuring that people can only think and act collectively. To say the word "I," which is all but forgotten, is the society's only capital offense (Rand 1938/2013, p. 20). Though the pull of a nameless and bewildering internal self is still felt by some people, the idea of individuality is literally inconceivable without the vocabulary to name it.

Despite his unnamable yearnings and numerous transgressions, Equality 7-2521 cannot stop believing that he exists solely as part of an interdependent society. His immersion in the cooperative runs so deep that when he conducts his experiments alone in the tunnel, even his own body appears alien to him: "And now there is nothing here save our one body, and it is strange to see only two legs stretched on the ground, and on the wall before us the shadow of our one head" (Rand 1938/2013, p. 5). Equality 7-2521's estrangement from his own body parallels his estrangement from his sexuality. He is psychologically unprepared for the sexual desire that soon overtakes him.

Equality 7-2521 cannot think of himself as a unique individual until he beholds his own reflection for the first time:

> And we came to a stream which lay as a streak of glass among the trees. It lay so still that we saw no water but only a cut in the earth, in which the trees grew down, upturned, and the sky lay at the bottom. We knelt by the stream and we bent down to drink. And then we stopped. For, upon the blue of the sky below us, we saw our own face for the first time. We sat still and we held our breath. For our face and our beauty were beautiful. Our face was not like the faces of our brothers, for we felt not pity when looking upon it. Our body was not like the bodies of our brothers, for our limbs were straight and thin and hard and strong. And we thought that we could trust this being who looked upon us from the stream, and that we had nothing to fear with this being.... We have much to speak of to ourselves, and we hope we shall find the words for it in the days to come. Now, we cannot speak, for we cannot understand. (Rand 1938/2013, pp. 35–36)

In a manner characteristic of the stock Rand hero, Equality 7-2521's moment of self-realization is a narcissistic one. The mythical Narcissus mistakenly believes that he sees the beautiful face of another person when he gazes into the reflective water, and he wastes away pining for love of that all too familiar, yet all too mysterious, stranger. The greater the fidelity of the mirror, the more perilous it becomes because it tempts us to confuse reflection with reality and perhaps prefer its image to the world around us. Like the naïve Narcissus, Equality 7-2521 on a basic level misapprehends his own face for that of a separate being from whom he may well have nothing to fear, but with whom he cannot as yet fully identify.

Equality 7-2521's moment of facial recognition readies him for the final stage of his individuation, the acquisition of language. For though his reflection allows him to imagine the potential power of individualism, without the necessary language to express individualistic thought, there can be no effective resistance to the common will. Very occasionally in this society, the word "I" fortuitously reappears, and the accidental guardian of the underlying concept of the autonomous self becomes a kind of doomed secular saint. As a child, Equality 7-2521 witnessed the execution of one such person:

> They brought the Transgressor out into the square and they led him to the pyre. They had torn out the tongue of the Transgressor, so that they could speak no longer. The Transgressor were young and tall. They had hair of gold and eyes as blue as morning [....] [T]heirs was the calmest and the happiest face. As the chains were wound over their body at the stake, and a flame set to the pyre, the Transgressor looked upon the City. There was a thin thread of blood running from the corner of their mouth, but their lips were smiling [....] And we thought then, standing in the square, that the likeliness of a Saint was the face we saw before us in the flames [....] But it seemed to us that the eyes of the Transgressor had chosen us from the crowd and were looking straight upon us. There was no pain in their eyes [...] only joy [...] and pride, a pride holier than is fit for human pride to be. And it seemed as if these eyes were trying to tell us something through the flames, to send into our eyes some word without sound. And it seemed as if these eyes were begging us to gather that word and not to let it go from us and from the earth. But the flames rose and we could not guess the word. (Rand 1938/2013, pp. 20–21)

The image of the serene Transgressor anticipates the Lacanian moment when Equality 7-2521 beholds the beauty of his own face for the first time. The reciprocal attraction between the narrator and the Transgressor also has a homoerotic undercurrent.

Rand envisions a continuing thread of holy transgressors surviving through the generations, akin to the little pockets of resistance imagined by Winston and Julia in *Nineteen Eighty-Four*: "It is whispered that once or twice in a hundred years, one among the men of the City escape alone and run to the Uncharted Forest, without call or reason. These men do not return [....] But our Councils say that this is only a legend" (Rand 1938/2013, p. 19). In the absence of sacred or subversive writings such as von Hess's historical record in *Swastika Night* or *the book* in *Nineteen Eighty-Four*, these renegades are surrounded by a ghostly oral culture about life in the nearly-forgotten twentieth century: "the Old Ones [...] whisper many strange things, of the towers which rose to the sky, in those Unmentionable Times, and of the wagons which moved without horses, and of the lights which burned without flame" (Rand 1938/2013, p. 6). Like the world of modernity, the political rebellion of the Transgressor is violently cut short, but his martyrdom shifts the hope of progressive change from the political to the ethical, which is why the novel ends not with the overthrow of the World Council but with the narrator assuming both the god-like stature of the Titan Prometheus and a new transcendent creed: "And now I see the face of god, and I raise this god over the earth, this god whom men have sought since men came into being, this god who will grant them joy and peace and pride. This god, this one word: 'I'" (Rand 1938/2013, p. 44).

For their commitment to the secular values of rational self-interest, individuals such as the Transgressor are entitled to the reverence that Rand believes is improperly accorded religious figures, which is why she chose to call this novel *Anthem*: "Q: Why did you choose the title *Anthem*? AR: Because this story is my hymn to man's ego" (1979/1998, p. 123). Nevertheless, although the Transgressor can inspire others as an iconic martyr, individual thought has been so effectively curtailed that the significance of his putative crime defies articulation.

The narrator's desire to acquire scientific knowledge, though a mortal sin, is inexpressible because it is rooted in the lost concept of personal ambition:

> The evil of our crime is not for the human mind to probe. The nature of our punishment, if it be discovered, is not for the human heart to ponder. Never, not in the memory of the Ancient Ones' Ancients, never have men done what we are doing. And yet there is no shame in us and no regret [....] [S]trange are the ways of evil! (Rand 1938/2013, p. 14)

The hero and heroine eventually escape with their electric wire to a forgotten house beyond the forest, a house fitted with every twentieth-century convenience, but they remain mentally and spiritually imprisoned within the confines of their abridged vocabulary. The scales do not fall from their eyes until they find the forbidden word that makes their individualism complete and their hope for revolution and renewal possible:

> It was when I read the first of the books I found in my house that I saw the word 'I.' And when I understood this word, the book fell from my hands, and I wept, I who had never known tears. I wept in deliverance and in pity for all mankind. (Rand 1938/2013, p. 45)

Anthem is the story of one man's quest for a word of superhuman power: the first-person singular pronoun, the word that makes personal autonomy conceivable and therefore possible.

This transformative adventure is catalyzed by lust for another, a particular woman whom Equality 7-2521 initially calls the Golden One. As it does in the projected political fictions of Huxley, Orwell, and Atwood, sexual desire for a transgressive woman provides the key to political consciousness. Gimpelevich notes that "Women play a similar role of instigator and inspirer for the transfiguration for the characters in *We* and *Anthem*. They also help to rediscover the souls of these individuals. The discovery is sweetly painful" (1997, p. 18). This rediscovery of the soul is essentially a rekindling of ethics, albeit from Rand's tendentious perspective. In Rand's projected political fiction, the penitent Equality 7-2521 is the conservative character who falls under the spell of the defiant Liberty 5-3000. Equality 7-2521's first desire to openly challenge the state is ignited by his refusal to share sexual access to her with other men during the state's annual procreation ceremony:

> [W]e had been thinking without reason of the Palace of Mating. And we thought that we would not let the Golden One be sent to the Palace. How to prevent it, how to bar the will of the Councils, we knew not, but we knew suddenly that we would [....] Still, without reason, as we stood there by the hedge, we felt our lips drawn tight with hatred, a sudden hatred for all our brother men. And the Golden one saw it and smiled slowly [....] We think that in the wisdom of women the Golden One had understood more than we can understand. (Rand 1938/2013, pp. 17–18)

Equality 7-2521's sexual longing engenders a moral responsibility to protect Liberty 5-3000 from rape and to ensure her right to self-determination.

Although he wants her for himself, the text is clear that she freely chooses him. Carnal desire also makes him aware of his responsibility to himself. No longer seeing humanity as simply an undifferentiated mass, Equality 7-2521, through his sexual awakening, understands ethical obligations in terms of a burgeoning network of relationships between unique individuals.

While Equality 7-2521 has spent his entire life trying unsuccessfully to conform to the collective will and obey the Council, Liberty 5-3000 is a born radical, a woman wiser than he, confident in an understanding of self that Equality 7-2521 previously shunned as evil. But Equality 7-2521's inference of Liberty 5-3000's unspoken knowledge is triggered by his physical attraction to her beauty:

> And there it was that we saw Liberty 5-3000 walking along the furrows. Their body was straight and thin as a blade of iron. Their eyes were dark and hard and glowing, with no fear in them, no kindness and no guilt. Their hair was golden as the sun; their hair flew in the wind, shining and wild, as if it defied men to restrain it. They threw seeds from their hand as if they deigned to fling a scornful gift, and the earth was a beggar under their feet. We stood still; for the first time did we know fear, and then pain. And we stood still that we might not spill this pain more precious than pleasure. (Rand 1938/2013, p. 15)

Though Rand is describing a beautiful woman through the eyes of a man, the image of Liberty 3-5000 is strangely phallic. Far from possessing womanly curves, her body is thin and straight as iron; her eyes are hard; and her demeanor is merciless, blending both pain and pleasure into a kind of sexualized sadism. Her body mirrors the "straight and thin and hard and strong" limbs of the male narrator, which he describes as his "beauty" (Rand 1938/2013, p. 36), indicating that it is Liberty 3-5000's severe, mannish attributes that make her beautiful to the narrator. Sexual desire emerges as male appreciation of a masculine build, revealing the novel's queer undertone. Even Liberty 3-5000's blond hair, a prized attribute of white femininity, recalls the "hair of gold and eyes as blue as morning" (Rand 1938/2013, p. 20) of the male Transgressor, who with his beseeching eyes is a much more stereotypically feminine figure than she. Liberty 3-5000 scornfully dominates the begging earth, evoking conventional masculinity. Whereas women, like the earth, are typically planted and impregnated, here the seed—the metaphorical semen—comes from her, again highlighting the self-love and homoeroticism of the narrator's fascination with her.

At the heart of the novel's philosophy of self-reliance is a masochistic love for masculinity, the very tendency that *Swastika Night* presents as the cause of totalitarianism. Equality 7-2521's fear and admiration for Liberty 3-5000's dark, pitiless eyes indicate that the mutual attraction these would-be lovers share is not necessarily comfortable. Their passion has the potential to accrue revolutionary as well as reproductive power; it must therefore be fundamentally challenging to the weak culture of a world which forces the individual to deny the self. Through his desire for Liberty 5-3000, Equality 7-2521 is able to question the validity of all that he has held holy, and reassess the value of what he has denied within himself. Mimi Reisel Gladstein (1999) recognizes Rand's presentation of sexual desire as a portal to liberation and transcendence: "Rand denies the existence of a split between the physical and the mental, the desires of the flesh and the longings of the spirit" (p. 52). Equality 7-2521's lust for Liberty 5-3000 provides him with the key to acquiring her innate revolutionary acumen.

The World Council tries to contain sexual desire by depriving it of an outlet. To prevent revelatory awakenings such as the one experienced by Equality 7-2521, the state strictly segregates the sexes: "For men are forbidden to take notice of women, and women are forbidden to take notice of men" (Rand 1938/2013, p. 15). Monogamy is, as in *Brave New World*, an unmentionable offense in Rand's projected political fiction. Intercourse, solely for the purpose of conceiving children, is an annual, compulsory group activity not unlike the periodic rape of Handmaids by Commanders in *The Handmaid's Tale*:

> [M]en may not think of women, save at the Time of Mating. This is the time each spring when all the men older than twenty and all the women older than eighteen are sent for one night to the City Palace of Mating. And each of the men have one of the women assigned to them by the Council of Eugenics. Children are born each winter, but women never see their children and children never know their parents. Twice have we been sent to the Palace of Mating, but it is an ugly and shameful matter, of which we do not like to think. (Rand 1938/2013, p. 16)

Through making sex a group activity, the Council of Eugenics degrades it from an act of private joy to a public embarrassment. Though sexual arousal undoubtedly occurs frequently among the citizens of Rand's dystopia, it is tainted by association with the state's demeaning mating ritual.

By satirizing eugenics prior to World War II, Rand appears to taking an enlightened position. But Richard Lawrence (2001) points out that Rand may not have been using the word in the scientific sense:

> It is not clear from this brief description whether the "Council of Eugenics" has retained any concept of eugenics in the usual sense of selective breeding. They may simply be arranging anonymous matings in order to remove any elements of personal relationships or individual feelings from the sex act. If they are engaging in selective breeding, one wonders whether a non-conformist like Equality 7-2521 would be allowed to have any children at all.

In addition to thwarting the emotional and psychological attachments that flow naturally from sexual contact, sequestering the offspring of these humiliating encounters also undermines the idea of the family unit. After all, the family is an exclusive, resource-pooling institution with the potential to take precedence over the communal whole within the hearts and minds of ordinary people.

Rand's faith in the traditional family model is affirmed at the conclusion of the novel when Equality 7-2521, who renames himself Prometheus, and Liberty 5-3000, now called Gaea, reunite in the wilderness beyond the city and aspire to start a nuclear family unit, situating within the remnants of traditional domesticity their eventual violent assault on the collectivist state:

> Gaea is pregnant with my child. Our son will be raised as a man [....] Here on this mountain, I and my sons and my chosen friends shall build our new land and our fort. And it will become as the heart of the earth, lost and hidden at first, but beating, beating louder each day. And word of it will reach every corner of the earth [....] And the day will come when I shall break all the chains of the earth, and raze the cities of the enslaved, and my home will become the capital of a world where each man will be free to exist for his own sake. (Rand 1938/2013, pp. 46, 48)

Rand's hero is confident not only that his children will be male—suggesting by implication that male children are more valuable—but that they and their descendants will produce economic self-sufficiency and military strength. The idea that the family is the seed from which the free market system grows can be traced to Marx and Engels's *Communist Manifesto*, which calls for the abolition of the family:

What is the present family based on? On capitalism, the acquisition of private property. It exists in all of its meaning only for the bourgeoisie [...] and will vanish when capitalism vanishes. Are you accusing us that we want to end the exploitation by parents of their children? We confess to that crime [....] The bourgeois sees in his wife nothing but an instrument of production. (1848/1998, pp. 56–57)

Like Marx and Engels, her philosophical adversaries, Rand traces capitalism, and the stable families on which it depends, back to the guiding will of individual patriarchs, the traditional heads of private households. This conception of the family is, of course, bogus. For the few at the top of the socioeconomic pyramid, capitalism may be conducive to familial stability. But for the countless workers who must prioritize making money above all else—including time with their families—capitalism subverts family cohesion.

Rand genuinely believed in the supremacy of the individual will. Yet the violent imagery of Equality 7-2521's ambition augurs an objectivist uprising of iron and blood against a pacifistic culture. Before his awakening, the narrator affirms the society's strict adherence to nonviolence: "There are few offenses blacker than to fight with our brothers, at any age and for any cause whatsoever" (Rand 1938/2013, p. 6). The World Council has so successfully secured global peace that, unlike every other speculative world discussed in this study, there is no longer a need for a standing army, police force, or proper prison system to enforce the law. Even when Equality 7-2521 is brought to the Palace of Correction for questioning, he is left essentially unguarded: "The locks are old on the doors and there are no guards about. There is no reason to have guards, for men have never defied the Councils so far as to escape from whatever place they were ordered to be" (Rand 1938/2013, p. 29). Gimpelevich maintains that Rand was an ardent pacifist: "According to her philosophy, a true radical will allow no place for any kind of destructive armament. She does not recognize physical force as even a slight possibility for any problem's solution. She is firm and fervent in her nonacceptance of physical violence" (1997, p. 15). But the tone of *Anthem* seems to suggest that there is something genuinely unnatural and emasculating about complete pacifism, that it somehow renders us docile and helpless in a way that terror never could. For Rand, violence is an aspect of human nature which has been employed for the sake of good as well as evil. When a culture becomes purely nonviolent, it can lose the will to identify and resist the stultifying oppression of total conformity. In other words, dissent sometimes properly depends on muscle. If collectivists do not wish to embrace Rand's notions of freedom and what must be done to achieve and preserve it, she feels that they are being willfully blind and must be forced to acknowledge her unvarnished "truths."

Rand's reductive approach to political theory and her investment in stereotypical gender roles have made her name anathema in most academic circles. Like Rand herself, Liberty 5-3000 is an independent woman who thrives in an androcentric culture. Yet rather than have her heroically braving the perils of capture or battle, Rand, as Lawrence makes clear, idealizes the notion of a magnificent woman joyously submitting to her god-like man: "It is typical of Rand that her main female character would be defiant of social conventions [...] and physically brave [...] yet at the same time would be submissive to her beloved [...] and would manifest a stereotypical feminine trait like vanity" (2001). In *Anthem* the triumphs of humanity's ultimate future are claimed by Rand's new Prometheus and his sons, while his wife—and any daughters she might bear him—remain happily sequestered in domesticity. By the final chapter, Rand has elevated the penitent Equality 7-2521 to a titan and reduced the once-steely Liberty 5-3000 to a frivolous trophy wife. As Equality 7-2521 begins to prepare his new house for occupancy, Liberty 5-3000 preens vainly before a bedroom mirror:

> We did this work alone, for no words of ours could take the Golden One away from the big glass which is not glass. They stood before it and they looked and looked upon their own body. When the sun sank beyond the mountains, the Golden One fell asleep on the floor, amidst jewels, and bottles of crystal, and flowers of silk. We lifted the Golden One in our arms and we carried them to bed, their head falling softly upon our shoulder. Then we lit a candle, and we brought paper from the room of the manuscripts, and we sat by the window, for we knew we could not sleep tonight. (Rand 1938/2013, p. 42)

The Golden One's evening in front of the looking glass parallels the narrator's moment of self-recognition at the stream. Yet the bucolic setting naturalizes his narcissism. By contrast, her mirror moment is artificial and materialistic, occurring among consumer goods and luxury items such as crystal bottles, jewelry, and artificial flowers. When the narrator finds her sprawled amid the detritus of femininity, he carries her off to the bedroom.

Though Liberty 5-3000, the narrator's Golden One, possessed a deeper knowledge of the correlation between sexual and political defiance than the narrator did when they lived within the confines of the city, the information discovered in the newfound manuscripts is apparently for men alone, to be shared with women as men see fit. While he writes and produces, she idles and consumes. In the end, her identity is equated with adornment and superficial materiality.

The narrator bestows the word "I" and the concept of individuality on his bride, impregnates her with a child that he is convinced will be male, and then, like Adam naming the subordinate creatures in Eden, christens his wife Gaea because she is to be the lucky mother of "a new kind of gods" (Rand 1938/2013, p. 45). Indeed, from the time Liberty 5-3000 enters her new home, she addresses her husband as though he were Jehovah himself: " 'Your will be done,' they said" (Rand 1938/2013, p. 41). In the city, Gaea was assaulted by the rhetoric of obedience to the collective, now she will live a life of obedience to her husband.

The alluring serpent in this reworked story of Adam and Eve is the long, smooth, narrow subway tunnel in which the narrator is tempted by the forbidden secret of the little wire's mysterious power, a discovery which—like Adam's ability to discern good from evil—nearly costs the narrator his life when discovered by the authorities. In place of the biblical cherub with the flaming sword standing watch over the entrance to paradise, Prometheus plans to employ an electric barrier to keep unwelcome trespassers out of his home:

> I shall build a barrier of wires around my home, and across the paths which lead to my home; a barrier light as a cobweb, more impassable then a wall of granite; a barrier my brothers will never be able to cross. For they have nothing to fight me with, save the brute forces of their numbers. I have my mind. (Rand 1938/2013, p. 46)

He and his lover may have been coconspirators while in the city of the damned, but Prometheus is the sole ruler of their gated castle.

Many critics, including me, are repulsed by Rand's insistence on a gender hierarchy in which women play the subordinate role. Susan Love Brown notes that *Anthem* presents a paradigmatic shift in Rand's fiction away from female protagonists: "*Anthem* shifts the focal point from woman to man, a focus that remains fixed in the last two novels. It is in this brief story, *Anthem*, that Rand establishes man as the discoverer and leader and woman as the acolyte or follower" (2006, p. 65). There is no way to defend Rand against a charge of sexism because, though a woman, she prized masculinity over femininity. She appears to satirize the idea of equality between men and women by making it a prominent feature of her dystopian society. Moreover, Rand never resolves the inherent contradiction between her valorization of the individual and her blanket preference for men over women.

A subtler bias embedded in the text is latent racial prejudice. Rand sensibly claims that she was deliberately vague about Equality 7-2521's ethnicity to emphasize that such an individual could emerge anywhere in the world: "Q: What race is Equality? AR: Any race—since he represents the best possible to all races of men" (1979/1998, p. 122). Yet the characters who are described have distinctly Northern European physical features. Liberty 5-3000 is nicknamed the Golden One because of her blond hair (Rand 1938/2013, p. 15), and the blond-haired, blue-eyed Transgressor looks stereotypically Aryan (Rand 1938/2013, p. 20). In Rand's universal parable of archetypal humanity, either white skin is the norm or only white characters warrant special attention. For Rand—and for most twentieth-century authors of dystopian fiction—whiteness is the default.

Although Rand disparages the idea that a life lived for others can be a happy life, concern for the well-being of humanity is at least a small part of her philosophy. When the hero of the story harnesses the power of electricity, his first impulse is to share it with his fellow citizens: "Tomorrow, in the full light of day, we shall take our box, and leave our tunnel open, and walk through the streets to the Home of the Scholars. We shall put before them the greatest gift ever offered to men" (Rand 1938/2013, p. 30). The narrator's achievement is clearly not motivated by what we normally call selfishness. He dreams about his discovery being used for the common good, and he appears free from any desire to aggrandize himself through its exploitation. James Montmarquet (2011) indicates that in Rand's fiction, pure self-interest cannot sustain innovation any more than self-abnegation: "If, as Rand admits, creators have persisted through the centuries, knowing that they are unlikely to benefit very much from their achievements, self-interest would not seem to have been their main motive" (p. 4). Moreover, when he is free and safe in his wilderness haven at the conclusion of the novel, Prometheus vows to put himself back in harm's way to help both the male and female friends he left behind escape from their totalitarian nightmare:

I shall steal one day, for the last time, into the cursed City of my birth. I shall call to me my friend who has no name save International 4-8818, and all those like him Fraternity 2-5503, who cries without reason, and Solidarity 9-6347 who calls for help in the night, and a few others. I shall call to me all the men and the women whose spirit has not been killed within them and who suffer under the yoke of their brothers. They will follow me and I shall lead them to my fortress [....] I and they [...] shall write the first chapter in the new history of man. (Rand 1938/2013, p. 46)

Objectivism is defined by individualism. But Rand, speaking through Prometheus, concedes—perhaps reluctantly—that we should help others and that positive social change requires collaborative effort. After all, Prometheus's ultimate success, though presented as a foregone conclusion, depends on the willing assistance of other like-minded men and women whom he plans to recruit. Even Equality 7-2521's use of the tunnel for his scientific experiments depends on the ongoing complicity of his friend International 4-8818, who theoretically could at any time do his legal duty by reporting Equality 7-2521 to the authorities (Rand 1938/2013, pp. 12–13). Even if Rand's point that special inspiration comes exclusively from gifted individuals is granted for the sake of argument, translating that inspiration into tangible benefits frequently requires either the assistance or the forbearance of others.

Prometheus's imperialistic talk of razing cities and founding a world capital (Rand 1938/2013, p. 48) likewise depends on the cooperation of a voluntary army. In theory, the communist city is established on principles of forced labor, which no able person with the ability to choose freely would consent to live under; but the persuasiveness of objectivism alone will be insufficient, even in Rand's opinion, to win enough converts to guarantee its success. Prometheus will have to transform his idyllic home into a "fortress" in preparation for what will eventually be a new world war, just as collectivism—though existing peacefully at the time of the story—was established by battles and purges in the distant past. This again undermines the dubious notion that Rand was a pacifist:

> We have heard the legends of the great fighting, in which many men fought on one side and only a few on the other. These few were the Evil Ones and they were conquered. Then great fires raged over the land. And in these fires the Evil Ones and all the things made by the Evil Ones were burned. And the fire which is called the Dawn of the Great Rebirth, was the Script Fire

where all the scripts of the Evil Ones were burned, and with them all the words of the Evil Ones. Great mountains of flame stood in the squares of the Cities for three months. (Rand 1938/2013, pp. 19–20)

Despite *Anthem*'s status as an outlier within the dystopian canon, Rand's portrayal of an apocalyptic war between good and evil echoes the sense of a near-cosmic struggle between competing ideologies in *The Iron Heel* and *We*.

In most projected-political fictions, goodness is equated with what a fully informed populace ought to embrace. Yet the dystopias of Rand and Zamyatin were knowingly established by majority rule, calling democracy itself into question as H. G. Wells did. Like the Mephi of *We*, the so-called Evil Ones in *Anthem* are the "good guys." Their theology is the worship of the individual spirit, which thrives, against incredible odds, in spite of so-called civilization. Ironically, the misguided many who fought for collectivism were actually fighting for a kind of freedom, not the freedom to choose, which Rand and Zamyatin believed was intrinsic to human dignity, but freedom from the responsibility of choice, like the freedom felt by a well-cared-for child. This appeal of "freedom from" is explored more fully by Atwood in *The Handmaid's Tale*. Like Atwood, Rand and Zamyatin understood that enough people could fear freedom of choice, and the risks that come with it, to strive successfully against it. But they, like the other major writers of projected political fiction, also realized that on an instinctive level, people would always desire the freedom to pursue their sexual lives and that this instinctive impulse could revive the hunger for greater personal autonomy and healthier communal relationships. Even in a world where the concept of having the freedom to make personal choices has been lost, the desire to take control of one's own life can be reawakened through sexual yearning for another person. Like the projected political fictions of London and Atwood, *We* and *Anthem* show great faith in the power of sexual desire to resurrect fallen humanity.

Rand's belief in the controlling and liberating power of language is central to *Nineteen Eighty-Four*, which leads Milgram to characterize Orwell's book as a kind of prequel to *Anthem*:

> Orwell's *1984*—unlike *We*—shares with *Anthem* the observation that a decline in the quality of human life is accompanied by a decline in language. Although the word "I" had not (yet?) disappeared, the language of this world is being drained of dangerous words in order to eliminate the corresponding ideas. The principles of "Newspeak" will lead eventually to the obliteration of the first person, which will be deemed inessential. Perhaps

the world of *1984* is similar to the "graceless years of transition" mentioned in *Anthem* (103), which would make Orwell's novel a sort of prequel to Ayn Rand's. (2005, p. 152)[2]

The claim that the values and beliefs of the Inner Party in *Nineteen Eighty-Four* are equivalent to those of the World Council in *Anthem* is undermined by the lack of a sadistic motive in Rand's dystopia. Rand's novel is a polemic against misguided principles rather than predatory ones. The lack of clear evidence that Orwell read *Anthem* makes the connection between the two novels more tenuous still, though Milgram points out that there is some reason to think that Orwell was familiar with *Anthem*: "It is possible and likely that he read *Anthem*. Because he was on the lookout for books like *We*, he might have been interested in reading *Anthem* if he had run across it. Malcolm Muggeridge, his friend, reviewed *Anthem* favorably in 1938, when it was published in England" (2005, p. 153). Yet even if he was unfamiliar with *Anthem* when he wrote *Nineteen Eighty-Four*, Orwell, like Rand, endorses the liberating power of sexual desire for the individual, even when political rebellion is seemingly impossible for the masses.

Notes

1. I use the 1937 edition of *Anthem*, published in 1938 in the UK. As Rand herself makes clear in her foreword to the 1946 printing, the differences between the UK and US editions are stylistic rather than substantive: "This story was written in 1937. I have edited it for this publication, but have confined the editing to its style; I have reworded some passages and cut out some excessive language. No idea or incident was added or omitted; the theme, content and structure are untouched. The story remains as it was. I have lifted its face, but not its spine or spirit; these did not need lifting" (2001/1946, p. 11). The earlier text arguably exerted greater cultural influence, since its critique of collectivism pre-dates World War II and the Cold War.
2. "(103)" refers to the 1946 US edition of *Anthem*, reprinted by Caxton Printers in 2001. The phrase in question is identically worded in both the UK and the US versions of the novel.

References

Brown, S. L. (2006). Essays on Ayn Rand's Fiction. *The Journal of Ayn Rand Studies*, 8(1), 63–84.
Claeys, G. (2017). *Dystopia: A Natural History*. Oxford: Oxford University Press.

Gimpelevich, Z. (1997). "We" and "I" in Zamyatin's *We* and Rand's *Anthem*. *Germano-Slavica: A Canadian Journal of Germanic and Slavic Comparative Studies, 10*(1), 13–23.

Gladstein, M. R. (1999). Ayn Rand and Feminism: An Unlikely Alliance. In M. R. Gladstein & C. M. Sciabarra (Eds.), *Feminist Interpretations of Ayn Rand* (pp. 47–55). University Park, PA: Pennsylvania State University Press.

Jacobs, N. (2007). Dissent, Assent, and the Body in *Nineteen Eighty-Four*. *Utopian Studies, 18*(1), 3–20.

Lawrence, R. (2001, May). Preface and Notes. *Anthem*. Ayn Rand. Retrieved from https://www.noblesoul.com/orc/texts/anthem/complete.html

Marx, K., & Engels, F. (1998). *The Communist Manifesto* (S. Moore, Trans.). London: Verso. (Original work published 1848)

Milgram, S. (2005). *Anthem* in the Context of Related Literary Works: We Are Not Like Our Brothers. In R. Mayhew (Ed.), *Essays on Ayn Rand's Anthem* (pp. 119–171). Lanham, MD: Lexington Books.

Montmarquet, J. (2011). Prometheus: Ayn Rand's Ethic of Creation. *The Journal of Ayn Rand Studies, 11*(1), 3–18.

Orwell, G. (1968). Wells, Hitler, and the World State. In S. Orwell & I. Angus (Eds.), *My Country Right or Left, 1940–1943: The Collected Essays, Journalism & Letters, Vol. 2* (pp. 139–145). New York, NY: Harcourt Brace Jovanovich. (Original work published August 1941)

Peikoff, L. (1995). Introduction. In A. Rand (Ed.), *Anthem: 50th Anniversary American Edition* (pp. v–xiii). New York, NY: Plume.

Rand, A. (1998). Questions and Answers on *Anthem*. In P. Schwartz (Ed.), *The Ayn Rand Column* (pp. 122–123). Irvine, CA: Ayn Rand Institute Press. (Original work published June 1979)

Rand, A. (2001). Foreword. In A. Rand (Ed.), *Anthem*. Caldwell, ID: Caxton Press. (Original work published 1946)

Rand, A. (2013). *Anthem*. Lexington, KY: Denton & White. (Original work published 1938)

CHAPTER 7

Desire and Empathy in George Orwell's *Nineteen Eighty-Four*

Nineteen Eighty-Four illustrates George Orwell's faith in sexual desire as a source of social responsibility. When considering the likely shape of things to come, Orwell looked backward to the sexual repressions of medieval Catholicism: "What we are moving towards at this moment is something more like the Spanish Inquisition, and probably far worse, thanks to the radio and the secret police. There is very little chance of escaping it unless we can reinstate the belief in human brotherhood without the need for a 'next world' to give it meaning" (1940/1968d, p. 17). Here, Orwell presents both the problem and the solution. As Ian Slater (1985) makes clear, Orwell believed that the empathetic sense of shared humanity and responsibility for each other that ideally flowed from belief in God must be restored without reviving faith in divinity:

> Orwell did not want to reinstate the Church's influence, for he believed that because the ideas of submission to God and of human control over nature are felt to be inimical, the Christian churches are on the whole hostile to reform [....] What needed to be done, said Orwell, was to "reinstate" the belief in brotherhood, the belief that no matter what differences exist between us, we are responsible for each other. (pp. 81–82)

A sense of "brotherhood" among people necessarily starts with trust between individuals, which is why the Party endeavors to keep personal relationships as adversarial as the basic functioning of society will allow. In

© The Author(s) 2018
T. Horan, *Desire and Empathy in Twentieth-Century Dystopian Fiction*, Palgrave Studies in Utopianism,
https://doi.org/10.1007/978-3-319-70675-7_7

Nineteen Eighty-Four the personal empathy that reignites social empathy originates in Winston and Julia's reciprocal erotic passion.

Certainly sexual desire for Julia's mind and body is the starting point of Winston Smith's tentatively hopeful outlook. Once they start seeing each other, Winston begins to imagine a whole network of illicit affairs that he thinks can germinate into actual pockets of political resistance:

> I don't imagine we can alter anything in our own lifetime. But one can imagine little knots of resistance springing up here and there—small groups of people banding themselves together, and gradually growing, and even leaving a few records behind, so that the next generation can carry on where we leave off. (Orwell 1949/1977, p. 156)

Winston's newfound sense of responsibility to himself, others, and future generations constitutes a burgeoning morality originating in eroticism. As his social conscience grows, his attention shifts from personal grievances to a cooperative struggle for change. Though his life is fragile, his situation precarious, and his chances of personal survival slim to non-existent, Winston's sexual desire leads him to do what he believes is right. This is the moral compass which Orwell, though an atheist, believed we lost with the decline of the Judeo-Christian tradition, and which—as he insisted in his column in *Tribune* from March 3, 1944—we must recover within ourselves:

> There is little doubt that the modern cult of power worship is bound up with the modern man's feeling that life here and now is the only life there is [....] I do not want the belief in life after death to return, and in any case it is not likely to return. What I do point out is that its disappearance has left a big hole [....] One cannot have any worth-while picture of the future unless one realizes how much we lost by the decay of Christianity. (1944/2000a, p. 103)

The Winston whom Orwell imbues with a belief in the spirit of humanity is a far cry from the restless man who believed at the beginning of the story that his diary would reach no one, apart from the Thought Police: "How could you communicate with the future? It was of its nature impossible" (Orwell 1949/1977, p. 9). His dreams of organized resistance are of course unrealistic, but they demonstrate how sexual desire changed him from a hapless victim of fear and propaganda into a daring revolutionary of sublime vision, inspiring him to openly confront O'Brien about the Brotherhood.

Eroticism fosters interpersonal trust and an open exchange of ideas. As Slater indicates, Orwell suggests that the individual's ability to think critically, imaginatively, and productively arises from their ability to trust and communicate honestly with others: "[T]he fundamental enemy of intellectual freedom, says Orwell, is the attempt to isolate oneself from one's fellows. The occasional need for solitude notwithstanding, he argues that while it is possible to work without thinking, 'it is almost impossible to think without talking,' which implies the company of others" (1985, p. 232). Bernard Crick (2007) posits that the development of Winston's and Julia's individuality, which blossoms in conjunction with their physical intimacy, arises out of the bond of trust between them, a connection initiated by sexual interest:

> Orwell believes that individuality can only be destroyed when we are utterly alone. While we have someone to trust, our individuality cannot be destroyed [....] If the affair is not a love affair in a genuine sense, it is, however, exemplary of 'mutual trust' right up to the end when they are tortured. Mutual trust, fellowship, fraternity and decency are recurrent themes in all of Orwell's writings after *The Road to Wigan Pier* and *Homage to Catalonia*. These themes qualify his earlier individualism. (pp. 150–151)

Crick's argument that the relationship between Winston and Julia "is not a love affair in the genuine sense" is premised on the fact that the bond between these characters is initially and primarily a sexual one:

> Some critics have argued that 'love' is asserted as a positive value in *Nineteen Eighty-Four* and is necessary for a good society, as shown by the love affair between Winston and Julia. They then say, not surprisingly, that the portrayal of love is clumsy and shallow. But it begins as sexual desire, a 'love affair'; anything like real love only grows on the toward the end. (2007, p. 151)

Crick's emphasis on sexual desire rather than romantic love agrees with what Orwell himself wrote while making revisions to the first manuscript of *Nineteen Eighty-Four*.

In an excerpt from a notebook from 1948, which is published in an appendix to the Clarendon Press reissue of the book, Orwell emphasizes the explicit connection between sexuality and rebellion in Winston's mind: "W's longing for a woman of his own—(connection in his mind between sexuality & rebellion?)" (1984, p. 142). It is sex, not love, that generates the bond between Winston and Julia, enabling their sociopolitical conspiracy. For Orwell, the trust between individuals that makes their individuality possible and ultimately facilitates a culture of ethics and justice originates with sexual desire, not the grace of a particular god, which is why the Party employs traditional mechanisms of institutional religion such as sexual repression.

Orwell, like the other authors in this study, asserts that as much as totalitarian regimes need to control the flow of desire, they can never do so absolutely. Sexual hunger always re-emerges as the catalyst for rejuvenating tendencies. Jenny Taylor (1984) points out that as with *We*, a sexual relationship is at the core of *Nineteen Eighty-Four*:

> It is the very centrality of the relationship between sexual and political repression in *1984* that makes the novel seem so recognisable today [....] Its plot is almost identical to [...] *We* [...] a futuristic dystopia in which the hero D-503 is moved by desire to political rebellion by the Other—E330—though he finally betrays her. (p. 26)

Taylor's claims about the plot similarities between *We* and *Nineteen Eighty-Four* are exaggerated, but she is right about the pivotal importance of desire in both novels. Like the relationship between D-503 and I-330, the sexual relationship in *Nineteen Eighty-Four* is again between an essentially orthodox character (Winston) and a radical seductress (Julia).

Calling Winston orthodox is admittedly surprising since he abhors Big Brother and disbelieves in the principles of INGSOC. But at the beginning of the novel, his helplessness and resignation ensure that he is no real threat to the Party: "Whether he wrote DOWN WITH BIG BROTHER, or whether he refrained from writing it, made no difference. Whether he went on with the diary, or whether he did not go on with it, made no difference. The Thought Police would get him just the same" (Orwell 1949/1977, p. 20). When we meet Winston, he is in a state of despair. He has decided that he is doomed to be arrested and shot, so the risks he takes are irrelevant.

Julia, on the other hand, firmly believes that she can get away with her subversive behavior and find happiness, not only for her but for Winston. Blu Tirohl (2000) rightly argues that though we first see Julia from the perspective of Winston's frustrated desire, it is she who takes the initiative to launch the sexual relationship:

Julia's seduction (it is she who makes the first move and subsequent liaison arrangements) of Winston serves three functions for him. Firstly, she provides an outlet for his sexual needs [....] Secondly, she demonstrates a failure in the Party to control her sexuality, since she adores intercourse and anything which corrupts The Party inspires Winston. Thirdly, she offers Winston loyalty and the message that he is not alone in his thoughts. (p. 58)

Tirohl could extend his perceptive analysis even further. The satisfaction of Winston's lust does more than provide him with a companion for his bed and thoughts—it transforms him from a restless defeatist into a willing soldier for the Brotherhood. The satisfaction of an erotic fantasy begets a pragmatic optimism:

> "In this game that we're playing, we can't win." She always contradicted him when he said anything of this kind. She would not accept it as a law of nature that the individual is always defeated [....] She believed it was somehow possible to construct a secret world in which you could live as you chose [....] "We are the dead," he said.
> "We're not dead yet," said Julia prosaically. (Orwell 1949/1977, pp. 136–137)

Both characters, of course, realize that organizing an open rebellion is impossible, but while Winston dwells on the hopelessness of overt resistance, Julia, perhaps naïvely, believes that they can beat the Party at its own game behind masks of apparent loyalty. In this, as Plank (1984) observes, Julia is admirably fearless: "[I]t is Julia who provided much of the courage to make the liaison last" (p. 37). Anne Mellor (1983) emphasizes Julia's insightful realization that her sexuality is a means to bring people together and generate ethical bonds:

> Julia recognizes that her sexuality threatens more than the Party's efforts to control the reproductive process. By giving immediate pleasure to the individual, sexuality also paves the way toward an experience of personal commitment, of a pair-bonding that is felt as a love for an individual and not for a system. (p. 120)

Mellor's analysis shows that Julia, perhaps inadvertently, emerges as the novel's moral voice and arguably the character who most threatens the Party. Before her relationship with Winston, she had led other Outer Party members to rebellion through her sexuality (Orwell 1949/1977, p. 126), enhancing her role as a leader and her attractiveness to Winston. Baruch (1983) sees her as the novel's true hero: "In this light, there is no question that the most courageous and admirable figure in the society of *1984* is Julia" (p. 51).

Yet *Nineteen Eighty-Four* is not a feminist novel. Julia's rebellion is limited to subverting the Party's code of sexual repression. Winston characterizes Julia's disobedience as purely sexual:

> With Julia, everything came back to her own sexuality [....] She had grasped the inner meaning of the Party's puritanism. It was not merely that the sex instinct created a world of its own which was outside the Party's control and which therefore had to be destroyed if possible. What was more important was that sexual privation induced hysteria, which was desirable because it could be transformed into war fever and leader worship. (Orwell 1949/1977, p. 134)

It is through her promiscuity that Julia seeks both to satiate herself and enervate the Party; Claeys (2017) describes her as "at one level, hedonism incarnate" (p. 439). Each orgasm Julia enjoys siphons away energy that would otherwise be spent buttressing Big Brother and the policies he represents. The damage she does to the body politic is small but real. She is a revolutionary but, as Winston boorishly says, a revolutionary only "from the waist downwards" (Orwell 1949/1977, p. 157).

Though this crude witticism is almost pejorative, Orwell uses it to convey Winston's frustration with Julia's lack of interest in political theory and the corresponding playful delight that she takes in this frustration. Yet, through Julia, Orwell may be questioning the value of theorizing and postulating rather than acting. For Paul Bail (2003), rampant promiscuity imbues Julia with a pragmatic wisdom that is far more valuable than Winston's intellectual theorizing:

> Julia bases her judgments on contextualized and experiential knowledge. Having had clandestine sex with scores of Party leaders, Julia sees through the hypocrisy and sham of the official social structure. As a result, she has the pragmatic realism of an outsider. In contrast, Winston, like many males, is enamored of abstract knowledge. Even after he rejects the official ideology of Big Brother, he still remains vulnerable to the lure of bankrupt political abstractions—the "ideals" of the Brotherhood—which O'Brien dangles before him as bait. (p. 217)

Thus, although Winston's conscious disaffection makes him appear to be an outside observer, Bail recognizes that Julia's perspective is more objective, accurate, and subversive. The reader can only speculate as to the amount of damage her extensive sexual experiences have done to the Party.

At the beginning of the novel, just as he accepts that achieving regime change is impossible, Winston believes that he will never sleep with Julia. His thoughts regarding her are a sexist mixture of frustrated lust and libidinal rage: "Vivid, beautiful hallucinations flashed through his mind [....] He would tie her naked to a stake and shoot her full of arrows like Saint Sebastian. He would ravish her and cut her throat at the moment of climax [....] He hated her because [...] he wanted to go to bed with her and would never do so" (Orwell 1949/1977, p. 16). Though these fantasies are appalling, the desire underlying them results in empathetic, compassionate behavior. When Julia falls on her injured arm, Winston instinctively helps her:

> In front of him was an enemy who was trying to kill him; in front of him, also, was a human creature, in pain and perhaps with a broken bone. Already he had instinctively started forward to help her. In the moment when he had seen her fall on the bandaged arm, it had been as though he felt the pain in his own body. (Orwell 1949/1977, p. 107)

Before he has time to think, Winston's sexual passion for Julia, an apparent mortal enemy, sparks empathy and socially responsible behavior.

Winston's desire for Julia soon changes his mind. Lurid and undeniably chauvinistic thoughts give way to dreams of consensual sex as he begins to recognize the utopian potential and significance of Julia's body. His fantasies about her begin to be set in the Golden Country, Winston's imagined, pastoral utopia reminiscent of the forest beyond the Green Wall in *We*:

> The girl with the dark hair was coming toward him across the field. What overwhelmed him in that instant was admiration for the gesture with which she had thrown her clothes aside. With its grace and carelessness it seemed to annihilate a whole culture, a whole system of thought, as though Big Brother and the Party and the Thought Police could all be swept into nothingness. (Orwell 1949/1977, p. 32)

Julia's exposed sensuality channels Winston's meek disaffection into impassioned hope. Whereas his heretical thoughts were previously vague and unfocused, they have now located themselves on Julia's body, which he recognizes as a potential substitute for the current body politic. By tearing off her Party uniform, she rends the fabric of cultural repression that binds the Party together, implicitly suggesting that she and Winston can create their own world beyond the grasp of the Thought Police. When he and Julia eventually have sex, they experience it as an act of sociopolitical resistance. "Their embrace had been a battle, the climax a victory. It was a blow struck against the Party. It was a political act" (Orwell 1949/1977, p. 128).

Daphne Patai takes issue with Orwell's "idealized portrayal of female maternal figures" in *Nineteen Eighty-Four* (1984, p. 88). Yet since all political dystopias need to regenerate, it is difficult to conceive of any kind of rejuvenating relationship without procreation because it alone affords the possibility of societal continuity into the future. Patai's claim that *Nineteen Eighty-Four* idealizes maternal figures is also complicated by the novel's presentation of Katherine, Winston's wife, who in her commitment to conceiving a child and becoming a mother serves as a foil to Julia.

Both Katherine and Julia are physically attractive, though Katherine is presented as more classically beautiful and dignified:

> Katherine was a tall, fair-haired girl, very straight, with splendid movements. She had a bold, aquiline face, a face that one might have called noble until one discovered that there was nearly as possible nothing behind it. Very early in their married life he decided [...] that she had without exception the most stupid, vulgar, empty mind that he had ever encountered. (Orwell 1949/1977, p. 67)

Despite her good looks, Katherine's banality and intellectual laziness make her unattractive to Winston. She is sexless because the Party has conditioned her to be stupid, and this deadening influence extends to every part of her personality.

Not surprisingly, just as sex brought about the liberation of Winston's spirit, it is the medium through which the Party reasserts its anaconda-like grip on his soul. Though Winston suffers physical torture at the hands of O'Brien, he responds with overwhelming feelings of desire: "He opened his eyes and looked up gratefully at O'Brien [....] [H]is heart seemed to turn-over. If he could have moved he would have stretched out a hand and laid it on O'Brien's arm. He had never loved him so deeply" (Orwell 1949/1977, p. 255). Here, probably without the author's cognizance, the undercurrent of queer desire running through the text, which Robert Currie (1984) analyzes in detail (pp. 64–65), fleetingly surfaces. Winston's interest in O'Brien is fundamentally irrational and manifests as a fixation on the torturer's body:

> O'Brien was a large, burly man with a thick neck and a coarse, humorous, brutal face. In spite of his formidable appearance he had a certain charm of manner. He had a trick of resettling his spectacles on his nose which was curiously disarming—in some indefinable way, curiously civilized. It was a gesture which, if anyone had still thought in such terms, might have recalled an eighteenth-century nobleman offering his snuffbox. (Orwell 1949/1977, p. 12)

Winston's attraction to O'Brien's style and urbanity reveals his own subconscious class prejudice—those who appear noble must on some level be of good character.

O'Brien also satisfies Winston's burning need to make a confession, one of the factors that initially inspired Winston to keep a notebook: "It had got to be written down, it had to be confessed" (Orwell 1949/1977, p. 69). Foucault addresses how societies that assert repressive controls over the sexual act often generate a network of erotic discourses, such as confession, which increase, rather than limit, sexual pleasure (1976/1978, p. 12). Under a sexually repressive regime, the aim of confession shifts from the utilitarian goal of finding out what the subject consciously knows to the sexually gratifying experience of revealing to the subject what they did not know about themselves. Ironically, confessions constitute an expansion of language in a society that seeks to limit the lexicon.

By the time he gets him strapped on the table, O'Brien knows about each of Winston's transgressions in detail. But he insists on listening to Winston confess them, helping him through the difficult areas with doses of corporal punishment. He truthfully explains the self-serving motive behind the Party's seizure of power and its draconian methods of preserving it. He also fills Winston in on what has been done to him in the past and what awaits him in the future:

> We shall crush you down to the point from which there is no coming back [....] Never again will you be capable of ordinary human feeling. Everything will be dead inside you [....] You will be hollow. We shall squeeze you empty, and then we shall fill you with ourselves. (Orwell 1949/1977, p. 260)

Winston is figuratively penetrated by the Party and becomes a receptacle for its dogma. In contrast to his joyously consensual liaisons with Julia, his re-education in the Ministry of Love assumes the brutal, psychologically destructive nature of rape.

O'Brien's startling revelation that he authored *the book* of political heresies supposedly written by Goldstein is crucial to Winston's re-education: "'I wrote it. That is to say, I collaborated in writing it. No book is produced individually, as you know" (Orwell 1949/1977, p. 264). Admittedly, we cannot tell if O'Brien is lying when he claims authorship of *the book*, yet its contents confirm O'Brien's claim. *The book* inveighs against the Party, yet reaches the conclusion that the Party cannot be overthrown: "Physical rebellion, or any preliminary move toward rebellion, is at present not possible. From the proletarians nothing is to be feared" (Orwell 1949/1977, p. 211). *The book* is cunningly crafted to seduce enlightened malcontents into hopelessness.

Given that *the book* is just more Party propaganda, how can we trust the validity of its claims? The Party may be far more vulnerable than it says and far more vulnerable than Winston believes. As Claeys points out, "Returning to the textual evidence, we see that, internally, clues of various kinds as to the possible instability of the system are indeed scattered throughout the book" (2017, p. 433). Effective resistance may therefore be possible. We cannot even be sure that Oceania is as vast as its leaders would have its citizenry believe it is. Airstrip One may be the whole of Oceania; Orwell's dystopian Britain may be an isolated pocket of totalitarianism like present-day North Korea. All that matters is that the people of this new Britain believe that their empire is great, giving them a jingoistic connection to their nineteenth- and early twentieth-century forbears.

Because Winston and Julia's own sexual revolution fails, many critics have concluded that *Nineteen Eighty-Four* refutes the idea that desire can effect change. Booker (1994), for example, argues that their ill-fated sexual relationship accomplishes nothing: "Indeed, the sexual rebellion of Smith and Julia turns out to be entirely ineffectual" (p. 76). Raymond Williams (1958/1983) goes further, claiming that the bleakness of *Nineteen Eighty-Four* reflects Orwell's supposedly nihilistic assessment of the twentieth-century political landscape. Politicians, like O'Brien, are consciously wicked, and the mass of simpletons they govern neither know nor want anything better:

In *Nineteen Eighty-Four*, [...] the hated politicians are in charge, while the dumb mass of 'proles' goes on in very much its own ways, protected by its very stupidity. The only dissent comes from a rebel intellectual: the exile against the whole system. Orwell puts the case in these terms because this is how he really saw present society, and *Nineteen Eighty-Four* is desperate because Orwell recognized that on such a construction, the exile could not win, and then there was no hope at all. (p. 293)

Williams distorts the message of the novel in many ways. Despite all that he experienced in the decade preceding World War II, Orwell never succumbed to pessimism and indeed rebuked others for doing so. Consider the following passage from his essay aptly titled "The Limit to Pessimism," in which he reviewed *The Thirties* by Malcolm Muggeridge:

What Mr. Muggeridge appears to be saying is that the English are powerless [...] because there is no longer anything that they believe in with sufficient firmness to make them willing for sacrifice. It is the struggle of people who have no faith against people who faith in false gods. Is he right I wonder? The truth is that it is impossible to discover what the English people are really feeling and thinking, about the war or about anything else. It has been impossible all through the critical years. I don't myself believe that he is right. (Orwell 1940/1968c, p. 535)

When Orwell speaks of the English people in this essay, he refers to common people everywhere. He does not pretend to know what the masses think or feel (or by extension what they are capable of), yet Williams accuses Orwell not only of knowing but also of taking the dimmest possible view of ordinary humanity. *Nineteen Eighty-Four* suggests otherwise. When a convoy of war prisoners with "Mongol faces" (Orwell 1949/1977, p. 118) passes through a large crowd, the proles—unlike the Party members—show no hatred: "At the start there had been a few boos and hisses, but it came only from the Party members among the crowd, and had soon stopped. The prevailing emotion was simply curiosity" (Orwell 1949/1977, p. 117). Here, the dingy, supposedly unenlightened masses react more naturally and humanely to ethnic difference than the comparatively privileged middle and upper classes.

Orwell consistently maintains that workers are not stupid: they simply lack the perspective that comes with education, leisure, and financial security—privileges in some measure enjoyed by the middle class. Though politically dormant, they are to Orwell fundamentally unconquerable and incorruptible. From his haven above Mr Charrington's shop, Winston, already anticipating that he and his lover will both be captured and put to death, realizes this truth while listening to the song of the washerwoman:

> Sooner or later it would happen: strength would change into consciousness. The proles were immortal [....] In the end their awakening would come. And until that happened, though it might be a thousand years, they would stay alive against the odds, like birds, passing on from body to body the vitality which the Party did not share and could not kill [....] Out of those mighty loins a race of conscious beings must one day come. You were the dead; theirs was the future. But you could share in that future if you kept alive the mind as they kept alive the body, and passed on the secret doctrine that two plus two make four. "We are the dead," he said. "We are the dead," echoed Julia. (Orwell 1949/1977, pp. 221–222)

All of these projected political fictions illustrate the process of strength becoming ethical consciousness through sexual desire. Jacobs (2007) identifies a link in the novel between sensuality and hope: "In the everyday resistances of Winston's protesting body, in the brief Utopia of eroticism when bodies are disrobed and touch each other tenderly, and in the vitality of the prole woman's sturdy physicality resistance seems possible" (p. 14). Crucially, it is in these moments of physical gratification that Winston feels that not only he but everyone is entitled to something better.

Jacobs argues that this connection between sexuality and solidarity is too fragile to be effective:

> In *Nineteen Eighty-Four*, Orwell's conception of human potential to resist oppression is limited by an ultimately imbalanced notion of the powers of the body. He seems capable of imagining only an intermittent and futile power in the body's capacity for connection and endurance—the powers not merely of sexual love but of communal solidarity. (2007, p. 15)

Jacobs's sense of the futility of the physical body as a locus of resistance is tied both to Winston and Julia's shared fate, and to Winston's belief that positive sociopolitical change depends on the workers' intellectual development. As a member of the de facto intelligentsia, it is unsurprising that Winston finds erudition indispensable to social evolution, but in this he reveals his own middle-class bias toward the intellect.

We should not mistake Winston's perspective for the author's. For Orwell, common decency is all that is required for meaningful change, and like the sex drive through which it emerges in the story, the virtue of the people is instinctive:

> My chief hope for the future is that the common people have never parted company with their moral code [....] I have never had the slightest fear of a dictatorship of the proletariat, if it could happen, and certain things I saw in the Spanish War confirmed me in this. But I admit to having a perfect horror of a dictatorship of theorists. (1940/1968b, p. 532)

Here we see Orwell's suspicion of the very intellectualism that Winston embodies. The Party has successfully manipulated Winston—and presumably people like him—for years, but its degenerating influence does not extend to its vast labor force.

Crick asserts that the proles are so immersed in a culture of debasement that the Party need not keep them under surveillance: "They did not need watching, they were so debased as to be no political threat" (2007, p. 153). Plank concurs, likening the proles to the sexually satiated citizenry of Huxley's World State: "Orwell's proles, erotically nourished with state-sponsored pornography, are the equivalent of the citizens of *Brave New World* who are encouraged to be openly erotic" (1984, p. 33). But Slater wisely points out that their lack of exposure to telescreens has kept the proles firmly grounded in reality: "Unlike the members of the Party, however, the proles' consciousness is not deliberately blunted by active ideological indoctrination—at least, not by anything beyond the standard news" (1985, p. 233). Although *the book* attributed to Goldstein would have its readers believe that the proles are ineffectual, *Nineteen Eighty-Four* suggests the opposite, which is why Slater describes Orwell's satire as "a return to Orwell's faith in the virtues of the working class" (1985, pp. 232–233). Even in *the book* we find inadvertent admissions that the proles are politically dangerous: "Proletarians, in practice, are not allowed to graduate into the Party. The most gifted among them, who might possibly become nuclei of discontent, are marked down by the Thought Police and eliminated" (Orwell 1949/1977, p. 210). If "nuclei of discontent" can arise among the proles, then there is no need for a middle-class vanguard of people like Winston. That gifted, potentially subversive individuals continue to emerge from the working class suggests that revolution need not stem from the middle class, despite the authors of *the book* attributed to Goldstein insisting that it must (Orwell 1949/1977, p. 203).

Even if, for the sake of argument, we accept the unsubstantiated claim that revolutions are always initiated by members of the middle class, Lawrence Phillips (2008) points out that the Party has failed in its attempt to segregate these groups:

> [T]he experimental fabric of London is a vast network of individual itineraries and stories that create, circulate and preserve a past that the Party attempts to rename, appropriate, or rewrite but clearly fails to repress entirely. That Party members can sally out into London (even at the risk of being picked up by a patrol) points to the potential development of individual consciousness of the past beyond Party control. Indeed the very scarcity of day-to-day consumables forces the outer-party member to undertake such expeditions [....] The failure by the Party to supply personal necessities draws Winston and presumably others before and, one must presume, after him into the streets of London and among the Proles. (p. 73)

Whether effective leadership emerges from either the working or middle class, the two groups maintain sufficient contact to allow for the possibility of collaboration. The nexus of the working and middle classes is also exemplified by Julia, a character who moves fluidly between different social environments.

In contrast to Winston's white-collar desk work, Julia, a machinist, labors with her hands: "[H]e had sometimes seen her with oily hands and carrying a spanner—she had some mechanical job" (Orwell 1949/1977, p. 11). Her employment is closer to a prole's than to Winston's. Like a prole, Julia is motivated by personal loyalty rather than political ideology. Claeys explains why Orwell's association of Julia with the proletariat and their instinctive wisdom demonstrates her superiority to Winston and calls into question the claim that Orwell's presentation of her is reductive:

> This is why she has to doze off while Winston reads to her from "the Book" which discloses the regime's inner secrets: it exhibits her impenetrability. She thus represents one of Orwell's key themes here, the instinctive continuity of the human [...] which the proles also embody. (This is also why he makes her clever with machinery.) This corresponds in part to Orwell's conception of nature, as does the large prole woman Winston observes frequently washing and singing as she works, who is also a crucial symbol. Julia's humanity is expressed through her animality. It is more material, more real than Winston's whimsical abstractions and metaphysical conundrums. (2017, pp. 412–413)

Linking both a young woman and the working class to animal tendencies is problematic. While I won't defend Orwell for doing so, his portrayal of these characters indicates at least that they are resilient figures who are less susceptible to ideological corruption than intellectuals such as Syme, Ampleforth, and even Winston. *The book* is party propaganda disguised as a revolutionary manifesto. Winston cannot see that and takes it at face value. Julia's indifference to *the book* shows her knack for instinctively discerning truth from falsehood. She is talented, resourceful, and nobody's fool. When necessary, she can also conceal her true feelings more successfully than can Winston. Crick observes that Julia rose from the proles via examination (2007, p. 151), bringing with her an intuitive sense of self-determination.

A radical prole would be in an even better position for subterfuge. The dearth of telescreens in proletarian neighborhoods may make it impossible for the Thought Police to eliminate or even identify every disaffected prole with the ability to organize and lead. William Casement (1989) argues that the Party is unlikely to spot every potential leader within the vast proletarian population:

> We must ask if the Party's strategies of eliminating intelligent proles or offering them Party membership will be fully effective. If not, the seeds of intelligence may grow, and from them, the shoots of political rebellion. We may wonder if intelligent proles could not find ways to escape detection, especially given the lax monitoring they undergo. (pp. 219–220)

Slater points out that what makes the proles fundamentally dangerous is the individuality arising out of their personal relationships, the individuality on which loyalties other than nationalism depend:

> [I]f there is hope in this matter, it lies in something that the proles have that no one else in Airstrip One possesses, and this is a strong sense of loyalty. This is not public loyalty, not a loyalty to the Party that has to adapt to each new policy, but a "fixed" loyalty to each other. By contrast, the Party members are marked by a lack of simple friendship for each other and by an acceptance of cruelty that reveals the divorce between the heart and the mind. (1985, p. 234)

Winston foresees a proletarian revolution that will eventually topple totalitarian regimes everywhere. His fate is never in doubt; he knows that he will be eradicated. But his story illustrates the kind of insight that is still possible and even probable within particular individuals in both the middle and working classes.

In addition to taking a reductive view of Orwell's portrayal of the proles, Williams is wrong to cast Winston as a discouraged exile from the community. From the beginning of the novel, Winston feels at home with his job at the Records Department and has friendly associates in Syme and Ampleforth, as well as a companion in Julia, with whom he believes he can attempt to subvert the machine from inside. He is secretly restive but not alienated. Williams's misunderstanding of Winston stems from his assumption that Winston is a proxy for Orwell. He uses the phrase "a rebel intellectual: the exile against the whole system" to refer to both the author and his character, and he tends to attribute Winston's observations to Orwell (1958/1983, p. 293). Referring to the scene in which O'Brien plays a recording of the atrocities Winston agrees to commit to help overthrow the Party, Whalen-Bridge (1992) rightly points out that Orwell intended for his readers to distance themselves morally from Winston:

> O'Brien plays back the tape to discredit Winston in his own mind and therefore to break him. But the reader is likely to understand the significance of the scene differently, and notice that, however true it may seem that one must "become a dragon to fight a dragon," those who would resist totalitarianism by becoming totalitarian forfeit the moral ground on which they have staked their resistance. (p. 74)

Ironically, this is a realization that London failed to make. As discussed in Chap. 2, he portrays his revolutionary terrorists as capable of maintaining their integrity despite engaging in tactics identical to those of the Iron Heel.

By misreading Winston as a representation of Orwell, Williams furthers his mistake by erroneously concluding that Orwell was an exile who could recognize and articulate the injustices of society but offer no viable solutions:

> Orwell's socialism became the exile's principle, which he would at any cost keep inviolate [....] The exile, because of his own personal position, cannot finally believe in any social guarantee [....] [A]lmost all association is suspect. He fears it because he does not want to be compromised [....] Because he is so quick to see the perfidy which certain compromises involve. (1958/1983, pp. 290–291)

Williams argues that Orwell was socially impotent because he would not compromise his personal independence by working for liberty within a group framework. Since Orwell was politically isolated from all segments of society, he lacked perspective and therefore accuracy: "His conclusions have no general validity" (Williams 1958/1983, p. 294). This, too, is untrue.

From the time of his return from Burma, Orwell saw himself as part of a modest-yet-vibrant community of English socialists, working for achievable, positive change in an emerging post-imperial Britain. Crick points out that Orwell was an active part of this group until his death and that *Nineteen Eighty-Four* does not show any loss of faith in democratic socialism: "[T]he book does not represent a repudiation of his democratic socialism as so many American reviewers assumed; for he continued to write for the *Tribune* and American left wing journals right up to his final illness, during the time of the composition of *Nineteen Eighty-Four*" (2007, p. 146).

Orwell, nevertheless, explicitly rejected the idea that progressive reforms could only result from participating in group efforts. The promise of socialism itself, as he wrote in 1945 in an unpublished letter to the editor of *Tribune*, had always depended on individual perseverance against overwhelming odds: "It is only because over the past hundred years small groups and lonely individuals have been willing to face unpopularity that the Socialist movement exists at all" (1945/2000c, p. 391). Orwell thus shows confidence in the efficacy of individual effort rather than isolationism.

Occasionally, Orwell did separate himself from certain people, not because of a tendency toward self-exile but on account of his loyalty to the left. In a letter to the Duchess of Atholl declining an invitation to participate in a speaking engagement, he makes his place and allegiances within English society and politics clear:

> I cannot speak for the League of European Freedom [....] Certainly what is said on your platforms is more truthful than the lying propaganda to be found in most of the press, but I cannot associate myself with an essentially Conservative body which claims to defend democracy in Europe but has nothing to say about British Imperialism [....] I belong to the Left and must work within it, much as I hate Russian totalitarianism and its poisonous influence in this country. (Orwell 1945/1968a, p. 30)

Orwell clearly had a place among the intellectuals of his generation as well as within the culture of his homeland. If he did enjoy a certain reputation as an uncompromising outsider, it gave him legitimacy within a network of liberal European activists and writers, heightening his efficacy as a catalyst for justice and reform. Contrary to Williams's supposition, Orwell did see himself as "belonging" to a social and political community.

Finally, Williams, like Patai and others, misinterprets the conclusion of *Nineteen Eighty-Four*, deeming it irretrievably hopeless. The book is a severe criticism of pervasive undemocratic attitudes among socialist and other self-described progressive elements, which is why—in both his fiction and essays—Orwell was so honestly and meticulously critical of the left. In a letter to H. J. Willmett dated May 18, 1944, Orwell discloses his motives:

> If the sort of world that I am afraid of arrives, a world of two or three great superstates which are unable to conquer one another, two and two could become five if the fuehrer wished it. That, so far as I can see, is the direction in which we are actually moving, though, of course, the process is reversible [....] I think and have thought ever since the war began, in 1936 or thereabouts, that our cause is the better, but we have to keep on making it better, which involves constant criticism. (1944/2000b, pp. 149–150)

Nineteen Eighty-Four is subtle enough to allow us to be both sympathetic to and critical of Winston. There is a sense of tragic loss when he is brutalized past the point of no return, but Crick points out that a conventional happy ending would have undermined the novel's satirical purpose (2007, p. 150).

Moreover, Winston's fate shows that in Orwell's dystopia the process of "curing" enemies of the state must still be conducted over long periods of time and on an individual basis. Mass reconditioning is beyond the power of the Party, and so minds can still be changed for the better. When released from the Ministry of Love, Winston and Julia are veritable zombies. Nevertheless, it would be wrong to argue that sex has no regenerative potential. *Nineteen Eighty-Four* portrays the worst kind of repressive police state, but it also—as Margaret Atwood points out—implies eventual deliverance (1987, p. 284). Like *The Iron Heel* and *The Handmaid's Tale*, the story is annotated by a scholar from a post-INGSOC society. As early as the beginning of the first chapter, the annotator refers to the institutions of the Party's government not only in the past tense but in a manner which suggests that the Party is an organization of the distant past, since the annotator assumes that the reader will be unfamiliar with Newspeak: "Newspeak was the official language of Oceania. For an account of its structures and etymology, see Appendix" (Orwell 1949/1977, p. 5).

Although Winston and Julia understand their likely fate, desire allows them to feel human, hopeful, and even redeemed under the bleakest possible conditions. As Laurence Lerner (1992/2007) points out, just how many other clandestine Oceanian couples are out there experiencing a sexual and ethical awakening of this kind is impossible to say: "As the story proceeds, the uniqueness of Winston and Julia seems to grow more and more marked, yet why should they be unique if they are so ordinary?" (p. 79) Positing that there may be others like Winston and Julia even within the Inner Party, Lerner concludes that "Ingsoc is not as stable as O'Brien asserts" (1992/2007, p. 79), a conclusion with which Craig L. Carr (2010) concurs:

> We might try to sustain a Hobbesian account of power in the face of O'Brien's remarks, however, if we suppose the inner party can never be completely secure in its power. Always there might be some deviant around, someone like Winston, willing to question the authority of Big Brother and inclined to incite others to stand against Him. (p. 113)

The most compelling testimony to the all-encompassing strength of the Party comes from O'Brien, when he re-educates Winston in the Ministry of Love: "There is no way in which the Party can be overthrown. The rule of the Party is forever" (Orwell 1949/1977, p. 265). Yet Claeys emphasizes O'Brien's unreliability: "Intoxicated with power, he too cannot see clearly, or at least clearly beyond power—and for a few moments—we grasp his own inner weakness" (2017, p. 414). According to Williams's own assessment, O'Brien is just another "hated"—and by implication dishonest—"politician." Just as by the year 1984 the Soviets were far weaker than they claimed to be, O'Brien's boastful rhetoric might be nothing more than empty, self-serving hyperbole. That the Party expends so much effort hunting, torturing, and murdering even loyal Oceanians such as Parsons may indicate hidden desperation and instability within the ruling elite.

In the face of governmental terror, potential revolutionaries (like the scores of men whom Julia once seduced) are still being born, growing up, discovering their sexuality, and—at least for a time—forming personal bonds beyond the reach of the Party. Despite O'Brien's self-assured claims about the self-restraint of the Inner Party, Casement (1988) notes that this subversive process of sociopolitical awakening through sexual desire is possible, and even likely, within the Inner-Party membership:

> Winston and Julia make love illicitly, and she not only intimates that she has done so with other Outer Party members, but avers that Inner Party members too would have her if they could [....] Although in theory Party members' sensuality is to be held in check, enforcement of this principle is sometimes lax or ineffective. (p. 48)

These radicals may eventually be caught and crushed, but more will follow; and their dreams remain realizable potentially on an individual level and ultimately on a societal one. This pattern of resilience also emerges in *The Handmaid's Tale*, which revisits the socioeconomic implications of misogyny central to Burdekin's *Swastika Night*.

REFERENCES

Atwood, M. (1987). Margaret Atwood/Interviewer: G. Hancock. In G. Hancock (Ed.), *Canadian Writers at Work* (pp. 256–287). Toronto: Oxford University Press.
Bail, P. (2003). Sexuality as Rebellion in George Orwell's *1984*. In J. Fisher & E. S. Silber (Eds.), *Women in Literature: Reading Through the Lens of Gender* (pp. 215–217). Westport, CT: Greenwood Press.
Baruch, E. H. (1983). The Golden Country: Sex and Love in *1984*. In I. Howe (Ed.), *1984 Revisited* (pp. 47–56). New York, NY: Harper & Row.
Booker, M. K. (1994). *The Dystopian Impulse in Modern Literature: Fiction as Social Criticism*. Westport, CT: Greenwood Press.
Carr, C. L. (2010). *Orwell, Politics, and Power*. New York, NY: Continuum.
Casement, W. (1988). Another Perspective on Orwellian Pessimism. *The International Fiction Review*, 15(1), 48–50.
Casement, W. (1989). *Nineteen Eighty-Four* and Philosophical Realism. *The Midwest Quarterly*, 30(2), 215–228.
Claeys, G. (2017). *Dystopia: A Natural History*. Oxford: Oxford University Press.
Crick, B. (2007). *Nineteen Eighty-Four*: Context and Controversy. In J. Rodden (Ed.), *The Cambridge Companion to George Orwell* (pp. 146–159). Cambridge: Cambridge University Press.
Currie, R. (1984). The Big Truth in Nineteen Eighty-Four. *Essays in Criticism*, 34(1), 56–69.

Foucault, M. (1978). *The History of Sexuality, Vol. 1* (R. Hurley, Trans.). New York, NY: Random House. (Original work published 1976)
Jacobs, N. (2007). Dissent, Assent, and the Body in *Nineteen Eighty-Four*. *Utopian Studies, 18*(1), 3–20.
Lerner, L. (2007). Totalitarianism: A New Story? An Old Story? In H. Bloom (Ed.), *Bloom's Modern Critical Interpretations George Orwell's 1984, Updated Edition* (pp. 71–81). New York, NY: Chelsea House Publishers. (Originally published in 1992)
Mellor, A. (1983). You're Only a Rebel from the Waist Downwards: Orwell's View of Women. In P. Stansky (Ed.), *On Nineteen Eighty-Four* (pp. 115–125). New York, NY: W.H. Freeman and Company.
Orwell, G. (1968a). Letter to the Duchess of Atholl. In S. Orwell & I. Angus (Eds.), *In Front of Your Nose, 1945–1950: The Collected Essays, Journalism & Letters, Vol. 4* (p. 30). New York, NY: Harcourt Brace Jovanovich. (Original work dated 15 November 1945)
Orwell, G. (1968b). Letter to Humphry House. In S. Orwell & I. Angus (Eds.), *An Age Like This, 1920–1940: The Collected Essays, Journalism & Letters, Vol. 1* (pp. 529–532). New York, NY: Harcourt Brace Jovanovich. (Original work dated 11 April 1940)
Orwell, G. (1968c). The Limit to Pessimism. In S. Orwell & I. Angus (Eds.), *An Age Like This, 1920–1940: The Collected Essays, Journalism & Letters, Vol. 1* (pp. 533–533). New York, NY: Harcourt Brace Jovanovich. (Original work published 25 April 1940)
Orwell, G. (1968d). Notes on the Way. In S. Orwell & I. Angus (Eds.), *My Country Right or Left, 1940–1943: The Collected Essays, Journalism & Letters, Vol. 2* (pp. 15–18). New York, NY: Harcourt Brace Jovanovich. (Original work published 6 April 1940)
Orwell, G. (1977). *Nineteen Eighty-Four*. New York: Harcourt Brace Jovanovich. (Original work published 1949)
Orwell, G. (1984). Appendix C: Notes of 1948 Towards a Revision of the First Manuscript of *Nineteen Eight-Four*. In G. Orwell (Ed.), *Nineteen Eighty-Four* (pp. 141–142). Oxford: Clarendon Press.
Orwell, G. (2000a). As I Please. In S. Orwell & I. Angus (Eds.), *As I Please, 1943–1945: The Collected Essays, Journalism & Letters, Vol. 3* (pp. 101–104). Jaffrey, NH: Nonpareil Books. (Original work published 3 December 1944)
Orwell, G. (2000b). Letter to H.J. Willmett. In S. Orwell & I. Angus (Eds.), *As I Please, 1943–1945: The Collected Essays, Journalism & Letters, Vol. 3* (p. 148). Jaffrey, NH: Nonpareil Books. (Original work published 18 May 1944)
Orwell, G. (2000c). Unpublished Letter to the Editor of *Tribune*. In S. Orwell & I. Angus (Eds.), *As I Please, 1943–1945: The Collected Essays, Journalism & Letters, Vol. 3* (pp. 389–391). Jaffrey, NH: Nonpareil Books. (26 June 1945)

Patai, D. (1984). Orwell's Despair, Burdekin's Hope: Gender and Power in Dystopia. *Women's Studies International Forum, 7*(2), 85–95.

Phillips, L. (2008). Sex, Violence and Concrete: The Post-War Dystopian Vision of London in *Nineteen Eighty-Four*. *Critical Survey, 20*(1), 69–79.

Plank, W. (1984). Orwell and Huxley; Social Control Through Standardized Eroticism. *Recovering Literature, 12,* 29–39.

Slater, I. (1985). *Orwell: The Road to Airstrip One.* New York, NY: W. W. Norton & Company.

Taylor, J. (1984). Desire is Thoughtcrime. In P. Chilton & C. Aubrey (Eds.), *Nineteen Eighty-Four in 1984* (pp. 24–32). New York, NY: Comedia.

Tirohl, B. (2000). We are the Dead… You are the Dead: An Examination of Sexuality as a Weapon of Revolt in *Nineteen Eighty-Four*. *Journal of Gender Studies, 9*(1), 55–61.

Whalen-Bridge, J. (1992). Dual Perspectives in *The Iron Heel*. *Thalia: Studies in Literary Humor, 12*(1–2), 67–76.

Williams, R. (1983). *Culture and Society.* New York, NY: Columbia University Press. (Original work published 1958)

CHAPTER 8

Ludic Perversions and Enduring Communities in Margaret Atwood's *The Handmaid's Tale*

Whereas Orwell portrays a revival of the tactics of the Inquisition in *Nineteen Eighty-Four*, Atwood presciently illustrates the cultural concerns of the early twenty-first century in *The Handmaid's Tale*. In Atwood's 1985 novel, the sociopolitical consequences of environmental degradation—a theme explored more fully in her MaddAddam Trilogy—allow the triumph of totalitarianism in what was America:

> The air got too full, once, of chemicals, rays, radiation, the water swarmed with toxic molecules, all of that takes years to clean up, and meanwhile they creep into your body, camp out in your fatty cells. Who knows, your very flesh may be polluted, dirty as an oily beach, sure death to shore birds and unborn babies. Maybe a vulture would die of eating you [....] Women took medicines, pills, men sprayed trees, cows ate grass, all that souped-up piss flowed into the rivers. Not to mention the exploding atomic power plants, along the San Andreas fault, nobody's fault, during the earthquakes, and the mutant strain of syphilis no mold could touch. (Atwood 1986, p. 112)

Just as our society has politicized climate change, Gilead looks to ancient scriptures in a vain attempt to find solutions to ecological woes. Atwood also predicted that the cultural concerns of the Cold War would give way to Islamophobia. In light of President Donald Trump's efforts to ban immigration from certain predominantly Muslim nations, it is unsettling how Atwood foresaw in the mid-1980s that the extreme right would exploit anti-Islamic xenophobia to advance its influence over middle- and working-class Americans: "It was after the catastrophe, when they shot the president and machine-gunned the Congress and the army declared a state of emergency. They blamed it on Islamic fanatics, at the time" (Atwood 1986, p. 174). President Trump's alliance with the evangelical right, his habit of casting opposition journalism as fake news, and his tendency to fill cabinet positions with former military personnel all resemble Orwellian facets of *The Handmaid's Tale*.

Orwell points out that since associations with divinity empower political leaders to revise and reshape history in the interests of the regime, religious faith prepares people to accept dictatorship:

> From the totalitarian point of view history is something to be created rather than learned. A totalitarian state is in effect a theocracy, and its ruling caste, in order to keep its position, has to be thought of as infallible. But since, in practice, no one is infallible, it is frequently necessary to rearrange past events in order to show that this or that mistake was not made, or that this or that imaginary triumph actually happened. (1946/1968, p. 63)

Following Orwell's lead, Atwood presents totalitarianism as inherently theocratic. In an article for the *Los Angeles Times* about the feature film adaptation of *The Handmaid's Tale*, Atwood explains to Gerald Peary (1990) that Puritan New England is the point of origin for totalitarianism in the USA: "The roots of totalitarianism in America are found, I discovered, in the theocracy of the seventeenth Century. 'The Scarlet Letter' is not that far behind 'The Handmaid's Tale,' my take on American Puritanism."

Atwood is right about the sexism and rigidity of Puritan culture, yet most nonwhite people would, I think, probably locate the genesis of US totalitarianism in the dispossession and liquidation of Native Americans by Europeans (including Puritans), slavery and the Middle Passage, or immigration restrictions, all of which were supported by the religious views and churches of many white people. While referencing the Puritans on one level, *The Handmaid's Tale* advocates female solidarity by implying that privileged Christian white women cannot assume that they are immune to the crimes historically inflicted on nonwhite women. What *The Handmaid's Tale* illustrates is closer to the horrific control over the sexuality of enslaved women in the American South than to the Puritans. For example, white Southern diarist Mary Chesnut (1981) writes:

Like the patriarchs of old our men live all in one house with their wives and their concubines, and the mulattoes one sees in every family exactly resemble the white children—and every lady tells you who is the father of all the mulatto children in everybody's household, but those in her own she seems to think drop from the clouds, or pretends so to think. (p. 29)

This antebellum family dynamic parallels the domestic situation for Wives and Handmaids in Gilead, indicating that it could arise in the progressive North as easily as in the conservative South.

The novel's geographical setting also, like Orwell's, undermines the it-can't-happen-here sentiment that makes liberal, secular bastions such as Harvard Square seem impervious to religious fundamentalism. Orwell wanted to show that there was nothing special about the so-called white race, specifically the English, by transforming England into Airstrip One. Atwood likewise highlights the insidious appeal of religious totalitarianism by demonstrating how it could take hold even in an extremely progressive community. She knew Cambridge, Massachusetts, well, having done her graduate work at Harvard University.

There are also ways in which Gilead differs considerably from Puritan New England. The patriarchy of the Puritans, particularly on sexual matters, is often overstated in comparison to other Christian communities of the time. Catholicism—a target of several projected political fictions—arguably exacted a heavier sexual burden on its adherents. Female literacy was emphasized, since Puritan women were supposed to read the Bible for themselves. As most New England economies during the time of the Puritans were still fundamentally local and trade based rather than dependent on monetary capitalism, the domestic production of women was arguably as much, or more, valued and respected than it was in most European nations. While drawing inspiration from the seventeenth century, *The Handmaid's Tale* anticipates the twenty-first-century worldview of Mike Pence. For Atwood, the real threat to civil liberties in the USA comes from the Christian right, who today are empowering and enriching themselves under the guise of protecting us from terrorism, and who seek to control women by alleging a spurious interest in the unborn.

Atwood's satirical take on the likely consequences of blending church and state should not be construed as an attack on faith itself. Unlike Rand, and even Orwell, Atwood does not see religion as inherently harmful. The narrator, who is also the hero of the story, believes in God (Atwood 1986, pp. 91–92). As her friend Moira tells her, many of those who help women escape from Gilead do so for religious reasons: "One of the hardest things was knowing that these other people were risking their lives for you when they didn't have to. But they said they were doing it for religious reasons and I shouldn't take it personally. That helped some" (Atwood 1986, p. 247). In certain contexts, faith can facilitate courageous and righteous action. But secularists also play an important role in helping Moira and women like her: "I was underground it must have been eight or nine months. I was taken from one safe house to another, there were more of those then. They weren't all Quakers, some of them weren't even religious. They were just people who didn't like the way things were going" (Atwood 1986, p. 247). Though she feels it should not play a role in political governance, Atwood appears to take a neutral view of religion. For her, religion is inherently neither productive nor destructive; it merely amplifies people's innate tendencies.

Still, like Orwell and Rand, Atwood suggests that as societies become less secular, quality of material life declines. Changes have occurred in Atwood's Gilead, but, as on Orwell's Airstrip One, these transformations constitute more of a reversal than an advancement of science: electric lights have been replaced by lanterns (Atwood 1986, p. 21); travel by automobile has become a novelty available only to members of the upper class; plastic and other synthetics are no longer used (Atwood 1986, p. 27). Atwood also revisits Huxley's parody of the scientific utopias of Wells. As in *Brave New World*, drugs are used to keep people docile: "We were tired there, a lot of the time. We were on some kind of pill or drug I think, they put it in the food, to keep us calm" (Atwood 1986, p. 70). When Atwood pointedly evokes Wells by writing about "the true shape of things to come" (Atwood 1986, p. 46) in *The Handmaid's Tale*, she depicts scientific knowledge not as something inherently progressive but as something that could actually facilitate degeneration.

Unlike her predecessors, Atwood also connects social regression to capitalism, an economic system that inculcates reductive reasoning yet enjoys sacred status in contemporary US culture. The narrator observes that preachers in Gilead are visually indistinguishable from businessmen (Atwood 1986, p. 82) and that Gilead's economy is an unregulated market: "Everyone's on the take, one way or another. Extra cigarettes? Extra freedoms, not allowed to the general run?" (Atwood 1986, p. 181). Government functions that determine the life or death of ordinary people have been privatized with horrific yet foreseeable results, such as "the idea of privatizing the Jewish repatriation scheme, with the result that more than one boatload of Jews was simply dumped into the Atlantic, to maximize profits" (Atwood 1986, p. 307). Even purely religious pursuits, such as prayer, have been commercialized to generate revenue:

> At the corner is the store known as Soul Scrolls. It's a franchise: there are Soul Scrolls in every city center, in every suburb, or so they say. It must make a lot of profit. The window of Soul Scrolls is shatterproof. Behind it are printout machines, row on row of them; these machines are known as Holy Rollers, but only among us, it's a disrespectful nickname. What the machines print is prayers, roll upon roll, prayers going out endlessly. They're ordered by Compuphone, I've overheard the Commander's Wife doing it. Ordering prayers from Soul Scrolls is supposed to be a sign of piety and faithfulness to the regime, so of course the Commanders' Wives do it a lot. It helps their husbands' careers. (Atwood 1986, pp. 166–167)

Under the auspices of piety, private enterprise flourishes in Gilead, bringing a result unlike the one predicted by Rand's libertarian writings. Immense wealth is concentrated in the hands of a handful of officials and entrepreneurs, while most people (regardless of gender) fill subservient roles and are dependent on the beneficence of the overprivileged. Amin Malak (1987) recognizes the duress underlying the narrator's putative choice to become a handmaid: "The dire alternative for the handmaid is banishment to the Colonies, where women clean up radioactive waste as slave labourers. The dictates of state policy in Gilead thus relegate sex to a saleable commodity exchanged for mere minimal survival" (p. 9). When she arrives at her Commander's palatial home, the narrator feels the financial rather than the spiritual underpinnings of her overtly ecclesiastic society: "The sitting room is subdued, symmetrical; it's one of the shapes money takes when it freezes. Money has trickled through this room for years and years, as if through an underground cavern, crusting and hardening like stalactites into these forms" (Atwood 1986, p. 79). By illustrating the ossification of wealth through capitalism—a system literally built on capital rather than merit—Atwood attacks the supply-side economics of the Reagan–Thatcher era. As in contemporary America, wealth in the Republic of Gilead remains concentrated in a few hands, "trickling through" the rarefied upper echelon rather than down to the masses.

More importantly, capitalism causes people to see the most basic human interactions as financial transactions. Booker (1994) points out that the restrictive labels put on specific categories of women recall the brand names of corporate trademarks: "Suggesting the paucity of roles available to women in our own contemporary world, women in this society exist not as individuals but as members of well-defined groups, corresponding almost to brand names" (p. 163). Offred characterizes her ceremonial sexual relations with the Commander not as rape or a sacred duty but as "serious business" (Atwood 1986, p. 95), just as their private assignations are bargaining sessions: "I won't give it away, this eagerness of mine. It's a bargaining session, things are about to be exchanged. She who does not hesitate is lost. I'm not giving anything away: selling only" (Atwood 1986, p. 138). Offred's relationships with the other women in the Commander's household become a form of debt requiring repayment through childbirth: "It's up to me to repay the team, justify my food and keep" (Atwood 1986, p. 135). Far from sanctifying human life, Gilead's corporate Christianity reduces it to a financial holding.

The consequences of profiteering, piety, and a pre-scientific outlook are most clearly apparent in the absence of modern obstetrics. Babies are born in homes without physicians or certified midwives rather than in hospitals and are delivered without access to analgesia or cesarean sections. Infants exhibiting any physical or mental defect are designated as unbabies or, as the Handmaids call them, "shredders" (Atwood 1986, p. 214). Such children are seen as valueless, denied medical treatment, and discarded. With regard to birth mothers, the state draws a correlation, backed by scriptural precedent, between health and suffering:

> It used to be different [...] a pregnant woman, wired up to a machine, electrodes coming out of her every which way so that she looked like a broken robot, an intravenous drip feeding into her arm. Some man with a searchlight looking up between her legs, where she's been shaved, a mere beardless girl, a trayful of bright sterilized knives, everyone with masks on. A cooperative patient. Once they drugged women, induced labor, cut them open, sewed them up. No more. No anesthetics, even. Aunt Elizabeth said it was better for the baby, but also: *I will greatly multiply thy sorrow and thy conception; in sorrow thou shalt bring forth children.* (Atwood 1986, p. 114, emphasis in original)

Given that the government of Gilead is committed to increasing its severely low birthrate, this suppression of natal technology seems counterintuitive. Moreover, since the status and professional advancement of the Commanders depend on their ability to impregnate either their Handmaids or their Wives (Atwood 1986, p. 116), they have a personal incentive to facilitate childbirth by any means necessary.

Fear of hard science, including obstetrics, is a shared facet of *The Handmaid's Tale*, *Anthem*, and *Brave New World*. If pregnancy is something that can be securely and predictably coped with, women might become more inclined to take control of their own reproductivity. Also, like the oligarchs in *The Iron Heel* who perceive themselves as the preservers of civilization, the Commanders actually believe that their faith-based cause is just and that their regime has improved life for the majority. According to their literal reading of scripture, God intends for women to bear children naturally and painfully, even though a man can never fully appreciate what that entails. Offred notes that her Commander "gave evidence of being truly ignorant of the real conditions under which we lived" (Atwood 1986, p. 159).

Here again we find a refutation of Wells's sanguine notion that privileging science will engender good governance. In Gilead, science, though valorized, has been debased as thoroughly as organized religion. The Commander, inaccurately presenting himself as a scientist, does not differentiate between scientific inquiry and market research: "'I was in market research, to begin with,' he says diffidently. 'After that I sort of branched out.... You might say I'm a sort of scientist,' he says. 'Within limits, of course'" (Atwood 1986, p. 185). Whatever his educational and career background, the Commander's emotional attachment to supernaturalism has eclipsed his empirical knowledge; in this he is not alone. Since the deity is the opener of wombs in the narrow minds of the Commanders, any reliance on technology becomes ideologically counterproductive blasphemy. In another subtle refutation of Wells, we find that the Marthas—who nurture women through their pregnancies—wear uniforms that look like physicians' operating-room scrubs: "She's in her usual Martha's dress, which is dull green, like a surgeon's gown of the time before" (Atwood 1986, p. 9). In Gilead, primitivism lurks beneath a thin veneer of modernity.

Despite the conscious abandonment of medical and technical science in the name of adhering to the laws of God, Jocelyn Harris (1999) maintains that Atwood's novel is a forward-looking book containing elements of science fiction. She justifies this claim by arguing that the development of the compubank did more for the Commanders of Gilead than the telescreen did for the members of the Inner Party in *Nineteen Eighty-Four*: "Not the new invention of television, as in Orwell, but the even newer one of electronic money management has brought this dystopia about. Women have been rendered powerless simply by the withdrawal of their credit at banks" (p. 272). However, three key facts undermine Harris's assertion: the compubanks were not developed by the rulers of Gilead; they were abandoned immediately after the revolution in favor of archaic colored pictures; and, most importantly, during their brief existence, they served a political and not a scientific purpose. Atwood does replace the home computer with the presumably more powerful computalk, but the specifics of this device are left undeveloped, and its presence has little impact on the story's plot. Gilead is deliberately more pre- than post-modern and, characteristically, only modern history and custom are suppressed: "They haven't fiddled with the gravestones, or the church [....] It's only the more recent history that offends them" (Atwood 1986, p. 31). Recent history would, of course, be particularly offensive to the Commanders because women attained full equality—at least nominally—only in the second half of the twentieth century. Gravestones and churches symbolically harken back to earlier times when, legally, women were little more than chattel.

The Handmaid's Tale provides another instance of sexual desire catalyzing political and moral consciousness, though this time from the narrative perspective of the revolutionary. Offred's affair with a high-ranking state official known only by the title Commander and the name Fred results in his execution as an enemy of the state (Atwood 1986, p. 309). On a superficial level, the relationship between Offred and Nick might seem to fit the paradigm of ethical awakening through desire better than what transpires between Offred and the Commander. Lucy M. Freibert (1988) asserts that Offred is empowered through her sexual relationship with Nick: "Offred's real breakthrough to her courageous sexual self comes not with the Commander, who soon bores her, but with Nick" (p. 288). From this perspective, Offred would be the conservative, subservient character and Nick would be the sexually liberated radical with whom she comes to identify politically through their illicit trysts. The Commander, meanwhile, would merely be a part of the repressive establishment along with his wife, the Aunts, and so forth. But Nick's personality and motives are largely undeveloped by Atwood. Unlike Offred's probing, and frequently subversive conversations with the Commander, Nick seems uninterested in what she has to say and volunteers little: "He on the other hand talks little: no more hedging or jokes. He barely asks questions. He seems indifferent to most of what I have to say, alive only to the possibilities of my body" (Atwood 1986, p. 270). Although Nick engineers her apparent rescue, Shirley Neuman (2006) points out that he may do so purely out of self-interest: "There is no evidence in the novel that Nick's 'rescue' of Offred is motivated by anything other than self-preservation" (p. 864). Nick has, after all, fathered Offred's child illegally and could be implicated either by her or Serena. Significantly, Nick's nocturnal encounters with Offred make her less interested in the May Day movement and more inclined to remain in Gilead, where they can share a sort of covert, quasi-marital relationship. Nick is such a shadowy figure that Booker theorizes that he may not care for Offred at all. Instead, he may be planning to exploit Offred's relationship with the Commander for political gain: "[H]e is apparently an agent of the 'Mayday" underground, and his interest in 'Offred' may be largely due to his understanding that she is in a position to extract useful information from her Commander" (1994, p. 165).

Conversely, Offred values her relationship with the Commander because his interest in her, unlike Nick's, extends beyond the possibilities of her body:

> [S]tupidly enough, I'm happier than I was before [....] I don't love the Commander or anything like it, but he's of interest to me, he occupies space, he is more than a shadow. And I for him. To him I'm no longer merely a usable body. To him I'm not just a boat with no cargo, a chalice with no wine in it, an oven—to be crude—minus the bun. To him I am not merely empty. (Atwood 1986, p. 163)

Even though he remains a monstrous sexist and delusional megalomaniac, through his desire for Offred the Commander can in some ways appreciate and bond with her. Just as the Commander no longer regards Offred as simply a receptacle for his sperm and an object for his lust, she comes to see him as more than a mere inseminator.

Through Offred's relationships with these two men, we see the bifurcation of the erotic self into separate physical and intellectual identities. Whereas the relationship with Nick is physical and almost entirely wordless, apart from clichés borrowed from films and popular culture, the badinage that occurs between Offred and the Commander is a sexual pleasure to him and a source of meager intellectual stimulation for her, even though she participates largely under duress. Offred and the Commander vigorously debate social and political issues. Offred's connection to the Commander even runs deep enough for her to become jealous of his wife, known to the reader as Serena Joy: "He was no longer a thing to me. That was the problem [....] Serena Joy had changed for me, too [....] Partly I was jealous of her" (Atwood 1986, p. 161). It is the bizarre erotic relationship between Offred and the Commander that generates their empathetic connection, awakens her consciousness, and inspires her to leave a record for the benefit of future generations. Offred and the Commander's secret meetings catalyze her sense of social responsibility.

Most importantly, these meetings give her the requisite information to tell her tale. Through the Commander she acquires information about the government and the motivations of those who run it, her ill-fated predecessor, and clandestine spaces such as Jezebel's where she finds out what becomes of both Moira and her mother. As Ginette Katz-Roy (2008) points out, the closer Offred gets to the Commander, the more power she has over him; though residing in a patriarchy of his own making, he comes to live both his public and his private life under the surveillance of women: "As a matter of fact, he is under the women's eyes constantly. Offred realizes that he is vulnerable and that she has power over him" (p. 123).

Offred is more subversive than she seems. At the start of the story, she has already attempted to escape from Gilead with her family; she is constantly on the lookout for sharp objects and other makeshift weapons; and she spends a great deal of time pondering sex and other forbidden bodily experiences. While her friends and family have died, vanished, or been indoctrinated, Offred, as she announces early in her account, is determined to survive: "Like other things now, thought must be rationed. There's a lot that doesn't bear thinking about. Thinking can hurt your chances, and I intend to last" (Atwood 1986, p. 8). Offred's desire to persevere matures into a belief that Gilead will fall and that she will escape from it: "I intend to get out of here. It can't last forever" (Atwood 1986, p. 134). In the meantime, she makes the best of a bad situation by choosing to be a Handmaid: "[N]othing is going on here that I haven't signed up for. There wasn't a lot of choice but there was some, and this what I chose" (Atwood 1986, p. 94).

Like Hitler's dream of breeding a master race, the Gileadians reduce sexual activity to a policy of crude eugenics. The most powerful, successful men are mated with the most nubile women to bear superior children who are then reared in the "best" households. To prevent the biological degeneration of future generations, sexual acts among racial minorities, social deviants, homosexuals, and those with physical or mental handicaps are criminalized. Even overtly patriotic citizens such as Nick, the Commander's guardian, are denied the opportunity to procreate if they have, or carry, any genetic health problems: "Low status: he hasn't been issued a woman, not even one. He doesn't rate: some defect" (Atwood 1986, p. 18). Much like Huxley and Burdekin, Atwood sees eugenics as the ultimate violation of the individual's reproductive rights.

But though Offred's Commander advances a form of eugenics in the face of the threat that unfettered procreation supposedly poses to the well-being of the state, he believes himself to be partially above the sexual restrictions that he helped create. Motivated by his lust for Offred, he begins to meet with her secretly at unauthorized times. In a society obsessed with regulating interaction between the sexes, the Commander's behavior might seem like disloyalty. But his rule breaking stems from his sense of security within the autocratic system he partially designed; it is a product of the special benefits he enjoys:

> He is demonstrating, to me, his mastery of the world. He's breaking the rules, under their noses, thumbing his nose at them, getting away with it. Perhaps he's reached that state of intoxication which power is said to inspire [...] in which you believe you are indispensable and can therefore do [...] anything you feel like, anything at all. (Atwood 1986, p. 236)

Here, the Commander is reminiscent of Huxley's Mustapha Mond with his library of proscribed texts: "But all around the walls there are bookcases. They're filled with books. Books and books and books, right out in plain view, no locks, no boxes. No wonder we can't come in here. It's an oasis of the forbidden. I try not to stare" (Atwood 1986, p. 137). Like Mond, the Commander believes that this literature, though harmful to most, is fit for him: "What's dangerous in the hands of the multitudes, he said, with what may or may not have been irony, is safe enough for those whose motives are... Beyond reproach, I said. He nodded gravely. Impossible to tell whether or not he meant it" (Atwood 1986, p. 158). The dialogue between the Commander and Offred is similar to Mond's extended conversation with John the Savage in *Brave New World*. Like Mond, the Commander never disavows the tenets of his society. But the Commander differs from Huxley's World Controller in that sexual transgressions inspire him to take unnecessary risks that bring about his eventual trial and execution for treason (Atwood 1986, p. 309). Reversing Orwell's gender roles, Atwood casts the Commander as a revolutionary from the waist downward. And though the trial itself may have been for show, he was in fact guilty of the acts for which he stood accused. We have here—as we do in the six other primary texts—a story that begins with a character, the Commander, securely ensconced within a dystopian world, who succumbs to sexual temptation and ends up a political outlaw.

Ironically, the primary radical in Atwood's dystopia often shows hardly more ideological awareness than the genetically programmed Lenina of *Brave New World*. In fact, Offred serves as something of a foil to more informed, perceptive women such as her mother and, especially, Moira. Moira is a committed feminist, yet, as the narrator notes when the coup that brings the Commanders to power begins, she appears pleased to have her critique of society validated: "She was not stunned, the way I was. In some strange way she was gleeful, as if this was what she'd been expecting for some time and now she'd been proven right. She even looked more energetic, more determined" (Atwood 1986, p. 178). Moira makes multiple attempts to escape from Gilead, occasionally resorting to violence, such as when she kidnaps and threatens to stab Aunt Elizabeth at the Rachel and Leah Center, which is nicknamed "The Red Center" (Atwood 1986, p. 96) by the women incarcerated there.

Moira, however, learns that overt aggression is easily crushed by retaliatory force. In the end, like others who refuse to be Handmaids, Moira ends up a self-loathing tool of the system as a resident sex worker at Jezebel's, a combination sexual resort and convention center where the Commanders negotiate with foreign dignitaries. Judging by her last conversation with Offred, her spirit has clearly been broken:

> "You should figure out some way of getting in here. You'd have three or four good years before your snatch wears out and they send you to the boneyard. The food's not bad and there's drink and drugs, if you want it, and we only work nights." [...] She is frightening me now, because what I hear in her voice is indifference, a lack of volition. (Atwood 1986, p. 249)

Both the openly rebellious and the abjectly obedient support Gilead whether they supply a uterus or hedonistic pleasure. As Baccolini (2000) makes clear, Offred's sexual recalcitrance provides a subtler, more effective challenge to the state: "The feminist mother and the lesbian friend represent two models of active resistance both in the pre-Gilead and Gilead society. They are both rebellious, impertinent women who refuse to collaborate with the system; however, neither is very successful because not enough women join them in resistance" (p. 22).

Offred is a reluctant revolutionary, even in a sexual sense, because she has been partially brainwashed by her jailers and thus occasionally displays aspects of their prudery. Even while training to be a Handmaid, she reacts disapprovingly to an expression of love carved into her desk: "On the top of my desk there are initials [...] joined by the word *loves* [....] These habits of former times appear to me now lavish, decadent almost; immoral, like the orgies of barbarian regimes" (Atwood 1986, p. 113). But while the sexual mores of her youth now seem alien to her, Offred clearly identifies her attractiveness as a source of political power:

> I enjoy the power; power of a dog bone, passive but there. I hope [...] [the soldiers] get hard at the sight of us and have to rub themselves against the painted barriers, surreptitiously. They will suffer, later, at night, in their regimented beds. They have no outlets now except themselves, and that's a sacrilege. (Atwood 1986, p. 22)

This concern with her own sexuality appears at times to lead Offred into an apolitical mindset. Although they confer secretly about the May Day movement, Offred shares neither all she knows nor the unlikely source of her information with Ofglen, her assigned shopping partner and a member of the organized resistance (Atwood 1986, p. 215). Indeed, willful abandonment of political awareness seems to be the result of her affair with Nick, the Commander's Guardian:

> The Commander is no longer of immediate interest to me. I have to make an effort to keep my indifference towards him from showing [....] The fact is that I no longer want to leave, escape, cross the border to freedom. I want to be here, with Nick, where I can get at him. (Atwood 1986, p. 270)

There is something almost aggressive, even prototypically masculine, in Offred's pursuit of Nick, particularly since their relationship is forbidden. Their trysts in Nick's garage apartment recall her adulterous rendezvous with Luke in hotel rooms. Offred's appetite for illicit sex is an endemic and empowering quality. Jamie Dopp (1994) attempts to depoliticize Offred through an analysis of her relationship with Nick: "Once she is with Nick, the handmaid renounces any desire for resistance" (p. 53). But Dopp's thinking overlooks the fact that Offred's desire to remain in Gilead with Nick signifies sexual self-determination, not political indifference. Offred's allegiance is to her desire. Her instinct is to remain where it can flourish, even after her relationship with the Commander has been discovered by Serena Joy and she faces arrest: "I could scream now, cling to the banister, relinquish all dignity. I could stop them, at least for a moment" (Atwood 1986, p. 294). Far from being passive, Offred tends toward forceful resistance when her sexuality is confined. It is her sexual desire, as Katz-Roy makes clear, that keeps her from becoming a victim: "Desire is still alive in her. Her priority is survival and the defense of her last territory, her own body. *Jouissance*, in the sense of 'enjoyment' of her full powers (to use a word used by French feminists) versus victimization" (2008, p. 125).

While she may not be planning political upheaval as she moves through the story, her sexual appetite motivates lurid, bloodthirsty fantasies which ultimately carry political implications:

> I could approach the Commander [...] kiss him, here alone, and take off his jacket, as if to allow or invite something further, some approach to true love, and put my arms around him and slip the lever out from the sleeve and drive the sharp end into him suddenly, between his ribs. I think about the blood coming out of him, hot as soup, sexual, over my hands. (Atwood 1986, pp. 139–140)

In the context of the Hebrew Bible, Gilead's source of temporal law, mortally wounding the Commander in the ribs is an act of women's liberation, since the source of Eve's subservience to Adam is her emergence from his ribs (Genesis 2:21–23). Offred's daydream recalls countless images of the highly sensual, highly lethal female leader perhaps best epitomized by the biblical Judith who beheaded Holofernes after maneuvering him into a compromising position (Judith 13:8).

Archetypal ideas of dangerous femininity emerge through stock elements of witchcraft, such as Offred's longing for familiars like those who attend the three weird women in Shakespeare's *Macbeth*: "I would like a pet: a bird, say, or a cat. A familiar [....] A rat would do in a pinch" (Atwood 1986, p. 111). Harris also points out that the name of Offred's lover, Nick, could be construed as an adaptation of a nickname for the devil: "Dark, secretive, sensual Nick, Old Nick, the agent of subversion" (1999, p. 275). In addition to the satanic allusion, Anne K. Kaler (1989) finds a reference to the infamous author of *The Prince* in the name: "The origin of the name of Offred's lover Nick may be found in the corruption of Nicolo Machiavelli's name, the 'old Nick,' an English nickname for the devil" (p. 58). Since it is through Nick that Offred presumably escapes at the end of the story, we find—as we did in *We*—a recasting of the devil as a quasiheroic figure. Just as witches were long believed to engage in sexual relations with the devil, Offred's intimacy with Nick develops a motif introduced by Zamyatin's I-330, who presides over the pseudosatanic cult of Mephi.

Although Offred resists the sexual and religious codes of Gilead, her suicidal impulses could be construed as mental surrender to the seemingly limitless power of the Commanders' dictatorship: "I think about the chandelier too much, though it's gone now. But you could use a hook, in the closet. I've considered the possibilities. All you'd have to do, after attaching yourself, would be to lean your weight forward and not fight" (Atwood 1986, p. 195). But as Pamela Cooper (1997) points out, these inclinations are aspects of self-preservation not self-destruction: "Suicide is one way to seize control of the body—a route to perverse empowerment which pushes the logic of the wounded body to its furthest limits of (self-) destruction" (p. 98). In a society where the principal governmental aim is to control women's bodies, suicide is a way for the individual to reestablish personal autonomy. As Cooper indicates, Offred "rejects this option" (1997, p. 98), choosing to give herself over into the hands of strangers on the final page instead. Nevertheless, Cooper notes that the death impulse is both realized and purged "through the symbolic suicide of a double" (1997, p. 98), since suicide is the route taken by both Offred's predecessor, who shares her name since Handmaids in Gilead take their legal identities from the first names of their Commanders, and by Ofglen, who mirrors her in the performance of official duties.

Doubling not only allows Atwood to explore alternate fates for her characters but also provides another example of how totalitarian regimes compel beleaguered citizens to assume the burdensome work of monitoring one another. Apart from perhaps the Wives, who to a certain extent share the reins of power with their husbands, and the Econowives, who are too overworked and underinformed to pose a threat (Atwood 1986, p. 24), each woman in Gilead is matched with a partner for whom she is responsible and to whom she is beholden:

> We [...] walk [...] towards the central part of town. We aren't allowed to go there except in twos. This is supposed to be for our protection, though the notion is absurd [....] The truth is that she is my spy, as I am hers. If either of us slips through the net because of something that happens on one of our daily walks, the other will be accountable. (Atwood 1986, p. 19)

Thus we find, in addition to Offred and Ofglen, Aunt Lydia and Aunt Elizabeth, and the Commander's two Marthas, Cora and Rita, each working alongside and spying on the other. These pairings inhibit revolutionary impulses by making life adhere to set patterns, resulting in a less spontaneous and less thought-provoking existence.

Labor, meanwhile, is so thinly divided between each pair that formerly active women find themselves stagnating under observation in an ocean of dead time: "This is one of the things I wasn't prepared for—the amount of unfilled time, the long parentheses of nothing. Time as white sound [....] Maybe boredom is erotic, when women do it, for men" (Atwood 1986, p. 69). Fertile women in Gilead are the ultimate fantasy for male chauvinists: idle and sexually submissive. The humdrum circumstances of leisure are clearly exciting to Offred's Commander. Far from indulging kinky sexual whims, he finds it deeply satisfying during their time alone to watch her reading with her clothing on: "While I read, the Commander sits and watches me doing it, without speaking but also without taking his eyes off me. This watching is a curiously sexual act, and I feel undressed while he does it" (Atwood 1986, p. 184). This encounter seems almost laughably banal at first glance, but in actuality it is deeply erotic and rebellious. With few exceptions, it is illegal for women in Gilead to read, yet the Commander is most attracted to Offred when he perceives her exhibiting this forbidden skill with its connotations of critical thought and agency.

Cooper (1995) points out that male surveillance is a cornerstone of the regime's authority and power, even to the point of constituting one of the most important and recognizable symbols of the state—the emblem of the eye: "In Gilead this male gaze, detached from the specificity of a body and so freed from any humanizing context, is rendered mechanical, impersonal, bureaucratic. Identified with a political authority figured in traditional terms as all-seeing, the eye becomes the Eye" (p. 50). By breaking from the sanctioned mode of supervisory male perception and viewing Offred with a sexual and social warmth approaching companionship, the Commander engages in societal disaffection. Looking at Offred in an almost conjugal way in his office, the Commander recreates an illegal atmosphere of domesticity. Located at the heart of the Gileadian police state, the Commander's office is configured as an anachronistic space filled with liquor, fashion magazines, beauty products, and other forbidden treats. The warm clutter of his office contrasts starkly with the cold opulence of the rooms he shares with Serena Joy.

Though the political implication of this behavior is somewhat encouraging, the sexual connotation is less positive. In the second of his *Three Essays on the Theory of Sexuality*, Freud (1915/2000) addresses this sort of compulsive voyeurism and the consequences that arise when it displaces actual lovemaking:

> Visual impressions remain the most frequent pathway along which libidinal excitation is aroused [....] The progressive concealment of the body [...] keeps sexual curiosity awake [....] On the other hand, this pleasure in looking [scopophilia] becomes a perversion [...] if instead of being preparatory to the normal sexual aim, it supplants it. (pp. 22–23)

Clearly the Commander derives more pleasure from watching Offred than from embracing her, and for a very good reason: sex has become so ceremonialized in Gilead that its playful, joyous aspects are lost. The erotic energy that once surrounded sex has not disappeared; it is merely relocated in the trivial games that Offred and the Commander play such as Scrabble, in casual conversation, and in the silent male gaze, which Offred realizes is sexually loaded.

In Gilead, the joy that once accompanied sex has been obliterated by the ritualization of intercourse, so privileged men derive perverse pleasure from courtship activities or everyday diversions that are mundane to us but carry an intense erotic charge for those who rule. Madonne Miner (1991) recognizes that when played by the Commander and Offred, a game of Scrabble is a sexual act: "As the Commander takes the Scrabble box from his desk drawer and dumps out the counters, Offred realizes that this game *is* forbidden sexual activity" (p. 148, emphasis in original). In Gilead, activities that allow women to read, write, and engage in other self-empowering pursuits have become perversions, as is clear from Offred's commentary:

> Scrabble! [...] This was once the game of [...] adolescents [...] long ago [....] Now of course it's something different. Now it's forbidden, for us. Now it's dangerous. Now it's indecent. Now it's something he can't do with his Wife. Now it's desirable. Now he's compromised himself. It's as if he offered me drugs. (Atwood 1986, p. 139)

The repetition of "now" stresses how the act of coming together to play Scrabble is as intense and immediate to both the Commander and

Offred as the act of climaxing together—more intense, actually, because while there are opportunities for physical union, opportunities for light social interaction are prohibited and scarce:

> What had I been expecting, behind that closed door, the first time? Something unspeakable, down on all fours perhaps, perversions, whips, mutilations? At the very least some minor sexual manipulation, some bygone peccadillo now denied him, prohibited by law and punishable by amputation. To be asked to play Scrabble, instead, as if we were an old married couple, or two children, seemed kinky in the extreme, a violation in its own way. (Atwood 1986, p. 155)

As Freud reminds us, it is not the form or substance of the forbidden game that makes it perverse; it is that the community in which the game takes place is not conducive to normal sexual relations: "The pathological character in a perversion is found to lie not in the *content* of the new sexual aim but in its relation to the normal [...] when circumstances are unfavourable to *them* [the normal sex aim and object] and favourable to it [the game]" (1915/2000, p. 27, emphasis in original). Routine has drained the pleasure out of procreative sexual relations, while Scrabble and other seemingly mundane activities have become the new forbidden fruit.

Just as banalities become sexual under repressive circumstances, they also acquire political significance. For instance, the pleasure which Offred and the Commander glean from an illicit boardgame is subversive because in a society where language is part of a fixed series of signs determined by the Bible, Scrabble allows the players to put flexibility and imagination back into words, rearranging their meaning in the process and allowing for the possibility of heretical thought, which is why these whimsical moments are often heightened by acts of political indiscretion:

> Sometimes [...] he becomes silly, and cheats at Scrabble. He encourages me to do it too, and we take extra letters and make words with them that don't exist, words like *smurt* and *crup*, giggling over them. Sometimes he turns on his short-wave radio, displaying before me a minute or two of Radio Free America, to show me he can [....] His head is a little below mine, so that when he looks up at me it's at a juvenile angle. (Atwood 1986, pp. 209–210, emphasis in original)

In addition to the blending of sexual and linguistic subversion, Offred and the Commander engage in a role reversal that subtly shifts the power dynamic. Spatially, he positions himself below her and gazes at her from a juvenile angle, implying that she is the figure of maturity and authority. Tara J. Johnson (2004) points out that by playing Scrabble with Offred, the Commander, though he might view the experience as primarily sexual, is "undermining the Gileadan theocracy" (p. 75), allowing the narrator not only to rediscover her creativity but also to recapture her command of language: "This behavior of the Commander's demonstrates his willingness for her to possibly relearn what she has forgotten and to increase her own vocabulary" (Johnson 2004, p. 75). It is unclear whether the Commander appreciates the sociopolitical empowerment that accompanies Offred's regained facility with language. Nevertheless, sexual banter over a gameboard veers quickly into listening to politically subversive radio broadcasts, showing that to control thoughts and behavior governments must tightly regulate and restrict even banal social interactions.

While *The Handmaid's Tale*, like *Swastika Night*, makes a compelling case for women's continuing political agency and empowerment, Atwood avoids bifurcating her characters into overlords and righteous rebels, a serious flaw in overly polemical works of dystopian fiction such as *The Iron Heel* and *Anthem*. The women in *The Handmaid's Tale* are far from ideal, and even the Commander, Offred concedes, is faintly sympathetic, not as a leader but as an individual: "I remind myself that he is not an unkind man; that, under other circumstances, I even like him" (Atwood 1986, p. 254). The Commander's illicit desires humanize and liberalize him, though admittedly not to the point where he accepts responsibility for his crimes. Though she shares her predecessors' interest in the potential for empathy and ethics in sexual passion, Atwood, writing *The Handmaid's Tale* in the conservative climate following the Sexual Revolution, shows less confidence in the strength of eroticism as a catalyst for social regeneration.

Miner ingeniously explains Offred's fondness for the Commander by highlighting the characteristics he shares with Luke. Milner argues that the two men "mirror one another" in "disquieting" ways (1991, p. 160): both share a personal interest in foreign languages and erudition (Miner 1991, p. 148); both men are interested in old things and seem emotionally invested in the past:

> We might discuss the narrator's antiquarian pleasures, but more important here, I think, is the association of Luke with items from the past; he likes old books, and, as we learn more about Luke we realize that he likes old ideas as well. Perhaps one of his favorite old ideas involves the differences between the sexes. (Miner 1991, p. 156)

Milner points out that when Offred travels to Jezebel's with the Commander, she recalls the hotel where she carried on her adulterous affair with Luke: "As if to underline the overlap between these two affairs, Offred comments on 'sameness' when she enters the hotel room with the Commander [....] The setting is the same, because the interaction is the same: unmarried woman with married man" (1991, p. 159). The indignities and abuses that Offred suffers in Gilead do not improve her questionable taste in men. Through this parallel the novel suggests that women, and arguably other minorities, can harm themselves through romantic involvement with otherwise attractive partners who are directly or indirectly hostile or indifferent to social equality.

Yet Atwood does not simply call for female solidarity. She cautions against appropriating traditional methods of oppression for progressive ends. The narrator's childhood memory of her mother burning pornographic books evokes both censorship and the immolation of transgressive women by civil and ecclesiastic authorities centuries ago:

> Don't let her *see* it, said my mother. Here, she said to me, toss it in, quick. I threw the magazine into the flames. It riffled open in the wind of its burning; big flakes of paper came loose, sailed into the air, still on fire, parts of women's bodies, turning to black ash, in the air, before my eyes. (Atwood 1986, p. 39, emphasis in original)

Here, the narrator's mother is no less censorious than the Aunts of Gilead. Even though her motive for doing so may be worthy, she destroys literature and suppresses suspect viewpoints.

Through the narrator's ambivalence toward her mother's zeal, Atwood suggests that if a women's culture does one day come about, the type of women's culture that emerges will depend on the methods used to initiate it: "Mother, I think. Wherever you may be. Can you hear me? You wanted a women's culture. Well, now there is one. It isn't what you meant, but it exists. Be thankful for small mercies" (Atwood 1986, p. 127). As Freibert notes, even the language of feminism has been coopted and distorted by the ruling elite: "Feminist campaigns against rape, child abuse, and pornography inadvertently give credence to rightwing calls for sexual control and book burning" (1988, p. 284). This inversion of female solidarity extends to further limiting women in the domestic sphere. Under the auspices of working together to lessen the burden on individuals and achieve greater freedom, women are urged to embrace their designated roles:

For the generations that come after, Aunt Lydia said, it will be so much better. The women will live in harmony together, all in one family [....] Women united for a common end! Helping one another in their daily chores as they walk the path of life together, each performing her appointed task. Why expect one woman to carry out all the functions necessary to the serene running of a household? It isn't reasonable or humane. Your daughters will have greater freedom. (Atwood 1986, pp. 162–163)

The oppression of women in Gilead depends on a caste system masked by egalitarian rhetoric. Exploitation masquerades as cooperation. As Dorothy Berkson (1990) notes, most women find themselves confined once again to the home: "Others fear that an emphasis on or idealization of women's cultures could backfire and create an ideological climate that could trap women once again in the private, domestic sphere. Margaret Atwood's brilliant dystopia, *The Handmaid's Tale*, is a chilling evocation of such a failure" (p. 112). In *The Handmaid's Tale*, the division of domestic labor into specific routine tasks likewise constitutes a kind of automation, alienating women from the fruits of their labor.

As with the appropriation and distortion of feminism, overtly liberal passages from both the Bible and Marxist theory are twisted to justify the regime's inequitable stratification of society: "Not every Commander has a Handmaid: some of their Wives have children: *From each*, says the slogan, *according to her ability; to each according to his needs*. We recited that, three times, after dessert. It was from the Bible, or so they said. St. Paul again, in Acts" (Atwood 1986, p. 117, emphasis in original). Through the gendering of pronouns, the Commanders change a utopian ethos of communalism attributed to Paul the Apostle into a divine injunction for women to serve the needs of men to the best of their ability. The biblical text, though similar in content, actually differs from the Commanders' propaganda: "There was not a needy person among them, for as many as owned lands or houses sold them and brought the proceeds of what was sold. They laid it at the apostles' feet, and it was distributed to each as any had need" (Acts 4: 34–35). The succinct language misappropriated by the Commanders surprisingly comes from Karl Marx's "Critique of the Gotha Programme": "from each according to his ability, to each according to his needs!" (1891/2009, p. 10). Marx's words highlight the similarities between his philosophy and the socialism envisioned by early Christians. More importantly, it illustrates the plasticity of both religious doctrine and political philosophy—either can be superficially valorized while the plain meaning of the actual doctrine is distorted almost beyond recognition. In keeping with Orwell's *Animal Farm*, in which laws are clandestinely rewritten to benefit the ruling class, the Commanders, as Booker notes, essentially rewrite holy scripture by misquoting it to an audience with no access to the original documents: "The official policies of Gilead are invariably justified by Biblical precedent, but since no one but the leaders of the 'republic' have access to the Bible they are able to claim biblical precedent for almost anything they want" (1994, p. 165). Through the manipulation of language, sexism and classism combine to form a sinister world where even the narrator begins to feel comfortable in spite of herself: "Already we were losing the taste for freedom, already we were finding these walls secure" (Atwood 1986, p. 133).

Harris argues that oppression in *The Handmaid's Tale* functions through gender rather than class boundaries: "Atwood seems to agree with [Virginia] Woolf that gender, not class, is the source of tyranny, and thus casts her vote against Orwell [...] for locating the origins of totalitarianism in class and among men only, and accuses him of underestimating the evil of misogyny" (1999, p. 276). But this line of thought ignores the significant attention Atwood pays to class issues. Like Winston Smith, the heroine of *The Handmaid's Tale* is middle class. The political machinery of Atwood's dystopia is largely geared toward controlling the middle class; and class distinctions, such as those between Wives, Aunts, Marthas, Handmaids, and Econowives, are the biggest impediment to female solidarity. Social class is marked via color-coded signs that strip women of their individuality and place them within specific class and employment categories. The use of colored clothing to convey status figures prominently in *Swastika Night*, but Harris is probably right to assert that Atwood's use of color coding is modeled on the colored overalls worn by Party members in *Nineteen Eighty-Four*: "The separate orders are marked by distinctive clothing as they were in *1984*, indeed as they are distinguished traditionally in utopian fiction as far back as More's use of the sumptuary laws in *Utopia*" (1999, p. 268). In *The Handmaid's Tale*, Wives are attired in blue (or black if their husbands die); Handmaids dress in red; Marthas wear green; Aunts are clad in brown. In this way a woman's function and class are identifiable at a glance, since Wives and Aunts are above Handmaids, who, in turn, outrank the Marthas (Atwood 1986, p. 213). Poorer women, known as Econowives, wear striped outfits, not unlike prison uniforms of old, encompassing all of the above colors, and they perform all of the tasks signified.

Competition for paltry class privileges undermines women's ability to unify, since venal members of disenfranchised groups often cooperate with the establishment in exchange for special privileges and limited power, a point made by Professor Pieixoto in the "Historical Notes" following Offred's narrative:

> As the architects of Gilead knew, to institute an effective totalitarian system or indeed any system at all you must offer some benefits and freedoms, at least to a privileged few, in return for those you remove. In this connection a few comments upon the crack female control agency known as the "Aunts" is perhaps in order. Judd according to the Limpkin material was of the opinion from the outset that the best and most cost-effective way to control women for reproductive and other purposes was through women themselves. For this there were many historical precedents; in fact, no empire imposed by force or otherwise has ever been without this feature: control of the indigenous by members of their own group. In the case of Gilead, there were many women willing to serve as Aunts, either because of a genuine belief in what they called "traditional values," or for the benefits they might thereby acquire. When power is scarce, a little of it is tempting. (Atwood 1986, p. 308)

Through her depiction of the Aunts, Atwood illustrates not only the intoxicating effects of power and privilege but the consequences of disunity among those subjected to discrimination.

Men in Gilead are subjected to institutional classism and sexism as well, even though the regime affords them certain powers and privileges:

> Men are sex machines, said Aunt Lydia, and not much more. They only want one thing. You must learn to manipulate them, for your own good. Lead them around by the nose; that is a metaphor. It's nature's way. It's God's device. It's the way things are. Aunt Lydia did not actually say this, but it was implicit in everything she did say. It hovered over her head, like the golden mottoes over the saints, of the darker ages. (Atwood 1986, p. 144)

By showing that the dehumanization of women depends in part on the idea that men only value them for sex, Atwood illustrates why men have a vested interest in being feminists. Nevertheless, men are still at a clear advantage. Their foibles are attributed to nature, not inferiority or wickedness:

"[Y]ou can't cheat Nature," he says. "Nature demands variety, for men. It stands to reason, it's part of the procreational strategy. It's Nature's plan." I don't say anything, so he goes on. "Women know that instinctively. Why did they buy so many different clothes, in the old days? To trick the men into thinking they were several different women. A new one each day."

He says this as if he believes it, but he says many things that way. Maybe he believes it, maybe he doesn't, or maybe he does both at the same time. Impossible to tell what he believes.

"So now that we don't have different clothes," I say, "you merely have different women." This is irony, but he doesn't acknowledge it.

"It solves a lot of problems," he says, without a twitch. (Atwood 1986, p. 237)

The new order may seem to stifle men as well as women, but privileged men have spaces—for example, Jezebel's—to which they can escape and where women are obliged to cater to their whims. Even for the Wives there is no escape from the confines of gender and class prejudice in Gilead.

Since, as suggested in *Nineteen Eighty-Four* in *the book*, revolution often depends on the middle class organizing and inspiring the workers, inter-class hostility is tacitly encouraged by the rulers of Gilead. This is evident when Offred encounters a group of Econowives on the street in a funeral procession for a miscarried fetus, a practice consistent with the belief that life begins at the moment of conception: "Coming towards us there's a small procession [...] Econowives [....] Beneath her veil the first one scowls at us. One of the others turns aside, spits on the sidewalk. The Econowives do not like us" (Atwood 1986, p. 44). A similar rift exists between Handmaids and Marthas: "The Marthas are not supposed to fraternize with us" (Atwood 1986, p. 11). Atwood's novel challenges traditional gender stereotypes while showing how the anxiety surrounding gender is intertwined with the tension between the classes. This allows for the possibility of gender liberation to bear with it the promise of class revolution. It also extends Orwell's class critique through the Sexual Revolution of the 1960s and 1970s.

Atwood, writing decades later in the wake of several major works of projected political fiction and in the midst of the Reagan–Thatcher era, directly acknowledges the pivotal nexus between classism and sexism. In her dystopia, class and gender frustrations must be released through "Salvagings" and "Particutions," which are organized, carefully contained mass murders and riots in which enemies of the state are publicly condemned before being turned over to the fury of the female middle class:

> I want to tear, gouge rend. We jostle forward, our heads turn from side to side, our nostrils flare, sniffing death, we look at one another, seeing the hatred [....] The air is bright with adrenaline, we are permitted anything and this is freedom, in my body also, I'm reeling, red spreads everywhere. (Atwood 1986, p. 279)

Harris shows how these terrible rituals again echo *Nineteen Eighty-Four*:

> Deliberate incitements to blood lust hold these societies together: Orwell's Two Minutes Hate and his Hate Week serve the same purpose of arousal as Atwood's Wall hung with the corpses of enemies of the state. Her Prayvaganza and Salvagings, or public hangings, recall Orwell's hangings which children clamor to attend. (1999, p. 268)

In both books, the primary aim of these ceremonies is to release otherwise dangerous sexual energy. Offred's reaction to the Partiticution not only bears this out but reveals the intensity of her sex drive: "My hands smell of warm tar [....] Death makes me hungry [....] I want to go to bed, make love, right now" (Atwood 1986, p. 281). Small wonder that the narrator of *Nineteen Eighty-Four* refers to Hate Week as "the great orgasm" (Orwell 1949/1977, p. 180).

In addition to similar methods of disempowering the middle class and directing sexual energy, there are, as Harris observes, many more ways in which Atwood's dystopia feels very like Orwell's:

> In both novels, a totalitarian society is divided by hierarchy; at a time of rations and austerity, only the privileged in Atwood receive real food, as in Orwell [....] The Commander's shoes, shiny like black beetles, especially recall Orwell's definition of tyranny as the boot stepping on the human face, forever. (1999, p. 268)

Such similarities also extend to the protagonists of each novel, both of whom, like Avis Everhard in *The Iron Heel*, live in the early years of their respective dystopias with lingering memories or notions of what existed before: "You are a transitional generation, said Aunt Lydia [....] For the ones who come after you, it will be easier. They will accept their duties with willing hearts. She did not say: Because they will have no memories, of any other way" (Atwood 1986, p. 117). As in *Nineteen Eighty-Four*, rewriting recent history positions the ruling class to shape the future. Just as they show an awareness of the past, the heroes in both *Nineteen Eighty-Four* and *The Handmaid's Tale* hope for the possibility of communicating with the future in a way that characters such as Huxley's John the Savage and Zamyatin's D-503 do not. Not surprisingly, the journal is the chosen medium for Avis, Burdekin's von Hess, Winston Smith, and Offred. Although Offred sometimes directly addresses her lost husband Luke in her "tale," the intended recipient of her narrative, like those of Winston and Avis, is a future generation: "A story is like a letter. *Dear You*, I'll say [....] You can mean more than one. You can mean thousands" (Atwood 1986, p. 40, emphasis in original). This progression from a narrative for her lost husband to a missive to a community of thousands demonstrates Offred's developing sense of social responsibility. Her sexuality largely defines her relationships with the Commander and even Nick, but it also engenders an appreciation for the importance of community.

Communication with future generations is fairly easy in *The Iron Heel*, since the oligarchs appear not to have recognized the connection between language control and thought control. Even in *The Handmaid's Tale* it is still a possibility, chiefly because the totalitarian government has only just begun to consolidate its power. Women, though forbidden to do so, probably still remember how to write. Yet it is revealing that Offred dictates rather than writes her record. An unused skill can, after all, be quickly lost. Moreover, the erosion of language as a method of limiting thought is becoming official policy in Gilead, just as in Oceania. Words relating to notions of freedom or even congeniality have been suppressed to distance people from self-worth and friendship: "*Amazing Grace* [...] such songs are not sung anymore in public, especially the ones that use words like *free*. They are considered too dangerous. They belong to outlawed sects" (Atwood 1986, p. 54, emphasis in original). Even the Commander's once common salutation, "hello," has fallen into near complete disuse: "'Hello,' he says. It's an old form of greeting. I haven't heard it for a long time, for years" (Atwood 1986, p. 137).

As Harris points out, Atwood shows her debt to Orwell by employing Newspeak words and grammatical structures: "Orwell famously simplifies the language of *1984* to Newspeak [...] and Atwood talks similarly of 'Unwomen' and 'Unbabies.' [...] Orwell's B vocabulary imposes desirable mental attitudes for political purposes, and obliterates value words such as free, honor, justice and morality. So does the official language of Gilead" (1999, p. 269). Still, though her use of language shows traces of Orwell's, Atwood's autocrats are more concerned with reviving biblical verse than with developing new speech patterns.

Given the ethnic and sexual prejudice found throughout the Bible, this works almost as well since it causes people to sanctify thinking along these narrow lines. The illegality of reading also allows the Commanders continually to revise scripture to serve as propaganda for their totalitarian ends:

> They played [the Beatitudes] from a tape, so not even an Aunt would be guilty of the sin of reading. The voice was a man's. "Blessed be the poor in spirit, for theirs is the kingdom of heaven. Blessed are the merciful. Blessed be the meek. Blessed are the silent. I knew they made that up, I knew it was wrong, and they left something out, too, but there was no way of checking. Blessed be those that mourn, for they shall be comforted. Nobody said when." (Atwood 1986, p. 89)

The Bible in *The Handmaid's Tale* works much like *the book* attributed to Goldstein in *Nineteen Eighty-Four*. On the one hand it provides a framework for the dictatorship of a priestly class. On the other it is a text with revolutionary ideas that are too combustive to be widely available to women: "It is an incendiary device; who knows what we'd make of it, if we ever got our hands on it? We can be read to from it, by him, but we cannot read" (Atwood 1986, p. 87). Reading the Bible could catalyze a reformation of Gilead's stringent theocracy.

Like reading, the study of mathematics is a seemingly innocuous activity considered too dangerous for women to engage in:

> I've never held a pen or a pencil, in this room, not even to add up the scores. Women can't add, he once said, jokingly. When I asked him what he meant, he said, For them, one and one and one and one don't make four. What do they make? I said, expecting five or three. Just one and one and one and one, he said. (Atwood 1986, p. 186)

In both *Nineteen Eighty-Four* and *The Handmaid's Tale*, the same simple addition is used to convey a state philosophy rooted in ancient modes of oppression. For Winston, agreement with O'Brien's assertion that two plus two can sometimes equal three and sometimes five signifies the importance of everyone accepting mutable party dogma as immutable truth. In *The Handmaid's Tale*, accepting that the same basic equation yields a different result based on one's gender signifies the importance of believing that men and women differ intellectually. Men can formulate reality, calculate accurately, and narrate coherently, while women are irrevocably impractical, inconsistent, and deluded.

But though Winston is eventually compelled to accept the prescribed way of thinking, Offred cleverly turns the Commander's statement upside-down, changing a joke aimed at conveying the uniformity of members of the same gender to an assertion of everyone's unique value as an individual: "What the Commander said is true. One and one and one and one doesn't equal four. Each one remains unique, there is no way of joining them together. They cannot be exchanged, one for the other. They cannot replace each other. Nick for Luke or Luke for Nick" (Atwood 1986, p. 192). Offred and the Commander's erotically charged conversations allow her to empathize with others and appreciate their irreplaceability. Here, Atwood breaks from Orwell by insisting on the occasional necessity of doublethink. One and one and one and one can, when necessary, equal four; they can also, if need be, remain four distinct units. Whereas for Orwell doublethink inevitably subverts the ability to reason clearly and logically, Atwood uses it to strengthen her protagonist's resolve, particularly when she considers the very different turns Luke's life might have taken following their capture:

> The things I believe can't all be true, though one of them must be. But I believe in all of them, all three versions of Luke, at one and the same time. This contradictory way of believing seems to me, right now, the only way I can believe anything. Whatever the truth is, I will be ready for it. This also is a belief of mine. This also may be untrue. (Atwood 1986, p. 106)

By leaving us open to various possibilities, Atwood counterintuitively presents doublethink as an enabler of truth and hope.

This comfort with inconsistency distinguishes *The Handmaid's Tale* from *Nineteen Eighty-Four*. The difference between the two novels is particularly evident in the dissimilar ways that the respective plots are resolved. Whereas Winston is compelled to adopt the principles of INGSOC at face value under torture, Offred may well be rescued. While Winston can only speculate about networks of resistance, Offred finds not only the May Day rebels but sympathetic affiliations among women and men everywhere:

"There can be alliances even in such places, even under such circumstances. This is something you can depend upon: there will always be alliances, of one kind or another" (Atwood 1986, p. 129). The eventual collapse of Gilead is finally confirmed in an epilogue in which historians from a subsequent republic discuss Offred's narrative in much the same way that Avis Everhard's journal is annotated for readers by the Brotherhood of Man in *The Iron Heel*.

Baccolini (2000) characterizes this open-ended conclusion as a departure from the traditional dystopian paradigm: "The space of ambiguity becomes a utopian space, and the novel's ending breaks dramatically with the absolute certainty of defeat in traditional dystopias" (p. 23). This reading both oversimplifies the standard resolution of dystopian fiction and overestimates the society that produces the "Historical Notes." Harris, for instance, reminds us that Atwood believed that *Nineteen Eighty-Four* was meant to be understood as having a positive ending because the past tense of the novel's postscript establishes that Newspeak is a thing of the past and thus, by implication, so is the Party (1999, p. 267).

Conversely, this idea of a positive dénouement is problematized by the fact that—in the spirit of Jonathan Swift—Orwell, as Larry W. Caldwell (1992) points out, may have meant for the appendix to *Nineteen Eighty-Four* to be read as a satire on the naiveté of intellectualism:

> Judging from the earnest, graduate-student voice of the Appendix narrator, it is a milieu which promotes scholarship and, by implication, the values of free inquiry and discourse; a milieu from which it is possible to look back upon twentieth-century totalitarianism as a rather quaint even ludicrous deviation [....] How would the humanistic epistemology of the scholar overcome the comprehensive ambitions of the Party? Contemplating this explicit polarization, Orwell satirizes the conventions of scholarship and finds the claims of academic scholarship incommensurate with the magnitude of the utopian problem. (p. 340)

Assessing the value of the "better" worlds that follow these dystopias is also tricky. Whalen-Bridge (1992) notes that men still appear to be more valued than women in Nunavit, since Professor Pieixoto shows greater interest in the Commander's identity and story than in Offred's: "The academics are less concerned by Offred's struggle than they are by the name of the Commander, a reminder to Atwood's readers that they do not have access to a transcendent plane of political correctness" (p. 74). For Dopp, Nunavit is more a continuation of Gildead than an improvement:

The "Historical Notes," rather than mitigating [a repressive] situation, reinforce it. They do so by presenting the regime that follows Gilead as quite as misogynist as the original [...] suggest[ing] that Gilead has in fact not "ended," at least not in any satisfactory sense; the forces underlying it have merely taken on a new form. (1994, p. 48)

Dopp supports her claim largely by emphasizing the crude insensitiveness of Pieixoto's remarks:

The keynote speaker, a supposed "expert" on Gilead, reveals himself during the course of his lecture to be politically uninformed and unrepentantly sexist [....] In explaining how his colleague came up with the title for the transcription, he says that "all puns were intentional, particularly that having to do with the archaic vulgar signification of the word *tail*. "The Underground Femaleroad," he tells us, has been dubbed by certain historical wags as "The Underground Frailroad," and so on (313). What is remarkable is not that the professor says these things but that they are accompanied by "laughter" and "applause" and that not a single voice is raised in objection. Nobody, not even the female academics demonstrably present, speak up to counter Pieixoto's tasteless comments. (1994, pp. 46, 48, emphasis in original)

Dopp is right to argue that both Pieixoto and Nunavit are far from perfect. But she disregards Atwood's rationale for these imperfections. To Dopp's thinking, *The Handmaid's Tale*, despite Atwood's best intentions, actually reinforces the patriarchy it seeks to undermine: "*The Handmaid's Tale* though intended to work against women's oppression, in fact reproduces the essentializing tendencies of a patriarchy that, as a feminist gesture, the novel should oppose" (1994, p. 43). The implication is that Atwood may have been unaware of the double standard presented by characters such as Pieixoto.

It is far likelier that Atwood intended Pieixoto's talk to generate uneasiness in the mind of the reader for the purpose of showing that the age-old struggle for gender equality would be an ongoing one and not a matter to be solved with the collapse of one tyrannical regime. In dismissing the waves of feminism that shaped the *fin de siècle* and much of the twentieth century, the Commander claims that male dominance is an indelible hallmark of human civilization: "Those years were just an anomaly, historically speaking, the Commander said. Just a fluke. All we've done is return things to Nature's norm" (Atwood 1986, p. 220). While there is nothing normal or natural about male supremacy, this kind of reasoning still occurs, as we realize when we compare both Gilead and Nunavit with our own androcentric society. As in Atwood's Gilead, Booker (1994) finds the lineaments of our cultural sexism in the Abrahamic religious traditions' influence on Western civilization:

> Indeed, the numerous parallels between the practices of the Republic of Gilead and those of the medieval Inquisition suggest that the oppressive religious energies that inform Atwood's dystopia have been present in Western civilization for centuries. That a resurgence of these energies like that embodied in the Republic of Gilead could occur this bespeaks an inability of Western society to learn the lessons of history. (p. 166)

In both the Abrahamic faiths and the Republic of Gilead, laws come from on high and heresy, which literally means choice, is anathema. *The Handmaid's Tale* points out that feminism, like any corollary of liberty and justice, depends on the right to choose.

Orthodoxy is also manifest in the disturbing cultural relativism that prevents Professor Pieixoto from condemning the crimes against humanity perpetrated by the rulers of Gilead, a troubling sentiment literally applauded by an audience of educated professionals:

> If I may be permitted an editorial aside, allow me to say that in my opinion we must be cautious about passing moral judgment upon the Gileadeans. Surely we have learned by now that such judgments are of necessity culture-specific. Also, Gileadean society was under a good deal of pressure, demographic and otherwise, and was subject to factors from which we ourselves are happily more free. Our job is not to censure but to understand. (*Applause.*) (Atwood 1986, p. 302, emphasis in original)

Pieixoto may be unaware of his own biases, but the narrator admits to being willfully blind during her youth:

> Is that how we lived then? But we lived as usual. Everyone does, most of the time. Whatever is going on is as usual. Even this is as usual, now. We lived, as usual, by ignoring. Ignoring isn't the same as ignorance, you have to work at it. Nothing changes instantaneously: in a gradually heating bathtub you'd be boiled to death before you knew it. (Atwood 1986, p. 56)

Even Moira, who presents as a vocal feminist, trivializes the militant activism of the narrator's mother by describing her as a "cute" person with "pizzazz":

"Your mother's neat, Moira would say, when we were at college. Later: she's got pizzazz. Later still: she's cute."
"She's not cute, I would say. She's my mother."
"Jeez, said Moira, you ought to see mine." (Atwood 1986, p. 253)

The risks and sacrifices born by the narrator's mother have made her adorable rather than admirable in the eyes of the very women she sought to help, a sad fact that she herself was well aware of:

You young people don't appreciate things, she'd say. You don't know what we had to go through, just to get you where you are. Look at him, slicing up the carrots. Don't you know how many women's lives, how many women's *bodies*, the tanks had to roll over just to get that far? (Atwood 1986, p. 121, emphasis in original)

These words about the sacrifices women make for each other illuminate generative networks among women, the moments of recognition and kinship, such as the signs through which Moira and the narrator silently communicate at the Red Center and later at Jezebel's.

The narrator's relationships with women in the novel span years, even decades; they are cyclical, digressive, moving through time in a way that her relationships with men do not. The narrator's memories from her life before Gilead of Moira and her mother merge with the dystopian present and shape her anticipations of the future. The novel, however, centers rebellion in the linear, heteronormative context of the narrator's relationships with men such as the Commander and Nick. We would think that the narrator's exchanges with Ofglen and Moira would be the novel's truly revolutionary moments, yet she feels more subversive playing Scrabble with the Commander than conspiring with Ofglen or hearing Moira disparage the Aunts at the Red Center. Offred's sense of power plays out in heterosexual relationships.

Still, her relationships with men are in the past, as with Luke, in the present, as with the Commander, or part of her transition to an uncertain future, as with Nick. These relationships with men, unlike those with women, do not span the length of her life and are therefore less meaningful to the reader. Offred's lifelong affiliative connections to women suggest the utopian possibility of a female network of love and ritual. But in Gilead, as in today's world, that is not where power lies. Sadly, the majority of societal power remains vested in men. The complacent attitude toward feminism expressed by the characters in the novel is their own, not Atwood's. It highlights the need for vigilance to advance the cause of gender equality and to protect women's hard-won sociopolitical gains.

The glimpses of life both before and after Gilead in *The Handmaid's Tale* emphasize the need for recurring revolutions expressed by I-330 in *We*. Whether the epilogues to *Nineteen Eighty-Four* and *The Handmaid's Tale* are meant to be taken seriously, as satire, or as a combination of the two, both draw heavily on London's prophetic notion that supposedly classless neo-utopias such as The Brotherhood of Man, Nunavit, or even the society that produced the retrospective analysis of Newspeak would be realized not through natural social evolution but only after a long, bloody struggle.

REFERENCES

Atwood, M. (1986). *The Handmaid's Tale*. Boston, MA: Houghton Mifflin.
Baccolini, R. (2000). Gender and Genre in the Feminist Critical Dystopias of Katharine Burdekin, Margaret Atwood, and Octavia Butler. In M. S. Barr (Ed.), *Future Females, The Next Generation: New Voices and Velocities in Feminist Science Fiction Criticism* (pp. 13–34). Lanham, MD: Rowman & Littlefield.
Berkson, D. (1990). So We All Became Mothers. In L. F. Jones & S. W. Goodwin (Eds.), *Feminism, Utopia, and Narrative* (pp. 100–115). Knoxville, TN: The University of Tennessee Press.
Booker, M. K. (1994). *The Dystopian Impulse in Modern Literature: Fiction as Social Criticism*. Westport, CT: Greenwood Press.
Caldwell, L. W. (1992). Wells, Orwell and Atwood (Epi)logic and (Eu)topia. *Extrapolation, 33*(4), 333–345.
Chesnut, M. (1981). *Mary Chesnut's Civil War* (C. V. Woodward, Ed.). New Haven, CT: Yale University Press.
Cooper, P. (1995). Sexual Surveillance and Medical Authority in Two Versions of *The Handmaid's Tale. Journal of Popular Culture, 28*(4), 49–63.
Cooper, P. (1997). A Body Story with a Vengeance: Anatomy and Struggle in *The Bell Jar* and *The Handmaid's Tale. Women's Studies, 26*, 89–123.
Dopp, J. (1994). Subject-Position as Victim-Position in The Handmaid's Tale. *SCL/ELC: Studies in Canadian Literature, 19*(1), 43–57.
Freibert, L. M. (1988). Control and Creativity: The Politics of Risk in Margaret Atwood's *The Handmaid's Tale*. In J. McCombs (Ed.), *Critical Essays on Margaret Atwood* (pp. 280–291). Boston, MA: Hall.
Freud, S. (2000). *Three Essays on the Theory of Sexuality* (J. Strachey, Trans.). New York, NY: Basic Books. (Original work published 1915)

Harris, J. (1999). *The Handmaid's Tale* as a Re-Visioning of *1984*. In P. Alkon, D. Chatelain, R. Gaillard, & G. Slusser (Eds.), *Transformations of Utopia: Changing Views of the Perfect Society* (pp. 267–277). New York, NY: AMS Press.

Johnson, T. J. (2004). The Aunts as an Analysis of Feminine Power in Margaret Atwood's *The Handmaid's Tale*. *Nebula, 1*(2), 68–79.

Kaler, A. K. (1989). A Sister, Dipped in Blood: Satiric Inversion of the Formation Techniques of Women Religious in Margaret Atwood's Novel *The Handmaid's Tale*. *Christianity & Literature, 38*(2), 43–62.

Katz-Roy, G. (2008). Sexual Politics and Textual Strategies in Margaret Atwood's *The Handmaid's Tale*. In M. Kneevi & A. Nikevi-Batrievi (Eds.), *History, Politics, Identity: Reading Literature in a Changing World* (pp. 111–133). New Castle: Cambridge Scholars Publishing.

Malak, A. (1987). Margaret Atwood's "The Handmaid's Tale" and the Dystopian Tradition. *Canadian Literature, 112*, 9–16.

Marx, K. (2009). *Critique of the Gotha Programme* (C. P. Dutt, Trans.). New York, NY: International Publishers. (Original work published 1891)

Miner, M. (1991). "Trust Me": Reading the Romance Plot in Margaret Atwood's *The Handmaid's Tale*. *Twentieth Century Literature, 37*(2), 148–168.

Neuman, S. (2006). "Just a Backlash": Margaret Atwood, Feminism, and *The Handmaid's Tale*. *University of Toronto Quarterly, 75*(3), 857–868.

Orwell, G. (1968). The Prevention of Literature. In S. Orwell & I. Angus (Eds.), *In Front of Your Nose, 1945–1950: The Collected Essays, Journalism & Letters, Vol. 4* (pp. 59–72). New York, NY: Harcourt Brace Jovanovich. (Original work published 2 January 1946)

Orwell, G. (1977). *Nineteen Eighty-Four*. New York: Harcourt Brace Jovanovich. (Original work published 1949).

Peary, G. (1990, March 4). *The Handmaid's Tale*: If Puritans Ruled... Atwood's Story on Screen. *The Los Angeles Times*. Retrieved from http://articles.latimes.com

Whalen-Bridge, J. (1992). Dual Perspectives in *The Iron Heel*. *Thalia: Studies in Literary Humor, 12*(1–2), 67–76.

CHAPTER 9

Conclusion

Twentieth-century projected political fiction and its assertions regarding the empathetic and ethical potential in sexual desire should be recognized as especially relevant to the current sociopolitical landscape, which in the new century is largely defined by anxieties about terrorism, and the power and prestige of Western nations. Donald Trump's election—along with his hostility to a free press and frequent mischaracterization of legitimate journalism as "fake news" and his administration's rampant xenophobia—shows the willingness of many people to support autocracy. Moreover, our increased comfort with racial profiling, heightened government and corporate surveillance, and socioeconomic inequity suggests that the projected political fiction of the last century is more relevant than ever.

The ongoing struggle of LGBTQ communities to secure full civil liberties, African-American communities' resistance to coercive policing, women's efforts toward greater de facto equality in public life, and other liberatory movements have produced a corresponding backlash among many other Americans who would prefer a return to white, heteronormative hegemony. Intoxicating notions of US exceptionalism recall the jingoism that fueled British imperialism, which Orwell criticized sharply in his fiction and essays:

> There is a habit of mind which is now so widespread that it affects our thinking on nearly every subject [....] As the nearest existing equivalent I have chosen

the word "nationalism" [....] The habit of identifying oneself with a single nation or other unit, placing it beyond good or evil and recognising no other duty than that of advancing its interests. (1945/2000, p. 362)

Whether the unit to which the individual wholeheartedly subscribes is a country, ideology, or religious faith, this kind of acritical, emotional reasoning generates policies and behavior that aggrandize ourselves and dehumanize our perceived enemies.

Although his dystopian satire differs considerably from Orwell's, Huxley identifies the same disturbing trend:

> Nothing is clearer in this present mid-point of the twentieth century than that its religion is idolatrous nationalism. There are nominal religions—Christianity, Mohammedanism, Hinduism, Buddhism, and so on; but it you inquire what the actions of people mean, it is perfectly clear that the real religion is nationalism; that we worship the nation state; that actually we make use of the traditional religions to buttress the nation state; and that new religions like Communism are also used in the service of great national idolatry. Karl Marx made a great mistake in underrating nationalism. (1992, pp. 48–49)

This broad conception of nationalism indicates that neither democracy nor a cultural history of egalitarianism is sufficient to prevent either the sudden or the gradual arrival of totalitarianism.

In analyzing *Nineteen Eighty-Four*, Christopher Hitchens (2002) draws special attention to the emergence through democratic channels of the INGSOC Party and its platform of brutality:

> The will to command and to dominate is one thing, but the will to obey and be prostrate is a deadly force as well [....] Nobody has ever made this point more forcibly than he does in *Nineteen Eighty-Four* [....] With a part of themselves, humans relish cruelty and war and absolute capricious authority, are bored by civilized and humane pursuits and understand too well the latent connection between sexual repression and orgiastic vicarious collectivized release. (p. 191)

Here, Hitchens hits on the most troubling facet of dystopian literature, the realization that most of us have an innate tendency to embrace totalitarianism, particularly under pressure. As Atwood illustrates in *The Handmaid's Tale*, this acceptance of repression is frequently misperceived as a kind of freedom: "There is more than one kind of freedom, said Aunt Lydia. Freedom to and freedom from. In the days of anarchy, it was freedom to. Now you are being given freedom from. Don't underrate it" (Atwood 1986, p. 24). While *The Handmaid's Tale*, in the tradition of London, Rand, Burdekin, and Orwell, is overtly repressive, Ní Dhúill (2010) finds the same wish for freedom from the obligations of self-determination in the indulgent frivolities of *Brave New World*: "In Huxley's dystopia, freedom *from* material scarcity, suffering, and adversity was acquired at the cost of freedom *to* question or think outside the fundamental premises, values, and methods of the social order" (p. 48, emphasis in original). This distinction between "freedom to" and "freedom from" suggests that the difference between dystopias and utopias is largely a matter of subjective preference. The tendency to embrace freedom from responsibility and to conform for the sake of security and, at times, material comfort is attractive. Even Orwell's Oceania is a utopia to characters as dissimilar as Parsons, Syme, Katherine, and O'Brien.

Beauchamp (1981) argues that it is the author's attitude toward the speculative world that determines whether it is a utopia or a dystopia: "It is no new discovery that one man's utopia will be another's dystopia: Perhaps the only really significant difference between *Walden Two*, for example, and *Brave New World* is each author's attitude toward his creation" (p. 104). Yet Claeys (2011) is right to stress that the reader plays an equal if not greater role in deciding whether an imagined world is a paradise or a prison: "just as one person's terrorist is another's freedom-fighter, so is one person's utopia another's dystopia. Indisputably, thus, whether a given text can be described as a dystopia or utopia will depend on one's perspective of the narrative outcome" (p. 108). As Philip Wegner (2014) points out, even overtly utopian novels frequently seem dystopian to readers: "But here is where difficulties begin to arise: for, as anyone who has ever taught these works will surely testify, what appears as a *eu*-topia, or a 'good place,' to one reader will seem utterly nightmarish to another" (p. 455, emphasis in original). After all, to differing extents, the various authors considered in this study all focused on what they perceived to be troubling elements in Wells's utopian fiction. Despite Wells's best intentions, for them his works and ideas were inherently dystopian.

For writers of projected political fiction, Wells's popularity and the wide influence of his beliefs showed that totalitarian systems can appeal to the majority and come about with its consent. As Allan Weiss (2009) observes, most citizens of dystopian worlds remain placid:

Contrary to the impression some historians of dystopian fiction [...] seem to have, dystopian regimes are not so much imposed from above as sought from below [....] The common image of a dystopian society is that it is the exact opposite of a utopia [....] Instead, the two genres mirror each other in many ways, particularly in that most residents of dystopias are happy or at the very least satisfied, and the (supposed) rebels are anomalies in their societies. (pp. 127–128)

The allure of losing oneself in the totalitarian hive clarifies why institutional control of sexuality can be appealing, even to those it stunts, harms, and disenfranchises. But hope consistently persists in this literature (and arguably in real life), embedded in the catalyzing, occasionally unwelcome effect of eroticism. Despite their ideological and stylistic differences, these novels find the hunger for self-determination, the ability to empathize and bond with others, and the impetus for moral renewal in sexual desire. It is out of the compulsion to pursue this visceral passion that the nobler aspirations flow and that these disparate works of twentieth-century speculative fiction coalesce as a distinct subgenre of enduring relevance.

References

Atwood, M. (1986). *The Handmaid's Tale*. Boston, MA: Houghton Mifflin.
Beauchamp, G. (1981). Jack London's Utopian Dystopia and Dystopian Utopia. In K. M. Roemer (Ed.), *America as Utopia* (pp. 91–107). New York, NY: Franklin.
Claeys, G. (2011). The Origins of Dystopia: Wells, Huxley and Orwell. In G. Claeys (Ed.), *The Cambridge Companion to Utopian Literature* (3rd ed., pp. 107–131). Cambridge: Cambridge University Press.
Hitchens, C. (2002). *Why Orwell Matters*. New York, NY: Basic Books.
Huxley, A. (1992). *The Divine Within* (J. H. Bridgeman, Ed.). New York, NY: HarperCollins.
Ní Dhúill, C. (2010). *Sex in Imagined Spaces: Gender and Utopia from More to Bloch*. London: Legenda.
Orwell, G. (2000). Notes on Nationalism. In S. Orwell & I. Angus (Eds.), *As I Please, 1943–1945: The Collected Essays, Journalism & Letters, Vol. 3* (pp. 361–380). Jaffrey, NH: Nonpareil Books. (Original work published 1 October 1945)
Wegner, P. (2014). The British Dystopian Novel from Wells to Ishiguro. In B. DeMaria, H. Chang, & S. Zache (Eds.), *A Companion to British Literature, Volume 4: Victorian and Twentieth-Century Literature, 1837–2000* (pp. 454–470). Chichester: Wiley-Blackwell.
Weiss, A. (2009). Offred's Complicity in the Dystopian Tradition in Margaret Atwood's *The Handmaid's Tale*. *Studies in Canadian Literature*, 34(1), 120–141.

Index

A
Ableism, 17, 121
Adorno, Theodor, 5, 71, 72, 75, 76, 82–84
Animal Farm, see Orwell, George
Annenkov, Yury, 58
Anthem, see Rand, Ayn
Anti-Semitism, 16, 17, 93, 98, 100, 110, 113, 120
Arendt, Hannah, 4
Atheism, 3, 11, 12
Atwood, Margaret, 2–6, 10, 11, 20–22, 29, 36, 74, 105, 106, 123, 135, 144, 164, 169–201, 204, 205
  Handmaid's Tale, The, 2, 3, 10, 11, 20, 22, 29, 36, 37, 46, 53, 74, 83, 105, 106, 123, 137, 144, 164, 166, 169, 204, 205; Antebellum South and, 171; capitalism, critique of, 21, 172–174; doublethink in, 21, 196–198; environmental degradation, critique of, 169; feminism in, 181–184, 191–194, 198–201; Huxley's influence on, 172, 179; *Iron Heel, The*, HT's similarity to, 194, 197; islamophobia, critique of, 169; language and thought in, 189–190; Orwell's influence on, 20, 169, 170, 193–201; Puritans and, 170; religion, attitude toward, 171–173; Wells, H.G., critique of, 172
  MaddAddam Trilogy, 169
  Oryx and Crake, 3
Auerbach, Jonathan, 25, 32, 33, 37–39, 43–45

B
Baccolini, Raffaella, 99, 105, 113, 180
Bail, Paul, 152–153
Baker, Robert S., 13, 75–77

Baker-Smith, Dominic, 74
Barley, Tony, 29, 30, 32, 34, 43
Barratt, Andrew, 63, 66
Baruch, Elaine Hoffman, 58, 152
Beauchamp, Gorman, 25, 29, 68, 205
Bellamy, Edward, 13, 17, 95
Berkson, Dorothy, 189
Berliner, Jonathan, 49
Bonifas, Gilbert, 106
Booker, M. Keith, 4–6, 8, 9, 11, 15, 16, 55, 80, 156, 177, 190, 199
Brave New World, *see* Huxley, Aldous
Briscoe, Erica, 48, 49
Brown, Clarence, 60
Brown, Susan Love, 17, 141
Browning, Gordon, 1
Buchanan, Bradley W., 85
Burdekin, Katharine, 2, 4, 10, 11, 16–18, 20, 21, 26, 28, 43, 44, 51, 73, 90, 93–125, 205
  Catholicism, critique of, 110–112
  Christianity, attitude toward, 95, 109–112
  English people, attitude toward, 119
  imperialism, attitude toward, 117–120, 124
  pacifism of, 95
  Swastika Night, 2–4, 7, 10, 11, 16–19, 21, 22, 26, 28, 51, 78, 79, 83, 90, 93, 134, 137, 166, 187, 190; Ableism in, 121; gay desire in, 97–105; Holocaust, portrayal of, 120; *Nineteen Eighty-Four*, *SN* as precursor of, 4, 104–109, 112–115, 124; racism in, 121; socialism in, 114–117; *The Handmaid's Tale*, *SN* as precursor of, 105–106; utopian aspects of, 94, 100, 125; Wells, H.G., influence on *SN*, 94–95
  U.S.S.R., attitude toward, 116, 117

C
Caldwell, Larry W, 197
Carr, Craig L., 165
Casement, William, 161, 166
Cather, Willa, 27
Chesnut, Mary, 170
Claeys, Gregory, 2, 5, 12, 16, 41, 129, 152, 156, 160, 165, 205
Common, Jack, 117
Connors, James, 65
Constantine, Murray, *see* Burdekin, Katharine
Cooke, Brett, 56, 57, 61, 66, 67
Cooper, Pamela, 183–184
Coughlin, John, 89
Crick, Bernard, 107, 149, 159, 161, 163, 164
Croft, Andy, 94, 105
Crossley, Robert, 94, 105, 106
Currie, Robert, 155

D
Deery, June, 76
Deleuze, Gilles, 8
Derrick, Scott, 39–40
Diken, Bülent, 9, 72
Duchess of Atholl, 163

E
Edelheit, Steven, 19
El Akkad, Omar, 2
Engels, Freidrich, 26, 138, 139
English, Elizabeth, 96, 97

F
Feminism, 3, 5, 16, 18, 21, 32, 93, 94, 111, 122, 123, 152, 188, 189, 198
Firchow, Peter Edgerly, 85, 89

Foucault, Michel, 5, 8–10, 12, 19, 59, 72, 155
Franco, Francisco, 110
Franklin, H. Bruce, 25, 28
Freibert, Lucy M, 176, 188
Freud, 5, 6, 9, 21, 80, 83, 185, 186
Frost, Laura, 86–87
Furer, Andrew, 49

G
Gilman, Charlotte Perkins, 94
Gimpelevich, Zina, 53, 135, 139
Gladstein, Mimi Reisel, 137
Goethe, Johann Wolfgang von, 64
Gollancz, Victor, 106
Goodwin, Sarah Webster, 3
Gorer, Geoffrey, 106
Gottlieb, Erika, 1, 6
Great Man Theory, 41, 124
Guattari, Felix, 8

H
Halbfass, Wilhelm, 81
Handmaid's Tale, The, see Atwood, Margaret
Harris, Jocelyn, 176, 182, 190, 193, 194, 197
Heje, Johan, 31
Herd mentality, appeal of, 52
    See also Oligarchy, appeal of; Totalitarianism, appeal of
Higdon, David Leon, 77
Hitchens, Christopher, 204
Hitler, Adolph, 28, 93, 95–98, 100, 101, 110, 112–114, 116–118, 121, 123, 178
Holden, Kate, 93, 98
Holzer, Angela C., 78
Homophobia, 16, 39, 94, 99, 100
Hopkins, Chris, 94–95
Horkheimer, Max, 71–73, 75

House, Humphry, 19
Hutchings, William, 61
Huxley, Aldous, 2, 4–7, 12–16, 18, 21, 28, 42, 44, 51, 65, 67, 68, 71–90, 135, 159, 204, 205
Brave New World, 2–4, 7, 10–12, 14–16, 19, 22, 28, 36, 42, 51, 53, 55, 68, 137, 159, 205; connection between language and thought in, 78–81; science in, 77
Brave New World: A Musical Comedy, 86
Brave New World Revisited, 78
Christianity, attitude toward, 81–83
Orwell's opinion of, 84
women, attitude toward, 75, 76, 90

I
Iron Heel, The, see London, Jack
Islamophobia, 169

J
Jacobs, Naomi, 129, 157, 158
Joannou, Maroula, 102
Johnson, Tara, 187
Jones, Libby Falk, 3

K
Kaler, Anne K., 182
Kant, Immanuel, 38
Katz-Roy, Ginette, 178, 182
Kipling, Rudyard, 119
Kumar, Krishan, 89, 95, 111

L
Lacan, Jacques, 18, 133
Lawrence, D. H., 36
Lawrence, Richard, 138, 140

LeFanu, Sarah, 10
Lenin, Vladimir, 15, 75
Lerner, Lawrence, 165
LGBTQ, 3, 203
London, Jack, 2–4, 7, 12–14, 21,
    25–49, 59, 73, 79, 110, 144,
    162, 205
  Catholicism, critique of, 41–43, 110
  charity, attitude toward, 35
  Iron Heel, The, 2–4, 12, 13, 18,
    25–49, 51, 54, 144, 164;
    queerness in, 41
  social class, conception of, 35, 46
  terrorism, attitude toward, 34
  women, attitude toward, 32, 46
Lothian, Alexis, 101, 102, 121

M
Madden, Deanna, 75–76
Malak, Amin, 173
Marcuse, Herbert, 14, 15, 20, 73, 74,
    90
Marx, Karl, 25, 26, 94, 131, 138, 139,
    189, 204
McCarthy, Patrick A., 64
McKay, George, 97, 105, 116, 117
Meckier, Jerome, 4, 84
Mellor, Anne, 151
Mihailovich, Vasa D., 67
Milgram, Shoshana, 129, 144, 145
Miner, Madonne, 185, 187
Montmarquet, James, 142
Moody, C., 56, 62, 67
More, Sir Thomas, 195
Muggeridge, Malcolm, 145, 157
Mussolini, Benito, 110

N
Nealon, Christopher, 100
Neuman, Shirley, 177
Ní Dhúill, Catríona, 5, 6, 54, 205

1984, see *Nineteen Eighty-Four*
Nineteen Eighty-Four, see Orwell,
    George
Norris, Frank, 27

O
Objectivism, 17, 35, 142–144
  contradictions in, 143
Oligarchy, appeal of, 85
  See also Herd mentality, appeal of;
    Totalitarianism, appeal of
Orwell, George, 2–9, 11–13, 16,
    18–22, 26–29, 31, 33–38, 43, 48,
    52, 59–61, 64–67, 73, 76, 84,
    87, 105–117, 119, 130–132,
    135, 144, 145, 147–166,
    203–205
  Animal Farm, 190
  Catholicism, critique of, 19, 20,
    110–112, 147
  Homage to Catalonia, 149
  Huxley, Aldous, assessment of, 84
  intellectualism, attitude toward,
    159–161
  Nineteen Eighty-Four, 2–4, 6–9, 11,
    12, 16–20, 22, 26–29, 31, 36,
    48, 51–53, 60, 66, 74, 78, 79,
    104–109, 111–115, 117, 124,
    134, 144, 145, 147–166, 204;
    hope in, 156–166; *Iron Heel,
    The*, influence on Orwell, 48;
    queerness in, 18, 155
  Road to Wigan Pier, The, 35, 106
  women, attitude toward, 151–155,
    161

P
Pagetti, Carlo, 10, 93, 113, 115, 122,
    123
Pareto, Vilfredo, 71
Parrinder, Patrick, 7

Patai, Daphne, 93, 97–99, 104, 106–108, 112, 114, 116, 117, 154, 164
Payne, Kenneth, 109–111
Peary, Gerald, 170
Peikoff, Leonard, 130
Pence, Mike, 171
Phillips, Lawrence, 160
Plank, William, 11, 151, 159
Portelli, Alessandro, 29, 37
Preslar, R. Mark, 54
Primitivism, 14, 49, 61, 175
Projected political fiction, 1, 2, 4–13, 18, 21, 29, 42, 51, 58, 67, 72, 75, 76, 83, 96, 135–137, 144, 158, 171, 192, 203, 205
  defined, 1
  sexism in, 10, 20

Q
Quakers, 119, 172

R
Rand, Ayn, 2, 11, 17, 18, 21, 22, 51, 63, 66, 73, 74, 76, 84, 129–145, 172–175, 205
  Anthem, 2, 17–19, 22, 36, 51, 63, 76–79, 83, 129–145; democracy, critique of, 144; Garden of Eden, references to, 141; homoeroticism in, 134, 136; imperialism in, 138–141, 143; language and thought in, 132–135; *Nineteen Eighty-Four*, *Anthem* as precursor of, 144–145; racism in, 142; sexism in, 137, 138, 140–142; Wells, H.G., influence on *Anthem*, 130, 144
Reich, Wilhelm, 19, 112
Reich, William, *see* Reich, Wilhelm
Reszler, André, 64, 67

Robinson, Paul, 6, 20
Rose, Jonathan, 19–20
Russell, Elizabeth, 96
Russian Revolution, 61, 130

S
Sargent, Lyman Tower, 4, 16
Sargisson, Lucy, 4, 16
Sedgwick, Eve Kosofsky, 102
Seed, David, 43–45, 49
Sexual Revolution, 9, 21, 156, 187, 192
Shakespeare, William, 78–82, 87, 88, 182
Shane, Alex M., 57
Shaw, George Bernard, 109
Shor, Francis, 28, 46
Slater, Ian, 147, 149, 159, 161
Social Darwinism, 17
Stec, Loretta, 99, 110, 122
Steinhoff, William, 4
Suvin, Darko, 14
Swastika Night, *see* Burdekin, Katharine

T
Taylor, Jenny, 150
Tirohl, Blu, 150
Totalitarianism, appeal of, 144, 190, 204–206
  See also Herd mentality, appeal of; Oligarchy, appeal of
Tower of Babel, 52
Trump, Donald, 2, 169, 170, 203

U
Utopia, *see* More, Sir Thomas

W
Walker, Jeanne Murray, 58
Watt, Donald, 80
We, *see* Zamyatin, Yevgeny

Wegner, Philip, 205
Weiss, Allan, 205
Wells, H. G., 13, 27, 29–31, 49, 77, 84, 94, 95, 130, 144, 205
Whalen-Bridge, John, 28, 32, 41, 45, 162
Williams, Raymond, 156, 157, 162–165
Willmett, H. J., 164
Witters, Sean A., 85, 86

Y
Yuknavitch, Lidia, 2

Z
Zamyatin, Yevgeny, 2–8, 13–15, 19, 21, 22, 28, 42, 49, 51–68, 72–77, 96, 106, 129, 131, 144, 194
    science and technology, attitude toward, 61–63
    We, 2–4, 7, 13–15, 18, 22, 28, 36, 42, 49, 51, 83, 104–106, 129, 135, 143–145, 150, 153; Catholicism, critique of, 59; ongoing relevance of, 51; Russian Revolution and, 61
    women, attitude toward, 60

CPI Antony Rowe
Eastbourne, UK
January 08, 2020